# The Mid-Appalachian Frontier:

## A Guide to Historic Sites
## of the
## French and Indian War

Robert B. Swift

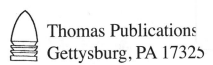

Thomas Publications
Gettysburg, PA 17325

D1225371

Copyright © 2001 Robert B. Swift

Printed and bound in the United States of America

Published by   THOMAS PUBLICATIONS
                P.O. Box 3031
                Gettysburg, Pa. 17325

ISBN-1-57747-070-2

Cover design by Ryan C. Stouch

Cover illustration, *Bushy Run*, by Don Troiani, www.historicalartprints.com

*To my wife Judy
and sons David and Brian*

# Acknowledgments

A debt of gratitude is owed the following individuals for their assistance in making this book possible. My wife Judy for her invaluable technical and editorial assistance, my sons David and Brian for help finding sites on the French and Indian War trail, my parents Robert and Ruth Swift for providing information concerning wester New York, John L. Moore for editorial advice, Joseph Dudick for research endeavors at the Library of Congress and elsewhere, Noel Carroll, Winston Wood, Craig Caba, and John Percy for providing helpful information in response to my queries and William Schmick for advice on writing technique.

# Contents

# Preface

The frontier throughout American history has been restless. People were continually on the move, social, economic and political changes occurred in rapid succession, and tensions and rivalries induced by all this ferment often exploded into armed conflict. The Mid-Appalachian frontier, a vast region bounded by mountain ranges and great waterways, was such a place during the first half of the 18th century.

During the period from 1720 to 1765, this region underwent a great transformation. The British and French struggled for supremacy, Native American tribes migrated westward from their homelands to escape white encroachment, and various ethnic and religious groups like the Scots-Irish and Moravian Brethren searched for a promised land.

The frontier was a fluid place where fixed boundaries meant little despite the edicts of royal officials in both London and Paris. But basically the region described herein is bounded by eight great waterways: the Delaware and Susquehanna Rivers in eastern Pennsylvania, the Potomac and Shenandoah Rivers in Maryland, Virginia and West Virginia; the Allegheny, Monongahela and Ohio Rivers in western Pennsylvania and the Niagara River in western New York.

From the Delaware Water Gap west to the Forks of the Ohio, a succession of mountain ranges made travel difficult. Migrating tribes and packhorse traders followed well-worn trails through mountain gaps and spots where the forest was so thick it was called the "Shades of Death." Later homesteaders and armies widened the trails so they could handle carts and wagons.

From the portages around the Niagara Falls south to the Shenandoah Valley, travel was made easier by the course of great river valleys that ran from the north to the south.

The paths along the valleys served for centuries as invasion routes for warriors from the Iroquois, Cherokee, and Catawba tribes and later accommodated a massive migration of the Germans and Scots-Irish.

The restless frontier was a magnet for strong-willed men and women who understood the ways of several cultures. Among these notables are: Conrad Weiser, the German emigrant who negotiated with the Iroquois on behalf of Pennsylvania authorities; Shikellamy, the Iroquois viceroy who was Weiser's diplomatic counterpart; Thomas Cresap, the trailblazer and sutler who lived along the Potomac River; Teedyuscung, the Delaware leader who sought to regain lost tribal lands; and Madame Montour, an interpreter at many conferences who was of French-Algonquian parentage.

The climactic event on the Mid-Appalachian frontier was the French and Indian War, or War for Empire, which started almost 250 years ago in the Pennsylvania backwoods in 1754 and concluded in 1763 with an international treaty signed in Paris. The war was brought on by the struggle between the British and French for control of the Ohio Valley, and by the desperate effort of Native Americans to preserve a way of life that was already in eclipse due to the introduction of European trade goods.

The final success of British armies after an initial series of debacles led to the fall of New France. But British mastery of the new domain was ensured only after the defeat of a pan-Indian uprising known as Pontiac's War in 1763-64.

The British victory was a short-lived illusion, however. The American colonists—the English, Germans, and Scots-Irish—now saw themselves in a new light as a result of their common wartime experience. They were starting down the road to independence.

Two of the men who played a prominent role in the creation of the United States—George Washington and Benjamin Franklin—were familiar figures on the Mid-Appalachian frontier and appear on the scene time and time again when key events unfolded. Following the exploits of these two men on both military and diplomatic missions, it becomes clear how actions taking place on one section of the frontier had an impact half a continent away. The geographic distances on the Mid-Appalachian frontier were great, but the people living along the region's great waterways were connected to each other in many ways.

This book is part narrative history, part travel guide to the Mid-Appalachian frontier. This format enables readers to visit the frontier sites on their own—the forts, battlegrounds, houses, churches, graveyards, tribal village sites, museums, and historic monuments as well as the many natural features that basically look the same as they did 250 years ago—and learn the story of what happened there. Interspersed throughout the book are short biographies of people who shaped or exemplified the frontier. The sites are grouped by ten different theaters of war or campaigns during the French and Indian War.

In many cases, you can stand at a frontier site, read a contemporary description and sense the curtain of the ages being lifted. In other cases, the man-made development of the 19th and 20th centuries has wrought its changes. The key topographical features may remain, but forested paths have given way to brick and asphalt. Here some imagination can help reclaim the past.

# 1

# The Native Americans, French and British move into the Ohio Valley, 1720s to 1759

## INTRODUCTION

The Ohio River Valley with its valuable resources of hardwood forest, fertile bottomland and fur-bearing animals beckoned both Europeans and Native Americans during the first half of the 18th century. Rivalries for control of this vast region located in Ohio and western Pennsylvania provided the spark that ignited a world war.

People entering the Ohio Valley were motivated by different desires. The Delaware, pushed out of their homelands in eastern Pennsylvania by English encroachment, settled in towns like Kittanning to plant crops and hunt game. The Shawnee, caught up in the same migration, returned to an area they had passed through 50 years earlier. The Iroquois colonized an area that had been depopulated as a result of warfare a generation before. The Iroquois who settled there became known as Mingos. Logstown was an important town where Delaware, Shawnee, and Mingos lived and where the Iroquois sent a viceroy named Tanacharison to oversee affairs.

The French called the Ohio River, "The Belle Riviere," or Beautiful River. Interested in the fur trade, they harbored imperial ambitions. The Ohio Valley was a strategic waterborne link between the French colonies in Canada and Louisiana. In 1727 the French took a first step at securing this link when they built a stronghold called Fort Niagara at the mouth of the Niagara River. Control of the Niagara portage was vital to keeping French trade goods and supplies flowing into the Ohio Valley; they strengthened their hold on this portage by building Fort Little Niagara at the southern terminus. French military expeditions, led by Baron de Longueuil in 1739 and Celeron de Blainville in 1749, demonstrated the importance the French attached to the region.

The first British to establish themselves in the region were noted Indian traders like George Croghan and Christopher Gist. But they were viewed as advance men for a larger purpose: the settlement and civilization of the Ohio Valley by settlers in the tidewater and piedmont regions who were already feeling hemmed in by the Allegheny Mountain barrier. Virginia sponsored a semi-official land company, the Ohio Company, to turn the Ohio forests into farmsteads.

In 1753-54, the imperial designs of the two European powers collided. The Mingos, Delaware, and Shawnee tried to determine which side best suited their interests.

The French sent an army of 2,000 soldiers from Fort Niagara into the upper Ohio Valley to build a string of log forts: Fort Presque Isle, Fort Le Boeuf, and Fort Machault. In December 1753, a young Virginian named George Washington went on a mission to Fort Le Boeuf to gauge French intentions.

In the spring of 1754, the French army ejected a small party of Virginia soldiers who were building a fortified post at the Forks of the Ohio where the Allegheny and Monongahela Rivers combine to form the Ohio. The Virginians were allowed to depart peacefully and the French built Fort Duquesne on the same spot. Shortly afterward, Washington arrived back in the region with a force of colonial soldiers. With Tanacharison's help, Washington ambushed a French party hidden in a ravine called Jumonville Glen atop Chestnut Ridge.

SITES AT A GLANCE—This map will give you a feel for the general locations of sites in this chapter. Some sites overlap and are not shown on this map.

Fort Niagara
Fort Little Niagara
La Belle Famille
Fort Presque Isle
Chautauqua Portage
Fort LeBoeuf
Venango/Ft. Machault
Logstown
Fort Duquesne
Jumonville Glen
Fort Necessity

Washington regrouped at a crude stockade called Fort Necessity and awaited a French counterattack. The French won that battle and got an unexpected bonus a year later when General Edward Braddock's army marched to ruin during a campaign against Fort Duquesne. Braddock's defeat convinced the Delaware and Shawnee to go on the warpath on behalf of the French.

But the French were stretched thin and they knew it. A large British army under General John Forbes marched on Fort Duquesne in 1758. Forbes' methodical advance convinced the Delaware and Shawnee to abandon the French. The French blew up the fort before it came under siege, and retreated north to Fort Machault along the Allegheny River. In the summer of 1759, French forces gathered at Fort Machault preparing to retake Fort Duquesne. But word came that a British army had placed Fort Niagara under siege. The French altered their plans and gathered a relief force at Fort Presque Isle. They moved north to break the British siege, but met complete defeat instead at a place near the Niagara portage called La Belle Famille. With the defeat of the relief party, Fort Niagara surrendered and the fleur-de-lis faded from the Ohio Valley.

## TRIBAL MIGRATIONS

In one sense, the migrations of Indian tribes along the waterways of the mid-Appalachian region were part of the cycle of life. The Delaware or Lenape (Real People) customarily moved in search of game or new fields to cultivate corn. The Shawnee were especially known for wandering great distances. Migrations were of a seasonal nature with the population of whole villages moving to the riverbanks to fish during the summer and back inland to escape icy blasts during the winter. Some migrations resulted from the intra-tribal wars that erupted at both ends of such major north-south trails such as the Warrior's Path.

The arrival of the Swedes, Dutch, and English along the bays and inlets of the Atlantic coast changed the nature of these tribal migrations. From the time the first European outposts were established along the Delaware, Hudson, and James Rivers in the early 1600s, the migrations reflected the dislocations brought on by a clash of cultures. European demand for beaver pelts resulted in the Beaver Wars of the 1670s. With the depletion of the beaver stock in their own lands, the Iroquois expanded their domain southward from the Finger Lakes region at the expense of the Susquehannocks. The dispersal of the Susquehannocks left the Susquehanna River Valley and the Shenandoah River Valley no-man's lands.

Meanwhile, Swedish authorities on the Delaware gave way to the Dutch, who in turn gave way to the English. But European powers shared one thing in common—they pushed their settlement lines steadily westward as new boatloads of immigrants arrived from Europe. Eventually the Delaware found themselves on the west shore of the Delaware River.

Traditional tribal ways also were disrupted by the introduction of European trading goods, alcohol, and the spread of smallpox and other new diseases for which the Indians lacked a natural immunity.

William Penn inaugurated a policy of land purchases after he founded Pennsylvania in 1681. Through a series of treaties with provincial officials, the Delaware found themselves dispossessed of their lands in Pennsylvania. They received desired trade goods—blankets, beads, gunpowder—for their land. But the Delaware and English harbored vastly different concepts of what land ownership meant. The Delaware viewed trade goods as payment for what today would be described as multiple use of the land; the English regarded the deeds written with pen and parchment as sealing their sole ownership.

One such deed—the Walking Purchase of 1737—exposed the gulf between English and Delaware land dealings. Charges of fraud connected with the purchase became a root cause of the Delawares' decision to side with the French and take to the warpath against the English 18 years later.

Not all migrations during this period followed a straight westward path, however. Bands of Shawnee actually migrated eastward over a period of decades from the Ohio River Valley, to Opessa's Town on the Potomac River and to spots along the Susquehanna and Delaware River. Their stay in eastern Pennsylvania was relatively short for English incursions set the Shawnee on a westward path again.

Iroquois diplomacy also played a role in tribal migrations. The Iroquois allied themselves with the British in their long rivalry with the French. But the Iroquois also sought to move dislocated tribes into the Susquehanna and Wyoming Valleys where they acted as a buffer against the steadily expanding English settlements. It took the Tuscarora, a defeated tribe, almost a century to migrate from North Carolina northward to the Finger Lakes region as proteges of the Iroquois. And for a time, from the 1720s to 1750s, the town of Shamokin (modern day Sunbury) at the Forks of the Susquehanna served as a refuge for displaced tribes under the protective eye of Iroquois overseers.

By the outbreak of the French and Indian War, many of the Delaware and Shawnee were living in the Ohio Valley towns of Kittanning and Logstown, where they broke the Iroquois hold and came under the influence of the French. Their warriors carried memories of lost homelands with them as they raided farms and frontier forts in Pennsylvania, Maryland, and Virginia.

## QUEEN ALIQUIPPA

The life of the Seneca Queen Aliquippa spans a period of tumultuous relations between Europeans and Native Americans in Pennsylvania. Aliquippa (16??-1754) was a young woman when she bade farewell to William Penn, founder of the colony of Pennsylvania, upon his return to England. During the last year of her life, Aliquippa received presents from a young Virginia colonel named George Washington. Daughter of a chief, Aliquippa is believed to have belonged to a tribe of Senecas that settled in eastern Pennsylvania. Her husband, a tribal leader, was prominent among those who signed peace treaties with Penn.

Aliquippa became tribal leader upon her husband's death. By the 1730s she was living near the Forks of the Ohio in western Pennsylvania. The accounts of traders and agents place her village at locations on the Monongahela River, Chartier's Creek, and the Youghiogheny River.

Aliquippa met virtually every prominent person who passed through the region, including diplomat Conrad Weiser, trader George Croghan, French expedition leader Pierre-Joseph Celeron de Blainville, and Washington. Aliquippa sided with the British in the imperial rivalry for control of the Ohio valley. She was proud of her social and political standing and took affront if slighted.

Washington learned that he had incurred Aliquippa's displeasure for not stopping to visit her while on his 1753 diplomatic mission to the French commander at Fort Le Boeuf. Thus, on the return trip home, Washington made it a point to pay a personal visit. "I went up about three miles to the mouth of the Youghiogheny to visit Queen Aliquippa, who had expressed great concern that we passed her in going to the fort," he wrote. "I made her a present of a match-coat and a bottle of rum, which latter was thought much the better present of the two."

Aliquippa's position was threatened after Washington was forced to surrender Fort Necessity in 1754 to a larger force of French troops. She moved east to George Croghan's trading post at Aughwick in central Pennsylvania and died shortly afterward. The city of Aliquippa in Beaver County is named for her.


## TANACHARISON

Tanacharison played a key role in events that pushed the British and French to the brink of war in the Ohio country. Tanacharison sided with the British, and because of this, he died an exile's death in late 1754 as the conflict whose birth he witnessed started to widen.

Tanacharison was also known as the Half-King, for the role he played as the Iroquois viceroy over the tribes of the Ohio valley. Like the viceroy Shikellamy who lived at the Forks of the Susquehanna River, Tanacharison was dispatched by the Iroquois council on Onondaga to oversee the tribes moving into the Ohio Valley. But it was more than just concern over vassal tribes that made Tanacharison's position an important one.

Many Iroquois, especially from the Seneca tribe, were migrating from southern New York into the Ohio country. They were known as Mingos and were not always keen on taking orders from Onondaga.

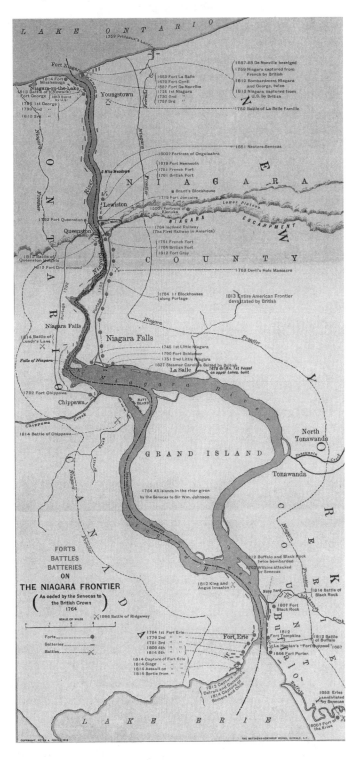

*Map of forts, battles, and batteries on the Niagara Frontier. This area was the scene of warfare for two hundred years.*

(Peter A. Porter, 1919)

Tanacharison arrived in 1747 as migration to the region increased. He made his home at Logstown on the Ohio River. The Iroquois initially sought a policy of neutrality between the French and British. This helped the Iroquois strengthen their position by playing one side off the other. But soon after Tanacharison's arrival, the European powers set their sights on the Ohio Valley.

Virginia formed the Ohio Company for the purpose of settling the region. In 1748, Tanacharison signed a treaty with Pennsylvania diplomat Conrad Weiser in which he promised to provide intelligence on French movements. A year later, the French sent a flag-waving expedition under Capt. Pierre Joseph Celeron de Blainville through the region.

Tanacharison encouraged the Ohio Company to build a fortified trading post in the region, but his response was different when the French sent an expedition in 1753 to build a series of forts between Lake Erie and the Forks of the Ohio. The Half-King sent three strong warnings to the French to desist; he accompanied George Washington on his mission to Fort Le Boeuf to protest the French invasion. After the French ejected the Virginians from the Ohio forks in April 1754, Tanacharison swung firmly to the British side. He informed Washington of the whereabouts of Ensign Jumonville's scouting force and joined in that attack.

But with Washington's surrender at Fort Necessity a month later, Tanacharison's position was jeopardized. The tribes living in the Ohio region were siding with the French. Tanacharison and his family fled to eastern Pennsylvania, stopping first at trader George Croghan's trading post at Aughwick and then seeking sanctuary with John Harris II at Harris Ferry on the banks of the Susquehanna River. There he took ill and died in October 1754. He was buried at an unknown location along the riverbank.

## FORT NIAGARA — YOUNGSTOWN, NEW YORK

*Directions: Take New York State Thruway north from Pennsylvania border. At Buffalo, take Exit 50. Follow I-290 west to I-190. Take I-190 north to Exit 25B. Follow fort signs on Robert Moses Parkway North to Fort Niagara.*

From the window of the officers' quarters at the French Castle here, the point where the mouth of the Niagara River meets Lake Ontario is visible. This was a chokepoint for New France, a strategic link that if severed would isolate the colony's political and population centers at Montreal and Quebec from a vast inland empire encompassing the Great Lakes and Ohio and Mississippi River Valleys. Fort Niagara controlled the water-and-portage route connecting the St. Lawrence River and Lake Ontario with the rest of the Great Lakes: Erie, Huron, Michigan and Superior. It served the French as a staging area and supply base for the expeditions that occupied the disputed Forks of the Ohio in the 1750s.

The British severed that lifeline when they captured Fort Niagara after a siege in July 1759. The fall of Fort Niagara left a network of western forts and trading posts, including Fort Duquesne at the Forks of the Ohio, to wither on the vine.

The French first realized the importance of this elevated peninsula jutting from the east bank of the Niagara River during LaSalle's explorations of the Great Lakes. Starting with a crude wooden stockade, Fort Conti, built at the site in 1679 and with another short-lived wooden post, Fort Denonville a decade later, the French kept a tenuous and shaky hold on the site.

As the French pushed westward to exploit the fur trade, they became aware of rival British designs to gain a foothold at Oswego at the eastern end of Lake Ontario. Fearing the British would supplant them, the French pressured the Seneca, an Iroquois tribe controlling the portage route around Niagara Falls, to agree to a more imposing and defensible stone fort at the site. With the Senecas withholding consent for a stone fort, the French engaged in a bit of trickery in 1727 when they secured approval from an Iroquois council to build a stone trading post, dubbed the House of Peace. The house actually doubled as a stronghold capable of resisting attack. Within its walls, the French located a powder magazine, guardhouse, barracks and storerooms. Overhanging dormers on the building's top floor shielded cannon.

As British-French rivalry over the Ohio country increased, Fort Niagara was strengthened. The French relied on the post to secure their claims to the Ohio Valley. In 1749, Pierre-Joseph Celeron de Blainville set forth from Niagara on an expedition down the Allegheny and Ohio Rivers to bury lead plates formally claiming the region for France.

*The French called this castle 'The House of Peace,' but in reality it was a fortified stronghold.*

*The Gate of the Five Nations was built in 1756 and served as the main entrance to Fort Niagara.*

In 1753-54, the fort commander Claude Pierre Pecaudy de Contrecoeur played a key logistical role in forwarding the soldiers, boats and supplies needed to build French Forts Presque Isle, Le Boeuf, Machault and Duquesne in the Ohio country. After a waterborne journey across Lake Ontario, the French troops regrouped at Fort Niagara before tackling the portage at Lewiston Heights and following it past Niagara Falls to Little Fort Niagara. From there they journeyed south to the Ohio country.

During the French and Indian War, the British set their sights on Fort Niagara early on. If General Braddock had succeeded in capturing Fort Duquesne, his next target—somewhat unrealistically considering the wilderness terrain—was to be Fort Niagara. After Braddock's defeat, the French under a new commander, Captain Pierre Pouchot, continued to boost Fort Niagara's defenses.

As it was, the British suffered many reversals before an army led by General John Prideaux and Sir William Johnson landed at Four Mile Creek, a sheltered inlet on Lake Ontario east of Fort Niagara, in July 1759 and began siege operations. The British conducted a classic artillery siege of the fort for several weeks; the breakthrough

came when a French relief force was defeated at the battle of La Belle Famille on the portage road leading to Fort Niagara. The relief force consisted of soldiers from the western posts that relied on Fort Niagara for supplies and provisions. When Pouchot learned of the defeat, he surrendered the beleaguered fort to Johnson. Prideaux had been killed when one of his army's mortars exploded.

Fort Niagara was one of a handful of frontier posts to remain in British hands during Pontiac's War in 1763-64. The fort served as a lifeline once again, this time to the British fort at Detroit, besieged by Pontiac's forces. The fort also played a key role in the American Revolution and War of 1812, and today, it is operated by the Old Fort Niagara Association and located within Fort Niagara State Park. The French Castle and many of the fort's buildings underwent a major restoration in the 1920s and 1930s.

A number of buildings from the colonial era can be visited, including the French Castle (1727), Powder Magazine (1757), Provisions Storehouse (1762), Gate of the Five Nations (1756), Bakehouse (1762), South Redoubt (1770), North Redoubt (1771).

A major French and Indian War reenactment takes place at the fort during the Forth of July weekend, and other special events are held. The fort is open at 9 a.m. daily year round with closing hours varying by season. Admission charged. Call 716-745-7611.

## LA BELLE FAMILLE—YOUNGSTOWN, NEW YORK

*Directions: From Fort Niagara, Take Route 18F south through Youngstown, past intersection with Route 93 to the spot with highway marker and monuments one mile south of Youngstown.*

The stakes could not have been higher for the French relief force headed for besieged Fort Niagara in July 1759. They were under orders to break the British grip on Niagara, the supply point to the French posts scattered along the waterways of the Great Lakes and Ohio River valley. If the British army outside Niagara could be defeated, the French could begin an offensive to recapture the Forks of the Ohio from another British army. If Fort Niagara fell, French posts as far west as Detroit and Michilimackinac would be isolated and subject to capture.

The French lost their gamble at the Battle of La Belle Famille on July 24. Just as French forces at Fort Machault were planning an attack on the Forks of the Ohio, they received word of the arrival of the British army outside Fort Niagara. A force of some 1,600 French soldiers and western Indian allies gathered at Fort Presque Isle on Lake Erie to march to Niagara's relief. Leading the army were names famous in frontier warfare: Capt. Francois Le Marchand de Ligneris,

Capt. Charles Phillipe Aubry and Capt. Francois Coulon de Villiers. The army crossed Lake Erie on boats, then headed downstream along the Niagara River to the southern end of the portage. The army marched along the Portage Road on the east shore of the river.

At a cleared spot in the forest known as La Belle Famille, the French encountered 450 British infantrymen behind a breastwork of logs. The British held their fire until the French were some 30 yards away and then shot volleys of musket fire into the overconfident French. The French lines were broken within twenty minutes, and the survivors fled towards Niagara Falls. British troops and Iroquois warriors chased the fleeing French. Some 500 French were killed or captured in the battle. At day's end, Ligneris, Aubry, and Villiers were prisoners in the British camp outside the walls of Fort Niagara.

The French commandant, Capt. Pierre Pouchot, sent an envoy to the British lines to confirm reports of the rout. When the envoy saw the captured French officers, he knew the end was near. Fort Niagara surrendered the next day.

Today the site of the Battle of La Belle Famille is marked by a highway marker and two stone monuments along Route 18F, one mile south of Youngstown. On the left side of the highway, you will see a blue-and-yellow state highway marker by a wooded area. One stone tablet is dedicated to French Chaplain Fr. Claude Francois Louis Virot, killed during the battle. The other gives a summary of the battle.

A History and Guide to Old Fort Niagara says the markers are placed incorrectly since the battle's main action took place in the center of Youngstown at the intersection of Route 18F and 93.

*La Belle Famille battlefield monument.*

# OLD STONE CHIMNEY & FORT LITTLE NIAGARA
## NIAGARA FALLS, NEW YORK

*Directions: Take Robert Moses Parkway north to Niagara Falls. Get off Quay Street exit to the right (Quay Street is marked on city maps, but there is no Quay Street exit sign. At point on expressway where sign says American Falls ahead, take exit with sign pointing to Downtown Niagara Falls/Information Center.) As you come to end of exit, observe park on right with mounted Civil War cannon in it. Take first right on Buffalo Ave. Circle around park a short distance to the parking lot. Chimney stands at end of parking lot on slope leading to expressway. A 1915 plaque is mounted on front of chimney.*

A slender stone chimney stands almost forgotten in a small park just east of the Robert Moses Parkway which brings thousands of visitors annually to Niagara Falls. The chimney is a surviving artifact of Fort Little Niagara, a French-built dependency of Fort Niagara. Fort Little Niagara or Fort du Portage occupied a strategic location in the water-and-portage route linking Lake Ontario and Lake Erie.

The outpost guarded the southern end of the portage road around Niagara Falls. The portage road started at Lewiston Heights where the Niagara River gorge develops and extended to Fort Little Niagara, just one and one-half miles north of the falls. The French and Seneca tribe used the portage road to carry bales of beaver, deer and bear skins from the western territories back east.

In the 1740s, as traffic on the portage road increased, French authorities decided they needed a fortified post at the head of the portage. They wanted to safeguard the French expeditions enroute to the Ohio country and make sure Indian fur traders did not bypass Fort Niagara in search of bargains at British Fort Oswego at the eastern end of Lake Ontario.

In 1745, a blockhouse was erected in the vicinity. Then in 1750 work began on a larger fort. The builder of the fort, Chabert Joncaire, was a member of an influential French frontier family deeply involved in the portage fur trade. Joncaire had close ties with the Seneca, the Iroquois tribe controlling the portage territory, and he used those contacts to gain tacit acceptance from the Seneca for the post.

Accounts describe Fort Little Niagara as consisting of a trading house and outbuildings surrounded by a triangular palisade with two types of bastions. The chimney was attached to the fort's mess hall and barracks.

When a British army laid siege to Fort Niagara in 1759, Joncaire was given orders to burn the fort. The chimney survived the fire. In 1761, the British built a new fort in the vicinity recognizing its importance to the

*The Old Stone Chimney in Niagara Falls city park is the surviving remnant of Little Fort Niagara.*

## CHAUTAUQUA PORTAGE—BARCELONA, NEW YORK

*Directions: Take Exit 60 off New York State Thruway. Turn right on Route 394. See sign for Barcelona. At first intersection, turn right onto Route 5 east. Look for historic 1829 Barcelona lighthouse and Barcelona Harbor on left. This is a boat launching facility and picnic area that provides public access to the Lake Erie shoreline. To reach Westfield, take Exit 60 off Thruway. Turn left on Route 394 which becomes Portage Street leading into Westfield.*

The Chautauqua or Chatakoin portage served as an important springboard for French expeditions into the Ohio region. At the small harbor town of Barcelona on the southeast side of Lake Erie the journey began.

The Chautauqua portage was one of several the French used to bring soldiers and supplies from their base at Fort Niagara into the Ohio region. Moving south from Fort Niagara, the French carried their canoes and watercraft on a portage around Niagara Falls and its gorge to Fort Little Niagara. At this juncture, they used water transportation again to enter Lake Erie. They sailed along the shoreline to a natural harbor where Barcelona now stands. There the French used an eight-mile portage generally following the course of Chautauqua Creek to reach the west shore of Lake Chautauqua.

They sailed eastward across the lake to its outlet on the east shore where modern-day Jamestown is located. The French then followed a water route linking the Chadakoin River and Conewango Creek to reach the Allegheny River, or to them "The Belle Riviere," at modern-day Warren, Pa.

The Chautauqua portage was used in 1739 when Baron de Longueuil passed through the Ohio region to join French forces fighting the Chickasaw tribe in the Mississippi River valley. When Pierre Joseph Celeron de Blainville led an expedition to assert French sovereignty over the Ohio region in 1749, he used the Chautauqua portage. Yet Celeron did not think much of the landing site at Barcelona, judging the lake waters too shallow, the harbor unprotected, and the beach subject to gales.

In 1753 when the French decided to occupy the Ohio region, the initial plans called for using the Chautauqua portage again. An advance party commanded by Charles Deschamps de Boishebert made a beachhead at Barcelona, but then word arrived from Quebec to move the main landing further south to Presque Isle (modern-day Erie) where a peninsula jutting into Lake Erie formed a bay that offered the French more protection.

Today the Barcelona harbor offers a good view of the start of the Chautauqua portage. The mouth of Chautauqua Creek is just west of Barcelona. In the nearby town of Westfield, the memory of the French is preserved in the French-Portage Road Historic District that includes Portage Street.

portage trade. This post was called Fort Schlosser; a new barracks and mess hall for British troops were built adjoining the chimney.

In later years, this building was used as a house for the British portage master John Stedman, then as a residence, and after that as a tavern. During the War of 1812, the British invaded the Niagara frontier and burned Fort Schlosser. Once again the chimney survived, and was utilized as part of a house constructed by General Peter B. Porter.

In the 1890s, a popular song called attention to the chimney as a silent witness to much of Niagara's history:

Long may the old stone chimney stand, upon Niagara's shore; the sons of France and Britain's band, they battle there no more; The pioneers and sweethearts dear, are sleeping on the hill, Where lone the Old Stone Chimney stands, in the evening gray and still.

The chimney has been moved twice from its original location to make way for industrial development and the expressway, but today it stands by itself at the south end of a small city park named for General Porter.

## FORT PRESQUE ISLE—ERIE, PENNSYLVANIA

The site of Fort Presque Isle has changed beyond recognition, but the natural feature that attracted the French to this area remains: Presque Isle Bay, the Lake Erie harbor formed by the 3,200-acre sand peninsula called Presque Isle. The peninsula is a state park and national natural landmark that provides habitat for a wide variety of plants and animals, and beaches and hiking trails along the bay and lakesides for people.

The French translation for Presque Isle means "almost an island." The peninsula offered natural protection for the French invasion army. They moved their base of operations in the spring of 1753 from the Chautauqua Portage thirty miles to here. An army of 2,000 French and Canadian soldiers landed at Presque Isle in June. Prior to their arrival, an advance detachment had already started work on a log stockade.

Fort Presque Isle was built on an elevation west of the mouth of Mill Creek on the landward side of the bay. The veteran officer commanding the expedition, Paul Marin de la Malgue, was in a hurry to build a portage road to the navigable waterway of French Creek. So shortly after he landed, Marin headed south to select a site for Fort Le Boeuf at the southern terminus of the portage road. But Marin was back at Fort Presque Isle to meet with several delegations of Delaware and Iroquois who visited over the next several months to gauge French intentions.

The French had mixed success in winning tribal leaders over. In September, Tanacharison, the Iroquois viceroy at Logstown, came to Presque Isle demanding that the French leave the region. But Marin rejected his demand and met later with a group of Shawnee who proved more receptive.

Fort Presque Isle's main role during the French and Indian War was as a supply-and-transfer point for troops and supplies heading south to Fort Duquesne. The size of the garrison increased during summer months and dwindled during the winter when food supplies were scant.

After the fall of Fort Duquesne to the British in 1758, Fort Presque Isle and Fort Machault served as staging points for a planned French counterattack to drive the British from the Forks of the Ohio. When word came of the siege of Fort Niagara in the summer of 1759, the French chose Fort Presque Isle as the gathering area for a relief force of 600 French troops and 1,000 warriors from throughout the Great Lakes region. The relief force met defeat at the battle of La Belle Famille. The French evacuated and burned Fort Presque Isle in early August.

The British built a new fort at Presque Isle, but it was burned to the ground during the first wave of attacks during Pontiac's War in 1763. The Americans built a Fort Presque Isle at a different site in the 1790s.

The site of Fort Presque Isle was greatly altered with construction of a brickyard in the 19th century. A state historical marker for Fort Presque Isle is located at 6th and Parade Streets, Erie. Presque Isle State Park can be reached by Route 832.

## FORT LE BOEUF MUSEUM
## WATERFORD, PENNSYLVANIA

*Directions: To follow the approximate route of the French portage road by car, take Route 97 exit off I-79. Go south on Route 97 to Route 19. Take Route 19 into Waterford. Museum located on the left side of Route 19 at south end of town.*

Fort Le Boeuf was one of a chain of posts the French built to secure possession of the upper Ohio Valley. But Fort Le Boeuf captures the imagination for other reasons as well. The fort is a reminder of the hardships the French suffered in trying to build a chain of posts as well as a portage road through the swamps of this region. The French invasion of the Ohio Valley stopped here in 1753 because of the toll that sickness and death took on the soldiers as much as anything else. The invasion resumed the next year with the occupation of the Forks of the Ohio.

Fort Le Boeuf is also where George Washington stepped onto the world stage. Washington, a young 21-year-old emissary of Virginia Governor Robert Dinwiddie, journeyed here in December 1753 to deliver a blunt diplomatic note to the French, warning them to evacuate the Ohio region. The French rejected Washington's ultimatum and he left empty-handed. But Washington wrote a journal of his trip and Dinwiddie arranged for it to be published in England and America bringing a first measure of fame to the young author.

When an army of 2,000 French and Canadian soldiers landed at Presque Isle in the spring of 1753, they did not anticipate the dangers awaiting them—not from hostile fire, but rather from illnesses caused by poor diet, unsanitary conditions, exposure to the elements, and back-breaking labor. When the campaign season ended in October 1753, only about 800 soldiers were still fit for duty. Many had been sent back to Fort Niagara to recuperate; the rest were buried in wilderness graves.

The French ran into untold difficulties building a 15-mile portage road between Fort Presque Isle and Fort Le Boeuf, the southern terminus located near French Creek which connects with the Allegheny River. The French converted an Indian path into a road for use by soldiers, wagons and cannon. But the heavy boots of the soldiers and the weight of the equipment turned the path that frequently cut across marshy areas into mudholes. The weather did not cooperate that summer either, being hot and dry and leaving many streams and rivers too shallow for military use. The expedition commander, Paul Marin de la Malgue, also complained to officials in Quebec that the supplies of salt pork and other food were found unfit for consumption when opened.

In June, Marin selected a location for Fort Le Boeuf on a knoll above Le Boeuf Creek, just north of Lake Le Boeuf in modern-day Waterford. With the arrival of hot weather, however, the number of sick men increased and work on building the fort and completing the portage road (overlaid with logs in some marshy areas) slowed. By fall, the French realized that dry weather and illness would prevent them from moving any farther south than Fort Le Boeuf that year. They sent most of the troops home for the winter, leaving garrisons at Forts Presque Isle and Le Boeuf. Marin, a veteran of many campaigns in the Great Lakes country, stayed at Fort Le Boeuf to recover from sickness. But he died on October 29 and was buried in the fort's cemetery.

Within six weeks of Marin's death, Washington arrived at Fort Le Boeuf to deliver Dinwiddie's message. Washington spent five days at the fort meeting with the commander, Legardeur de Saint Pierre, and making careful observation of what he saw. Here is Washington's description of Fort Le Boeuf from his famous journal:

> ...four Houses compose the Sides; the bastions are made of Piles driven into the Ground, and about 12 feet above, and sharp at Top, with Port-Holes cut for Cannon and Loop-Holes for the small Arms to fire through; there are eight 6 lb. Pieces mounted, two in each Bastion, and one piece of four Pound before the Gate; in the Bastions are a Guardhouse, Chapel, Doctor's Lodging, and the Commander's private store, round which are laid Plat-Forms for the Cannon and Men to stand on: There are several Barracks without the Fort, for the Soldiers Dwelling, covered, some with Bark, and some with Boards, made chiefly of Loggs: There are also several other Houses, such as Stables, Smiths Shop.

During the French and Indian War, Fort Le Boeuf served as a French supply post supporting Fort Duquesne. The French burned the fort in August 1759 after the fall of Fort Niagara rather than let it fall into British hands. But the British built a blockhouse at the site in 1760. This blockhouse was attacked and burned during Pontiac's War. The Americans also built a blockhouse at the same site in 1796.

Today the site of Fort Le Boeuf is well marked on a knoll on the south end of Waterford on the left side of Route 19, the main street. The Judson House, an 1820 Greek Revival home, occupies much of the fort site. Next to the Judson House is the Fort Le Boeuf Museum which

*The Judson House occupies much of the site of Fort Le Boeuf.*

offers unique and interesting exhibits about the beaver fur trade, portages, Native American life and the French, British and American forts as well as a slide show about Washington's trip. The museum is owned by the Pennsylvania Historical and Museum Commission, but administered by Edinboro University. Edinboro students have conducted extensive archaeological digs at the site and some of the artifacts are displayed in the museum.

The fort is open on some weekend afternoons in the summer and fall months, but it is best to call ahead for a schedule. To arrange a tour call the Department of Sociology, Anthropology and Social Work, Edinboro University, Edinboro Pa., 814-732-2573.

## GEORGE WASHINGTON DELIVERS MESSAGE TO THE FRENCH — FORT LE BOEUF, WATERFORD, PENNSYLVANIA

The French occupation of the upper Ohio Valley in the fall of 1753 set off alarm bells in Williamsburg, the capital of colonial Virginia. Virginia hoped to colonize the Ohio region; the French incursion threw a roadblock into the plans by Ohio Company, a group of wealthy Virginian investors, to settle homesteaders on lands granted them by the British government. Virginia's governor Robert Dinwiddie decided to issue a warning to the French to peacefully withdraw from their newly built forts at Presque Isle and Le Boeuf. Dinwiddie found his messenger in George Washington, a young adjutant with the Virginia militia but an experienced wilderness hand through his land surveying work for the Virginia baron, Lord Fairfax.

Washington eagerly volunteered for this choice assignment. He left Williamsburg on October 31 on a momentous ten-week adventure that would lift him from obscurity and launch him on a 40-year career as a provincial commander, leader of a revolutionary army, and the first president of the United States.

Washington assembled a traveling party along the way that included Christopher Gist, a seasoned trader working for the Ohio Company, Jacob Van Braam, a Dutchman who spoke French, and four helpers. He stopped at Wills Creek, an English trading post on the Potomac River, where he met Gist and then went to the Forks of the Ohio. He described the spot prophetically as a good location to build a fort.

Washington's first diplomatic foray came at Logstown on the Ohio River, the headquarters of the Iroquois viceroy Tanacharison. During a visit that lasted five days, he strengthened British ties with Tanacharison. The viceroy had already voiced his displeasure to the French about their invasion.

Tanacharison and three other villagers joined Washington on the journey north from Logstown. This set the stage for a three-way round of diplomacy at Fort Le Boeuf. Washington first met the French at Venango, a strategic point where French Creek enters the Allegheny River. Here Washington met with Captain Phillipe Thomas de Joncaire, a member of a famous French trading family based at Niagara. This encounter is memorable for Washington's famous observation about the effect of wine upon tongues:

> The Wine, as they dosed themselves pretty plentifully with it, soon banished the Restraint which at first appear'd in their Conversation and gave a License to their Tongues to reveal their Sentiments more freely. They told me, That it was their absolute Design to take Possession of the Ohio, and by G—, they would do it; for that they were sensible the English could raise two Men for their one; yet they knew, their Motions were too slow and dilatory to prevent any Undertaking of theirs.

But Joncaire lacked the authority to respond to Dinwiddie's message and Washington set out on December 7 for Fort Le Boeuf by way of French Creek to meet someone who did. The French commanders at Fort Le Boeuf treated Washington courteously, but the written answer to Dinwiddie's ultimatum was a firm no. The French said they were not obliged to obey Dinwiddie's summons.

At Le Boeuf the interplay between the French, Virginians, and Tanacharison was spirited during the five days Washington spent there. The French commander, Legardeur de Saint Pierre, sought to win over Tanacharison and his party with gifts and liquor. He also offered to send shipments of trade goods to Logstown.

Once he had the French response, Washington wanted to depart Le Boeuf promptly, but he ended up staying longer. Tanacharison dallied and Washington did not want

to leave him entirely to French blandishments. The entire party left for Venango on December 16. There Joncaire proved more adept than his colleagues at Le Boeuf in getting Tanacharison to stay longer. Washington and Gist left on their own on December 23, but with the horses tiring, they decided they could make better time if they set out on foot. They faced danger twice during this part of the journey, once when an Indian whom they met along the way and traveled a short distance with fired a shot at them, and the second time when Washington fell off a homemade raft into the partly-frozen Allegheny River.

Washington arrived in Williamsburg on January 16, 1754 and delivered his journal, a map of the Ohio region, and observations of French movements to Dinwiddie. Dinwiddie decided to print the journal to call attention to the French invasion and Washington had his first taste of worldwide fame.

A statue of Washington delivering the message to the French stands today in a small park in Waterford, Pa. adjacent to the site of Fort Le Boeuf. The statue is on the right side of Route 19 on the south end of town across the street from the Fort Le Boeuf Museum. The statue was dedicated in 1922 and moved to its current site in 1952 by the Fort Le Boeuf chapter of the Daughters of American Colonists.

To follow the route of Washington's journey from Pittsburgh (Forks of the Ohio) to Waterford (Fort Le Boeuf) by car, consult "Indian Paths of Pennsylvania" by Paul A. W. Wallace. This is a publication of the Pennsylvania Historical and Museum Commission.

*George Washington statue in Waterford, PA. Washington journeyed to Fort Le Boeuf in 1753 to deliver an ultimatum to the French.*

## CUSSEWAGO—MEADVILLE, PENNSYLVANIA

Directions: Go to Allegheny College campus on Park Avenue extension on north side of Meadville. Stone monument is just north of Lords Gate, the main entrance to the campus, and east of Reis Hall, a red brick building.

Cussewago was a town inhabited by Delaware and Iroquois in the 1750s at the juncture where Cussewago Creek enters French Creek. Washington visited this town in 1753 on his way to deliver the ultimatum to the French at Fort Le Boeuf. Cussewago was one of two towns in the region associated with Custaloga, a Delaware chief who was considered pro-French. Colonel Henry Bouquet reported seeing cabins at the site of Cussewago in 1760. Custaloga is reported to be one of the chiefs who signed a peace treaty with Bouquet in 1764 to end Pontiac's War.

Located on the campus of Allegheny College in Meadville, a stone monument marks Washington's stay at Cussewago. The plaque reads:

> In December 1753, George Washington, then a youth of 21, on the historic mission from Governor Dinwiddie of Virginia to the French commander at Fort Le Boeuf, followed the eastern bank of French Creek and camped overnight opposite the mouth of the Cussewago, near the foot of this campus.
>
> Accompanied by his trusty guide, Christopher Gist, an interpreter, Indian trader, frontiersman, three friendly Indians chiefs and a convoy of French soldiers from the fort at Venango, making a party of 16, Washington traveled in five days from the mouth of French Creek to Fort Le Boeuf, now Waterford, 24 miles north of this place.
>
> "Saturday Dec. 8 'We set out and traveled 21 miles to Cussewago, an old Indian town.'" (Diary of Gist.)
>
> His horses having become disabled, the return trip down French Creek was made in canoes obtained at Le Boeuf, and owing to the ice in the stream, six days were covered in reaching Venango, the present site of Franklin.

## VENANGO/FORT MACHAULT FRANKLIN, PENNSYLVANIA

Directions: To reach Franklin from Meadville, take Route 322 east into downtown. Turn left on Elk Street and follow east past Washington Crossing Road (Routes 8/62) and Eighth Street Bridge to fort monuments on left side of Elk Street. These are small curbside monuments.

Venango was a strategic spot on the network of waterways in the Upper Ohio Valley, the place where French Creek enters the Allegheny River. Iroquois and Delaware villages were located there in the 1740s and 1750s. Venango gained status as a place where council fires were lit and important matters discussed.

In 1741, John Fraser, an English trader and blacksmith, established a post at Venango. Fraser carried on a trade with Indian villages long cultivated by the French; he also operated a blacksmith shop that repaired guns. Fraser posed a threat to French designs to increase their influence in the region.

In 1753 the French sent Capt. Phillipe Thomas de Joncaire, the scion of a French trading family, to Venango to establish a base. Joncaire occupied the cabins built by Fraser. The Englishman relocated south to an outpost along the Monongahela River near the spot where General Edward Braddock's army crossed two years later. When George Washington visited Venango in December 1753, he noticed that the French colors were hoisted above one of Fraser's cabins. The delay in building the portage road between Fort Presque Isle and Fort Le Boeuf in the fall of 1753 meant that Venango remained little more than a French outpost under Joncaire's command.

But in the summer of 1755 the French started work to transform the trading post into Fort Machault, named for the French government minister Jean-Baptiste Machault d'Arnouville. The French commander at Fort Machault, Lieutenant Michel Maray de La Chauvignerie, reported difficulties in finding suitable timber and tools for building a fort. Fort Machault was a typical log stockade, rectangular-shaped with four bastions, and stood on the west shore of the Allegheny River about a quarter-mile from the mouth of French Creek or River au Boeuf. Fort Machault was used primarily as a supply depot for Fort Duquesne. The French built a sawmill nearby so they could build river rafts to transport troops and supplies down the Allegheny.

Fort Machault was also a launching point for a number of raids by mixed parties of French soldiers and Delaware and Shawnee warriors on homesteads in the Susquehanna Valley and Blue Mountain region of Pennsylvania. On one of those raids a family drama ensued. Ensign Michel La Chauvignerie, the 17-year-old son of the fort commander, became separated from the other members of his raiding party in the Blue Mountains and after several days wandering in the wilderness he approached provincial Fort Henry and surrendered in October 1757. La Chauvignerie was interrogated about French strength at Fort Machault by no less than Pennsylvania Chief Justice William Allen. He was eventually put on parole in Philadelphia and exchanged.

With the fall of Fort Duquesne in November 1758, Fort Machault became the southernmost French post in the Ohio Valley. French troops gathered there to prepare for an attack to retake Fort Duquesne. But the French themselves conceded that this log fort was too weak to withstand enemy cannon fire. When Fort Niagara fell to the British in July 1759, the French evacuated and burned Fort Machault.

*The Fort Machault monument.*
*The French built Fort Machault where French Creek*
*enters the Allegheny River.*

The British built a post called Fort Venango near the site in 1760. But it was overrun and the garrison was wiped out during Pontiac's Rebellion in May 1763.

Today the sites of Fort Machault and Fort Venango are located in a residential neighborhood on the east side of Franklin. But it is possible to walk down to the Allegheny River at several spots and get a good sense of the terrain. The mouth of French Creek is visible from the left on the west shore. The door to Fort Machault faced the river and the garrison looked out at a ring of forested hills on the river's east shore.

A small stone monument marking Fort Machault is located in front of a house at 616 Elk Street, three houses from the intersection of 6th and Elk Streets. Access to the undeveloped river bottom is afforded by the street leading past Wegel Brothers Marina at 704 Elk Street.

A small stone monument marking Fort Venango is located near the intersection of 8th and Elk Streets. This monument is located in front of a vacant lot and across from Evangelical Lutheran Church.

# KING BEAVER'S TOWN
## SAUCONK — SAWCUNK — SHINGAS TOWN
## BEAVER, PENNSYLVANIA

*Directions: State historical marker on Route 68 (3rd St.) at Wilson Avenue on east side of Beaver. Turn left at Wilson Avenue for two blocks. A Greenbelt park in residential neighborhood overlooks the Ohio River at this spot.*

This Delaware village was an important fur trading center and base for many of the raids against English settlements east of the Alleghenies following the defeat of Braddock's expedition. It was situated west of where the Beaver River empties into the Ohio River and along the Great Path which connected the Forks of the Ohio with the French settlement and fort at Detroit. The Beaver River takes its name from the plentiful supply of beaver trapped in the area.

This village was known by several different names, but the state historical marker refers to it as King Beaver's Town. King Beaver was the leader of one of the Delaware clans and a brother of Shingas. King Beaver and Shingas sided with the French when war broke out. Shingas gained notoriety among the English for his raids on forts and settlements in eastern Pennsylvania. Both King Beaver and Shingas resided here for periods during the 1750s, but they also based their operations out of other villages such as Kittanning and Kuskuski. Also living here for a time was Killbuck, a Delaware chief who led raids against English settlements in the Potomac and Shenandoah Valleys of Virginia.

Hugh Gibson, an English prisoner captured in a raid on Fort Robinson in the Shermans Creek area of the Susquehanna Valley, spent portions of 1757 and 1758 living at King Beaver's Town. Gibson, a 15-year-old youth, was taken when a raiding party attacked Fort Robinson in 1756 while the local militia was gathering the harvest. Gibson was led first to Kittanning where he was adopted as a member of the Delaware. When Kittanning was attacked by Pennsylvania troops, Gibson was removed to Kuskuski and then to King Beaver's Town.

Gibson fell in and out of favor with his captors during his stay at King Beaver's Town. They suspected him (with good reason) of plotting to escape. Once when Gibson heard of preparations for a raid on settlements in central Pennsylvania, he asked to go along. But Shingas sent him on a mission to Kuskuski instead, and he was later moved to a village along the Muskingum River in Ohio. He escaped from there in 1759 with two girls captured in one of the first raids on Pennsylvania settlements, Barbara Leininger and Marie LeRoy. They made their way to British-held Fort Pitt and eventually went back to their homes.

18

## Logstown—North of Ambridge, Pennsylvania

Directions: Take Route 65 north of Ambridge along the Ohio River to Logan Lane by a Sheetz store. Turn right on Logan Lane to Duss Avenue also known as old Route 65. Turn right on Duss Avenue. Pass by state historical marker for Logstown on right side and small white monument for Legionville, the camp in 1792 of the American army under command of General Anthony Wayne. Continue short distance until you spot 15-ton boulder with Logstown plaque in front of red brick Byers building on right side. A good view of the Ohio River can be found by going to a small cemetery across Route 65 from Sheetz at Logan Lane. A small blue marker noting the location of Logstown is here.

Logstown was one of the principal Native American villages in the Ohio Valley, a place where the Iroquois sought to exert influence over the region and the site of important diplomatic parlays with the French and British. Logstown, or Chiningue as the Native Americans and French called it, was situated on a plateau on the north side of the Ohio River, 18 miles downstream from the Forks of the Ohio. Its name stems perhaps from a pile of half-sunken logs in the Ohio at this spot or the log cabins that provided shelter for the village inhabitants. In any event by 1754, the French decided that available timber was so scarce at Logstown that it was not the best place to construct a new fort. They turned their sights on the Forks of the Ohio instead.

Founded by the Shawnee in the 1720s, Logstown evolved into a multi-ethnic village with Delaware, Seneca, Mohawk and Wyandot living there. The town gained stature after 1747 when Tanacharison, the newly appointed Iroquois viceroy for the region, made his headquarters there. Indian traders such as George Croghan for the British and Phillipe Thomas de Joncaire for the French extended their operations to Logstown. In 1748, Conrad Weiser, the Pennsylvania Indian emissary, journeyed to Logstown to strengthen ties with the tribes that had migrated westward and advance British claims to the Ohio Valley. Weiser took a rough survey of the town's fighting strength and concluded it could field nearly 800 warriors from ten tribes: Seneca, Shawnee, Wyandot, Mississauga, Mohawk, Mohican, Onondaga, Cayuga, Oneida and Delaware.

The French expedition leader, Pierre-Joseph Celeron de Blainville, visited Logstown in 1749. He reported that it was one of the largest villages on the Ohio, numbering 50 cabins, and also noted that both French and British flags were flying conspicuously above the town. Celeron ordered the British flag taken down.

Agents of Virginia's Ohio Company came to Logstown in 1751-52 to gain permission from Tanacharison to build a storehouse at the Forks. In November 1753, enroute to Fort Le Boeuf, George Washington spent five days at Logstown meeting with various chiefs and enlisting Tanacharison as a travel partner for the rest of his journey to deliver an ultimatum to the French. Within a month after Washington's departure from Fort Le Boeuf to return home to Williamsburg, the French dispatched an advance party under Lt. Michel Maray de La Chauvignerie to Logstown to reconnoiter the site for a fort. But La Chauvignerie reported that the timber in the area had already been used for firewood and to build cabins. The French decided to build Fort Duquesne at the Forks after it was learned the Ohio Company was building a storehouse there.

After Tanacharison's departure into exile in 1754 and the fall of Fort Duquesne in 1758, Logstown's importance declined, and later observers reported it in ruins. Today, despite some industrial activity in the area, you can still get a good geographical sense of the plateau on which Logstown was situated overlooking the Ohio River and a series of hills on the south bank.

The main Logstown monument is a large boulder on Duss Avenue north of Ambridge in front of a red brick building currently occupied by Oneal, a metals company, and the Ambridge school teachers association. This building at one time headquartered A. M. Byers, a steel company. The inscription on the monument reads:

> Logstown 1725-1758 An historic Indian village was located a short distance northwest of this spot. It was founded by Shawnee and later occupied by Delaware, Seneca, Mohawk and Wyandot. Here in 1748 Conrad Weiser, agent of Pennsylvania, negotiated a treaty that opened the region west of the Alleghenies to Anglo-Saxon influence and development. June 11, 1752, the Treaty of Logstown was made between the Iroquois Indians and the Virginians, giving the latter the right to build a fort and establish a trading post at the Forks of Ohio. Major George Washington held council at Logstown with Tanacharison, Scarouady, Shingas and other chiefs Nov. 24-30, 1753 while on his important mission to Fort Le Boeuf.
>
> —Fort McIntosh Chapter of the Daughters of the American Revolution 1932.

## Fort Duquesne—Point State Park, Pittsburgh, Pennsylvania

Directions: Point State Park is reached from the east and west by Interstates 376 and 279, by Route 8 from the north and Route 51 from the south.

The French achieved an important objective in April 1754 when they occupied the Forks of the Ohio and built Fort Duquesne to guard this gateway to the Ohio region. The Forks is the triangle of land, now in the city of Pittsburgh, where the Allegheny and Monongahela Rivers meet to form the Ohio River. From there the Ohio River flows 987 miles to the Mississippi River. For the French, occupation of the Forks was necessary to secure the links between their colony of Canada and possessions in Louisiana and the Illinois territory and keep the British out of the Ohio Valley. They wanted to stop the incursions of English traders and agents of the Virginia-based Ohio Company into the region.

The strategic importance of the Forks was not lost on those who passed by the spot. Virginia emissary George Washington surveyed the place enroute to Fort Le Boeuf in November 1753 and was impressed by the command it had over both rivers, plentiful timber supply and fertile river bottom land. "I spent some Time in viewing the Rivers, and the Land in the Fork, which I think extremely well situated for a Fort," he wrote in his journal.

The French had actually considered building their fort at the Iroquois village of Logstown 18 miles downstream on the Ohio. But their plans were delayed in the fall of 1753 by the slow progress on the portage road between Fort Presque Isle and Fort Le Boeuf. Their attention was drawn to the forks when word came that the Ohio Company was building a small storehouse there known somewhat grandly as Fort Prince George. This was a countermove ordered by Virginia Gov. Robert Dinwiddie after Washington's trip revealed the full nature of French designs in the Ohio Valley. Ensign Edward Ward commanded a party of 41 workers and soldiers hurrying to finish work on Fort Prince George when the French came. An army of 500 French soldiers and Indian allies arrived on a flotilla of 300 canoes and 60 bateaux that sailed down the Allegheny. Ward was in no position to offer resistance to the French who vastly outnumbered his party and were armed with cannon; the French expedition leader, Claude Pecaudy de Contrecoeur, arranged terms whereby Ward departed peacefully the next day.

Tanacharison, the Iroquois viceroy, had supported the Ohio Company's efforts to build the storehouse. He was on the scene when the French arrived and strongly protested the occupation.

The French named Fort Duquesne, for Marquis Duquesne, governor of Canada. Fort Duquesne was located on the Allegheny River shore of the Forks. The earth-and-log fort was square-shaped with four bastions enclosing the commandant's quarters, guardhouse, shops, barracks and a small parade ground. The bastions contained such buildings as a blacksmith shop and powder magazine. Defensive outer works were also constructed as well as a palisade located east of the fort.

Fort Duquesne occupied a strategic spot, but French officers considered it a difficult place to defend. The fort was subject to flooding and vulnerable to bombardment if cannon were placed atop the hills on the Monongahela River side.

The French were prepared to evacuate the fort when Gen. Edward Braddock's army approached in 1755. But they met with unanticipated success when a mixed force of French and Indians sallied out into the forests to meet Braddock and brought his army to ruin. Three years later the French evacuated and blew up the fort when a much more powerful army under General John Forbes approached the Forks.

During the war, Fort Duquesne was a gathering place for France's Native American allies. These tribes included not only the Delaware and Shawnee, but also warriors from a number of distant Great Lake tribes such as the Ottawa, Huron, Potawatomis and Mississauga. After the French left, the British built a larger and more imposing fortification at the Forks and named it Fort Pitt.

Today the historic Forks area is part of Point State Park, a 36-acre park of fields, walkways, fountains and historical markers. The park was created forty years ago in an area cleared of slums and warehouses and excavated by archaeologists. The outline of Fort Duquesne's walls is traced in stone in a field just east of the fountain. In the center of the outline is a bronze marker showing the plan of Fort Duquesne. You can look west from this spot at the beginnings of the Ohio River, the Gateway to the West for the French and British. The names of the commanders of Fort Duquesne and other French military leaders in the Ohio region are inscribed in a tablet at the entrance to the Fort Pitt Blockhouse, a surviving structure of Fort Pitt.

The Fort Pitt Museum, administered by the Pennsylvania Historical and Museum Commission, is located in the restored Monongahela bastion of Fort Pitt near the blockhouse. This is one of the premier museums in the mid-Atlantic region for interpreting the French and Indian War. The museum features two stories of exhibits, dioramas, and models exploring every facet of the Great Power rivalry for the Ohio Valley.

## FORT NECESSITY NATIONAL BATTLEFIELD
## FARMINGTON, PENNSYLVANIA

Fort Necessity's appearance belies the important role it played in the French and Indian War. This rudely built circular log fort in a marshy clearing was the scene of a desultory battle in the rain between two combatants not even officially at war with each other. The fighting involved only about 1,000 soldiers and earned few heroics for anyone, but echoes from the volleys fired here were heard around the world and pushed Great Britain, France, other European powers and dozens of Native American tribes into a worldwide war for seven years.

The Fort Necessity campaign began in April 1754 when Colonel George Washington led 132 Virginia soldiers from Alexandria, Virginia, toward the Forks of the Ohio. A French army had occupied the forks earlier that spring and ejected a Virginia garrison that was building a fort there. Governor Robert Dinwiddie ordered Washington's expedition to regain the strategic spot. But this was a tall order given the French superiority in troops and arms. Washington's men trekked over the Allegheny Mountains without all the supplies promised by Dinwiddie. But the Virginians benefitted from the information about French movements and counsel provided by Tanacharison, or Half King, the Iroquois viceroy in the region, and the English trader Christopher Gist who had a plantation nearby.

Washington picked a site six miles east of the imposing Chestnut Ridge for a base camp. This area known as Great Meadows provided forage for the horses and a "charming field for an encounter," according to Washington in a letter to Dinwiddie. In late May shortly after arrival at camp, Washington's men ambushed a French scouting party and killed their commander, Ensign Coulon de Jumonville, at nearby Jumonville Glen. Washington then built the log stockade called Fort Necessity and encircled it with trenches and embankments. A reinforcement of 250 Virginia and South Carolina soldiers arrived. They were equipped with much-valued swivel guns. Washington's troops spent two weeks building a road to Gist's plantation.

Reports of French troops on the march prompted the Virginians to withdraw to Fort Necessity where the reinforcements were stationed. On July 3, an army of 600 French soldiers and 100 pro-French Indians under the command of Captain Louis Coulon de Villiers, Jumonville's half brother, attacked the fort. The French were content to fire on the fort's defenders from the safety of the woods. They had an easier time finding targets and British casualties mounted. The attackers killed all the livestock and horses. After several hours of fighting, heavy rains dampened the powder supplies and made it impossible for either side to fire. The British trenches were swamped with water and the defenders' situation was getting desperate. At about 8 p.m. Villiers called to the British asking if they wanted to negotiate. Washington dispatched a Dutchman, Jacob Van Braam, to the French lines, and a surrender document was agreed upon that allowed Washington's force to depart with the honors of war and bearing their arms. Two British hostages, Van Braam and Capt. Robert

*The author's son stands at the gate of the reconstructed Fort Necessity. This is a premier site for learning about the French and Indian War.*

Stobo, remained with the French. But the surrender terms caused an international controversy. Van Braam and Washington had unwittingly agreed to a phrase that stated they had assassinated Jumonville at the ambush a month earlier.

The fall of Fort Necessity resulted in the British expulsion from the Ohio country and the decision by the wavering Delaware and Shawnee tribes to side with the French. Tanacharison and other pro-British Indians fled to the east.

Within a year, Gen. Edward Braddock's army marched by the burnt ruins of Fort Necessity on their way to another debacle. In 1770, long after the war ended, Washington purchased Great Meadows and remained in possession of the land until his death in 1799.

Fort Necessity today is the only federal historic site in the mid-Atlantic region that interprets the French and Indian War. As such, it tops the list of places to visit to learn about the period. The park visitor center has a movie and fine exhibits. The reconstructed Fort Necessity and entrenchments sit on the site of the original stockade. Visitors can also walk the trace of Braddock Road still visible in the woods near the stockade. The Fort Necessity National Battlefield also administers the related nearby sites of Braddock's Grave and Jumonville Glen.

## WASHINGTON SPRING/HALF KING'S ROCKS MOUNT SUMMIT, PENNSYLVANIA

*Directions: From Route 40 at the Mount Summit Inn, take Jumonville Road north one mile. Look for signs for Washington Spring and Rock Fort Camp on right. State highway marker Braddock Road (Rock Fort Camp) on Route 40 at Summit.*

Chestnut Ridge is one of the Allegheny Mountain ranges, the last mountain barrier on the eastward journey along Nemacolin's Path and Braddock Road to the Forks of the Ohio. Along the top of the imposing 2,500-foot ridge are several historic sites where scouting parties and armies camped.

Washington Spring is a spot where George Washington camped several times on his journeys into the Ohio country. Washington first stayed at the spring in November 1753 on his way to Fort Le Boeuf, then again in May 1754 on the Fort Necessity expedition. He stayed there a third time in June 1755 as he accompanied General Edward Braddock's army on the march to Fort Duquesne. This is also the vicinity of Braddock's Rock Fort Camp, the army's tenth stop on that expedition.

Washington Spring is located on private property and "no trespassing" signs are posted. But the spring and a remnant of Braddock Road are visible through the woods on the right side of Jumonville Road. Two blue and gold historical markers for Washington Spring and Rock Fort Camp mark the spot.

On the left side of Jumonville Road in this vicinity is Half King's Rocks, where Tanacharison, the Iroquois viceroy, was camped on May 28, 1754, the eve of the Battle of Jumonville Glen. Washington's force met Tanacharison at this camp before making the final approach to the French camp at Jumonville Glen, 1.5 miles to the northeast.

## JUMONVILLE GLEN—MT. SUMMIT, PENNSYLVANIA

*Directions: From Fort Necessity National Battlefield, drive 4.9 miles west on Route 40. Turn right on Jumonville Road at Mount Summit and drive 2.5 miles north. Jumonville Glen is located on right side. A half-mile access roads leads to the Glen.*

In 1754, Jumonville Glen was a secluded spot off the beaten path on Chestnut Ridge. It remains that way today under the care of the National Park Service. Junmonville Glen takes its name from the French officer, Ensign Coulon de Jumonville, killed there in a skirmish on May 28, 1754, with Virginia troops led by Col. George Washington. The brief fight that resulted in Jumonville's death is shrouded in mystery and controversy, but historians agree it was one of the flashpoints leading to the French and Indian War.

Jumonville led a scouting party of 50 French soldiers on May 23 from the French-held Forks of the Ohio to search for British troops and give them a summons to leave the territory of the French King. But he was also under orders to send a runner back to his superiors with word of his findings before he presented such summons to the British. In the meantime, Tanacharison and other Indians friendly to the British tracked Jumonville's movements. Washington had arrived at Great Meadows on May 24 and soon he received word from Tanacharison about the French party. The trader Christopher Gist also reported that French soldiers had reached his plantation and seemed intent on wrecking it, but were dissuaded by Indians guarding it.

On May 27, Tanacharison sent word that about 30 French soldiers were camped at a hidden ravine one-half mile off the main trail on Chestnut Ridge. The French camp was about seven miles west of the British base at

***Washington Spring. George Washington camped here several times on his travels.***

Great Meadows. Colonel Washington resolved on an all-night march to confront them. His force of 40 men tramped through dark woods during a heavy rain and reached Tanacharison's camp on the ridge at Half King's Rocks near dawn. From there, Tanacharison led Washington to the French camp in the ravine beneath a large rock cliff. The French were cooking breakfast; security at the camp was lax with no guards posted.

Washington divided his force, and directed one group under Captain Adam Stephen to surround the French on the left side of the ravine. As he positioned his men, the French spotted them and fired a volley. After this first volley, accounts differ. The French claim Jumonville yelled out that he was on a diplomatic mission and demanded a cease-fire.

Washington said he heard no call from Jumonville and ordered his men to return fire. After fifteen minutes of firing, the French surrendered, with 10 killed including Jumonville and 21 captured. One Frenchman escaped and gave the alarm at the Forks. Washington went back to Great Meadows and set about building Fort Necessity.

The skirmish sparked an international controversy over whether Jumonville was engaged in a diplomatic or military mission, or both. The French published pamphlets to buttress their position; Washington questioned why the French employed secrecy and kept hidden if they were truly diplomats.

The National Park Service maintains the Jumonville Glen site today. Visitors can get a good flavor of wilderness battle by taking the steps down the rock cliff, and into the ravine with the small stream where the French camped. The area looks much the same as in 1754. The Glen is open 10 a.m. to 5 p.m., but closed in the winter.

## CAPTAIN FRANCOIS—MARIE LE MARCHAND, SIEUR DE LIGNERIS AND THE FRENCH MARINES

Many French soldiers in the Ohio Valley were members of a military force known as the Marines or Compagnies Franches de la Marine. The marines were stationed in the colonies of Canada and Louisiana. They manned the chain of French forts protecting the fur trade and were under the administration of King Louis XV's naval minister who oversaw overseas affairs. The first marines were recruited in France in the late 17th century and encouraged to become permanent residents of New France when their six-year term of enlistment was up. By 1750, many of the marines—especially the officers—were Canadian born. In 1753-54, the French sent an invasion force comprised of marines and Canadian militia to the Ohio Valley. During the French and Indian War, it was common practice for one or two marine officers to accompany the Delaware and Shawnee on their raids along the Pennsylvania and Virginia frontiers.

The marines' regulation uniform was a grey-white coat with blue cuffs and coat lining, a blue waistcoat, breeches and stockings, and tricorn hat. In the forest wilderness, uniform standards were more lax especially during the harsh winters when coats made of blankets called capotes were worn.

Captain De Ligneris (sometimes spelled Lignery) was an officer with Baron de Longueuil's military expedition into the Ohio Valley in 1739. Ligneris (1704-59) was commander of French Fort Ouiatenon on the Wabash River in the Illinois territory in 1752. By 1755, he was in the Ohio Valley serving as second-in command at Fort Duquesne and fighting at the Battle of the Monongahela. Ligneris succeeded as commander of Fort Duquesne in 1756 and it became his lot to preside over the waning of French power in the Ohio Valley.

Ligneris abandoned and destroyed Fort Duquesne in 1758 with the approach of a powerful British army under General John Forbes. He retreated to Fort Machault on the Allegheny River and made preparations to drive the British from the Forks of the Ohio. Just when his plans for a counterattack at the Forks were nearing completion in the summer of 1759, the French faced a dire threat with the British siege of Fort Niagara. Ligneris led a relief force of troops from the upper Ohio Valley forts and the western territories north to Niagara. But the relief force met defeat at the Battle of La Belle Famille on July 24. Ligneris was mortally wounded in the battle and captured by the British; he died of his wounds on August 29 at Fort Niagara, a month after the French surrendered the post to the British.

# 2

# Braddock's March to Disaster, March–July 1755

## INTRODUCTION

On paper, the battle plan looked easy. General Edward Braddock was to lead an army of British regulars to oust the French from the Forks of Ohio and swing north to conquer Fort Niagara, the chokepoint for supplies moving from Quebec to the western territories. The grandiose plans, however, were drawn up by men half a world away in London who knew little about the North American frontier. In reality, the great distances involved in traversing the wilderness interior of the continent, logistics of moving men and supplies across daunting mountain ranges, and unfamiliarity with forest combat combined to turn Braddock's expedition into an epic military disaster.

Braddock's army met its ruin near the banks of the Monongahela River in modern-day North Braddock almost 250 years ago. But military historians still point fingers and cast blame for the many things that went wrong for the British on that hot summer day, July 9, 1755. To set the record straight, Braddock's 1,400-man advance guard did not stumble into an ambush, as many assume. On a narrow woodland path, troops ran headlong into a force of some 400 French and Native American warriors rushing from Fort Duquesne to engage them.

The French recovered quickly from the shock even though their dashing commander, Captain Daniel Beaujeu, was killed in the initial volley. The British did not adapt their European-style battlefield tactics to suit the forested terrain. Even though they fought bravely at first, their ranks were decimated by fire from an unseen foe and two-thirds of the soldiers were killed or wounded. The remnants of a proud army fled in retreat. Braddock died of wounds sustained in the battle and was buried in an unmarked grave along the line of retreat.

While Braddock's defeat had dire consequences for English settlers of Pennsylvania, Maryland, and Virginia, the real blow to the colonies came when surviving elements of his army left the frontiers undefended. Colonel Thomas Dunbar, commander of a 1,000-man rear guard, decided to withdraw from Fort Cumberland and retreat to winter quarters in Albany, New York even though it was the middle of summer. By October, Delaware and Shawnee raiding parties attacked the Great Cove and Susquehanna Valley and found few equipped to offer resistance.

When Braddock landed the previous March at Alexandria, Virginia, few could have foreseen this melancholy fate. British regulars, thought many on both sides of the Atlantic, were sure to vanquish a backwoods foe. Braddock huddled with the colonial governors and arranged for the arrival of the 44th and 48th regiments from Ireland. He also invited George Washington, the young Virginia colonel who had fought the French at Fort Necessity the previous year, to join his staff.

The army split in two for the first leg of the march. The 44th regiment under Sir Peter Halkett headed northwest from Alexandria to Winchester, Virginia. Dunbar and the 48th regiment headed north to Frederick, Maryland, and then west to cross the Potomac River at the mouth of Conococheague Creek at modern Williamsport. Braddock rode in a chariot to Frederick where he attempted to deal with the army's considerable logistic and supply problems. Braddock's soldiers faced

SITES AT A GLANCE—This map will give you a feel for the general locations of sites in this chapter. Some sites overlap and are not shown on this map.

Ft. Duquesne ◆ ◆ Braddock's grave
◆ Ft. Necessity
Ft. Cumberland ◆
Potomac crossing
Hopewell Meeting House

the herculean task of hauling heavy cannon over mountain ranges and through miles of wilderness so they could breach the walls of Fort Duquesne. Braddock borrowed seamen skilled in the use of block and tackle to assist in this task.

Braddock was short of wagons to carry equipment and provisions. Here Benjamin Franklin, a prominent member of Pennsylvania's provincial assembly, entered the picture. Franklin met Braddock at Frederick and offered his assistance to round up horses and wagons from the farmers of Lancaster, York, and Cumberland Counties. Franklin made a crafty appeal to the German farmers of that region, mixing the carrot of the King's payment for those who offered their wagons with the threat that soldiers would come to seize that not volunteered. Within two weeks, a convoy of wagons was on its way to join Braddock.

During his meeting with Braddock, Franklin observed that Indians lying in ambush in the woods could pose a threat to troops marching in formation. But Braddock dismissed his concerns, and Franklin reported him saying: "These savages may, indeed be a formidable enemy to your raw American militia but upon the King's regular and disciplined troops, sir, it is impossible they should make any impression."

In his autobiography, Franklin gave this assessment of Braddock: "This general was, I think, a brave man and might probably have made a figure as a good officer in some European war. But he had too much self-confidence, too high an opinion of the validity of regular troops, and too mean a one of both Americans and Indians."

## DUNBAR'S REGIMENT CROSSES POTOMAC
## WILLIAMSPORT, MARYLAND

*Directions: To reach the visitor center at Cushwa Warehouse, take exit 2 off Interstate 81. Take Route 11 south to downtown Williamsport where it becomes Potomac Street, and look for park area at river. For a panoramic view of the Potomac River, visit the earthworks of Fort Doubleday, a Civil War era fort in Williamsport, located one block south of Potomac Street at the intersection of West Salisbury and Commerce Streets. Climb the stone steps uphill to the fort.*

A late spring snowstorm greeted Col. Thomas Dunbar's 48th regiment as it headed to Frederick, Maryland, in April 1755. General Braddock followed his troops days later in a horse-driven carriage. Leaving Frederick, the British regulars marched on a road roughly paralleling modern Alternate Route 40 and crossed a summit known today as Braddock Heights. Halfway up the heights on the south side of Alt. Route 40, a stone monument visible from the

road notes that both Braddock and George Washington traveled this route in 1755. Dunbar's regiment followed Alt. Route 40 to South Mountain, the first of many major mountain barriers facing the British. At this point, there is disagreement among historians as to whether Dunbar's regiment crossed South Mountain via Turner's Gap (Alt. Route 40) or via Fox's Gap (Reno Monument Road) to the south on its westward march.

The next physical barrier facing Dunbar's soldiers was the Potomac River at modern Williamsport. In the 1750s, this place was known as Conococheague, for it is where the Conococheague Creek enters the Potomac. Indian traders were based here and in 1744 Evan Watkins got permission from the Virginia Assembly to establish a ferry across the Potomac from the mouth of the Conococheague on the Maryland side to his landing on the Virginia side.

Some conjecture exists as to why Dunbar even crossed the Potomac here. British officers may have mistakenly believed that a road led to Fort Cumberland at this crossing. Others suggest that Dunbar was searching for supplies and forage for horses. And some see a political motive to drum up support for the expedition in Maryland and Pennsylvania. Once Dunbar crossed the Potomac, he marched south to meet Sir Peter Halkett's regiment at a location north of Winchester. Braddock himself crossed the Potomac at Swearingen Ferry at modern Shepardstown, West Virginia. A Maryland highway sign on Route 34 in Sharpsburg notes his travel along this route.

*Roadside marker for Swearingen Ferry.*
*Braddock crossed the Potomac at this historic ford.*

Today the public has ample access to the riverside area at Williamsport where Dunbar crossed the Potomac. The area is part of the Chesapeake and Ohio Canal National Park. The park's Williamsport Visitor Center is located in the Cushwa Warehouse, a building next to the Cushwa boat basin. The C & O Canal towpath runs by the distinctive 1834 stone Conococheague Aqueduct that spans the mouth of the creek. Other walkways lead to the river flats area.

## SPRINGFIELD FARM—WILLIAMSPORT, MARYLAND

*Directions: Take Exit 2 off I-81 south. Go south on Route 11 to Springfield Lane. Turn left by Maryland historical marker for Springfield Farm. Springfield Lane leads to white barn/museum.*

Springfield Farm served as a supply depot for Col. Thomas Dunbar's regiment. It has its beginnings in the 1720s as an Indian trading post situated along the Great Trail, a warpath used by the Iroquois, Cherokee, and Catawba in their respective campaigns against each other. The land on which Springfield Farm is located was part of the land manor of Conococheague created in 1736 by Lord Baltimore, Maryland's proprietor. Baltimore leased tracts to various traders and settlers. During the Braddock campaign, Conococheague was used as a place to store flour and other provisions sent from Pennsylvania.

Two fieldstone buildings on the Springfield Farm, the springhouse and the storehouse (or stillhouse), are associated with this period. The storehouse was used to store provisions for Braddock's army. The springhouse is linked to Col. Thomas Cresap, a colorful Indian trader and commissary to Braddock's army. Cresap moved his base of operations from Oldtown, Maryland, to Conococheague after Braddock's defeat left the frontier exposed to raiding parties. Cresap reportedly lived in the springhouse although some dispute that. George Washington is supposed to have pointed to the structure as Cresap's abode when he visited Williamsport as president in 1790 to inspect it as a possible site for the nation's capital.

Today a section of Springfield Farm is open to the public as a town museum and park. The springhouse and storehouse are in the section of the farm still in private hands, but the buildings can be seen from the public area. The town maintains a museum adjacent to the barn with exhibits on Williamsport's history from Native American habitation through the Civil War and Chesapeake and Ohio Canal era. The museum is open Sundays from 1 p.m. to 4 p.m.

## BRADDOCK'S ARMY PASSES HOPEWELL MEETING HOUSE—CLEAR BROOK, VIRGINIA

*Directions to Hopewell Meeting House: Take Route 11 north of Winchester to Clear Brook. Turn left on Route 672. Look for stone monument for Hopewell Meeting House. Go west on Route 672 until Hopewell Road. Look for meeting house sign, building in grove of trees on hill, south side.*

Sir Peter Halkett led the 44th regiment from Alexandria and west across Virginia to the Shenandoah Valley. The army's route of march roughly parallels modern Routes 7 and 9 passing modern Leesburg, Virginia, Key's or Vestal's Gap across the Blue Ridge and modern Charles Town, West Virginia. From Charles Town, the route parallels modern Route 51 part of the way and then cuts south to modern Clear Brook at the junction of Routes 11 and 672 about eight miles north of Winchester, Va. This is where Col. Thomas Dunbar's regiment joined Halkett's after it left Conococheague. The army then marched west along modern Route 672 which even today is also known as Braddock's Road, or Sir John's Road for Braddock's quartermaster general Sir John St. Clair.

The Hopewell Meeting House and graveyard is a landmark on Route 672 that witnessed the passage of both Halkett's and Dunbar's regiments. The Meeting House has served the Quaker population in the area since 1734. A log meeting house stood on the spot when Braddock's troops marched by. The log house burned in 1757 and was replaced by the current grey stone house. This building has three chimneys and is surrounded by a stone wall. The east end was built in 1759; the west end in 1789.

The Meeting House is a peaceful spot on a tree-shaded knoll. The march of Braddock's army can be followed along a six-mile stretch of Route 672, which passes apple orchards enroute to Apple Pie Ridge. Follow Route 672 through a gap in Little North Mountain to Route 654. Turn left on Route 654 to join Route 522.

*Hopewell Meeting House.*

Head west on Route 522 which roughly parallels the army's line of march. Then head west on Route 127 through Bloomery Gap to the Forks-of-the-Cacapon River, both natural landmarks in Braddock's day. The army's route then headed north along Little Cacapon River to Col. Thomas Cresap's trading post at Oldtown and then west along the Potomac River to Fort Cumberland. The route of Braddock's army is hard to follow in this region because many sections of the old road have been abandoned and modern roads go elsewhere. The main source for tracking the road in this area is Braddock's Road through the Virginia Colony by Walter S. Hough. This book was published in 1970 by the Winchester-Frederick County Historical Society, but the reader should be cognizant that thirty years of road work and development have intervened since Hough traced the route.

One thing to remember is that Braddock's army was spread out. Various detachments marched along these routes at different intervals so the movement of the entire army occurred over a period of weeks.

## BRADDOCK'S MARCH:
## FORT CUMBERLAND AND THE NARROWS
## CUMBERLAND, MARYLAND

*Directions to Fort Cumberland: Take I-68 west to Exit 43B to downtown Cumberland. Turn left on Harrison Street, right on South Mechanic Street, then left at Baltimore Street, and park at Western Maryland Station Visitor's Center. Walk across Baltimore Street bridge over Wills Creek to start walking tour in Riverside Park. Then follow along Washington, Greene, and West Streets.*

*Directions to The Narrows. Take Exit 44 off Interstate 68. Follow Alternate Route 40 through Narrows. At east end, there is a pullover where Wills Creek flows through Narrows. Driving westbound look for Maryland State highway sign for "The Narrows." This sign is by parking lot for Kline's Restaurant on right side. There is a small picnic area by sign overlooking a flood-channeled Wills Creek. At one time, people could drive to the top of Wills Mountain to get a bird's eye view of The Narrows, but that route has been closed for a number of years, according to local tourism officials.*

Fort Cumberland, a provincial Maryland post, served as the staging point for Braddock's army. It was the army's last breathing space before making the hard 110-mile trek across mountains to the Forks of the Ohio. In 1750, the Ohio Company established a trading post at this spot where Wills Creek enters the Potomac River. Maryland troops under orders of Gov. Horatio Sharpe built a palisaded log fort here in 1754.

Braddock arrived at the fort on May 10, 1755, and spent a month dealing with the supply and logistics problems that had beset him since he landed in America. His entire

*Fort Cumberland marker.*
*A walking tour explains the fort's history.*

army was camped at the fort and this necessitated a never-ending search for food for the men and fodder for the horses. The prospect of having Indian allies with the expedition fizzled here. Braddock alienated the pro-British Indians when he ordered their women away. The action was taken to break up romances between the soldiers and women, but it left Braddock with but a handful of scouts for the rough road ahead.

A glimpse of fort life is found in the diary of a Mrs. Browne, a widow who accompanied her brother on the expedition from London to Fort Cumberland. Mrs. Browne served as a nurse and reached Fort Cumberland after the army had passed through. Her brother served as a commissary and died of illness at Fort Cumberland. Mrs. Browne's diary is full of interesting observations about the lodging, food, and entertainment she encountered. She wrote on June 13, 1755:

At 6 we came to Fort Cumberland, the most desolate Place I ever saw. Went to Mr. Cherrington who receiv'd me kindly, drank Tea, and then went to the Governor to apply for Quarters. I was put into a Hole that I could see day light through every Log, and a port Hole for a Window; which was as good a Room as any in the Fort.

The Fort Cumberland site is on a hill overlooking the juncture of the Potomac River and Wills Creek. The area is a residential neighborhood, but the city of Cumberland has established a walking tour of several blocks that explains the fort's history. The city has installed 28 interpretive plaques at points and a reconstructed section of the fort palisade along the tour.

On June 7, Braddock's troops began moving west from Fort Cumberland. Days earlier, the army's road builders had encountered a major obstacle trying to clear a route for the army across Wills Mountain. A naval officer named Ensign Spendelow found a better route between Wills Mountain to the north and Haystack Mountain to the south.

This route became known as the "Gateway to the West" to future generations of travelers. Today it is called The Narrows, one of the major natural landmarks associated with the Braddock campaign.

## BRADDOCK'S MARCH:
### ACROSS THE ALLEGHENIES TO THE YOUGHIOGHENY RIVER — WESTERN MARYLAND & PENNSYLVANIA

Once Braddock's army left Fort Cumberland, the soldiers faced a tough march across the mountain ranges of the Alleghenies until they reached the Great Crossing of the Youghiogheny River. The line of march closely parallels modern Alt. Route 40. Maryland highway signs mark several of the army's encampments, but the geographical features provide the best testament to the challenges facing the army on this march. West of The Narrows at modern La Vale, Alt. Route 40 parallels a stream called Braddock Run. This is the vicinity of Spendelow Camp, an encampment named for the young ensign who discovered The Narrows. The army made slow progress marching steadily uphill to Martin's Plantation (modern Frostburg) where another encampment was made. A state marker on a traffic island along Alt. Route 40 on the eastern edge of Frostburg notes this.

Crossing the 3,000-foot high summit of Big Savage Mountain west of Martin's Plantation posed a major problem. This mountain is named for John Savage, member of a surveying party in 1736. Several army wagons broke away from their handlers on the steep grades and plunged down the western slope of Big Savage Mountain. Braddock's army made a camp at Savage River in a pleasant valley between Big Savage Mountain and Little Savage Mountain. A state highway marker for "Savage River Camp" marks this still bucolic site.

The army marched over Meadow Mountain (elev. 2790) and camped at Little Meadows four miles east of modern Grantsville. Here the decision was made to speed up the march. An advance column of troops was formed, and most of the wagons and packhorses were relegated to a rear column commanded by Colonel Dunbar.

Braddock's army forded the Casselman River at a place known as Little Crossings just east of Grantsville. Today travelers can get a sense of the landscape at Casselman Bridge State Park. This four-acre park provides public access to the Little Crossings and an eighty-foot stone arch bridge built in 1813 across the Casselman River. The park is on Alt. Route 40 just east of Grantsville.

Braddock's army then crossed Negro Mountain (elev. 3075) and headed north across the modern state line into Pennsylvania. They crossed the Youghiogheny River at Great Crossing, an age-old ford used by Native Americans

*This bridge, built in 1813, marks a historic ford where Braddock's army crossed the Casselman River.*

and a place familiar to aide-de-camp George Washington from his journeys into the Ohio country in 1753 and 1754. The creation of the 16-mile Youghiogheny River Lake by the U.S. Army Corps of Engineers in the 1940s greatly altered the landscape here even to the point of submerging a 19th century stone bridge. But Braddock's Run, which the troops marched by, still flows east of the river from a point just south of Route 40. The Corps-run Jockey Hollow Visitor Center on Route 40 on the west side of the river has exhibits and photos showing what the crossing looked like before the lake was created.

## BRADDOCK'S CAMPAIGN:
### SITES ALONG CHESTNUT RIDGE JUMONVILLE ROAD, PENNSYLVANIA

The most distinct traces of Braddock's road are preserved off Route 40 leading to the 2,500-foot summit of Chestnut Ridge, the last mountain barrier before the Forks of the Ohio. Braddock's army advanced along a road that closely parallels Route 40 between modern Addison and Summit, but the sites along this stretch of road are associated more with the backwash of defeat as the remnants of Braddock's army retreated eastward after the July 9 battle along the Monongahela.

A Pennsylvania historical sign on Route 40 three miles east of Farmington marks the site of an army encampment on June 24. This is known as Twelve Springs Camp for the numerous springs in the vicinity.

### Fort Necessity

Braddock's troops marched past the ruins of George Washington's Fort Necessity in the Great Meadows; a fine stretch of Braddock's road is preserved as a hiking trail in Fort Necessity National Battleground west of Farmington on Route 40.

The Braddock Road Trace runs south of the reconstructed Fort Necessity. This section of road started as a trail blazed by trader Christopher Gist and a Delaware named Nemacolin. Washington converted the trail into a road during the 1754 Fort Necessity campaign. Braddock's troops widened this road and it later served as a major transportation route to the west until 1817 when it was abandoned.

*Braddock's final grave.*
*This monument was erected in 1913.*

**The National Park Service maintains traces of Braddock Road.**

## BRADDOCK'S GRAVE

About one mile west of Fort Necessity on Route 40 is the site of Braddock's Grave and the army's Old Orchard encampment. The grave monument and a 23-acre tract of land that preserve traces of Braddock's Road are part of the National Park Service holdings. Braddock's army first camped at this site on June 25; the Old Orchard camp was also the army's first bivouac on the retreat after the panic-stricken flight from the Monongahela. Here General Edward Braddock, the commander-in-chief of British forces in North America, died on the evening of July 13 of wounds sustained four days before in the battle. Braddock's death came unexpectedly even though the wound to his lungs was considered severe.

Washington officiated at a brief burial ceremony. Braddock's body was buried in the middle of the road so the passing army wagons would obliterate signs of the grave. The British feared that marauding warriors would dig up the body and scalp it.

In 1804 workmen repairing Braddock Road found a human skeleton in the middle of the road near the east bank

of a small stream called Braddock Run. Because of military insignia, the body was identified as Braddock's. The remains were interred 100 feet southeast on a knoll; in 1913 a white granite monument was erected over this second grave. The National Park Service has also marked the site of Braddock's initial grave just east of Braddock Run on the road trace to the right of the monument.

## ROCK FORT CAMP

From Old Orchard Camp on June 25, Braddock's army advanced to the crest of Chestnut Ridge at the modern Mount Summit Inn, then turned north along the ridge using a route that parallels the modern Jumonville Road. The army encamped June 26 at the Rock Fort Camp, also known as the Half King's Rock. This is the same area where the Iroquois leader Tanacharison camped prior to Washington's attack on a French party at nearby Jumonville Glen in 1754. A state highway marker for Rock Fort Camp is located on Route 40 at Summit. Heading north on Jumonville Road one mile, additional signs for Washington Spring and Rock Fort Camp are on the right side of the road. The privately owned property in this area is posted for no trespassing.

## DUNBAR'S CAMP

Braddock's road continues past Jumonville Glen, which is administered by the National Park Service. Two-tenths of a mile north of Jumonville Glen is Dunbar's Camp, where the 850-man rear guard commanded by Col. Thomas Dunbar set up camp with a storehouse of military supplies. The survivors of the July 9 battle fled to this camp. Dunbar had sent wagons loaded with provisions to meet the survivors when he first heard of the disaster. But the panic that seized the army on the battlefield spread to

Dunbar's Camp. Dunbar ordered the destruction of the supplies so they would not fall into the hands of the French and Indian army that the soldiers imagined was hot on their heels. The arms destroyed included four cannon, 300 rounds of canister, 3,000 cannon balls and 16,000 pounds of powder. The wounded Braddock was brought here in a litter and on July 13 the retreat began.

Today the site of Dunbar's Camp and another woodland trace of Braddock's Road is part of the Jumonville Training Center, a 270-acre retreat run by the Western Pennsylvania Conference of the United Methodist Church. The Jumonville Preservation Association holds a seminar on the French and Indian War each November at the training center. The 50-acre section of the retreat where Dunbar camped has yielded a treasure trove of artifacts over the years. The camp site is protected from development through a conservation easement held by the Archaeology Conservancy, a national non-profit group devoted to protecting archaeological sites.

The public has access during the day to the hiking trails in the King Wood area, a forest of hemlock and pine trees that covers the camp site and Braddock Road trace. This public access area is to the right of the training center off the main entrance road. The Half King trail leads south to Jumonville Glen.

From Chestnut Ridge, Braddock's main army passed Christopher Gist's plantation and crossed the Youghiogheny River for a second time at Stewart's Crossing or modern Connellsville at Route 119. The army headed northwest and crossed the Monongahela River twice. Just after the army forded the Monongahela River west of Turtle Creek, the advance guard encountered the French and their Indian allies that had rushed eight miles out from Fort Duquesne to stop them.

From Chestnut Ridge, Braddock's army marched another 50 miles to the battlefield. The landscape of Braddock Road's along this stretch has been greatly altered with the development of the Pittsburgh metro area and thus will not be covered in this book.

## BRADDOCK'S FIELD—BRADDOCK CARNEGIE LIBRARY, BRADDOCK, PENNSYLVANIA

Can an 18th century wilderness battlefield be reclaimed from the site of the Edgar S. Thomson steel plant, one of the massive industrial complexes built in the Pittsburgh region in the late 19th century? This is the ambitious goal of the Braddock's Field Historical Society, a local history group that wants to clear a portion of the old mill and build a visitor center and museum to interpret the battle.

The battlefield on which Gen. Edward Braddock fell mortally wounded was transformed into a maze of steel foundries and railroad tracks by the industrialist Andrew Carnegie. The Thomson plant closed down in the early 1980s with the collapse of the region's steel industry, but the buildings remain. And now the steel towns of Braddock and North Braddock are struggling to survive and looking to both their colonial and industrial heritage for answers.

The Braddock's Field Historical Society and Allegheny County were awarded a state grant in 1998 to conduct a study to determine whether a visitor center and museum can be built on the battlefield site and serve as a tourist attraction. As a first step, the society has opened an 18th century history room devoted to the Braddock campaign. This is located in Braddock's 1889 Carnegie Library that is being renovated.

Robert Messner, the society's secretary, says the goal is to bring one of the French and Indian War's premier sites the recognition it deserves. He points out that a host of famous historical figures were at the scene, including frontiersmen Daniel Morgan and Daniel Boone who drove supply wagons. In the vicinity of Braddock and Center Avenues and 6th Street in North Braddock is where Braddock's army met defeat eight miles east of Fort Duquesne on July 9, 1755.

Braddock's army forded the Monongahela River near the cabin of English trader John Fraser (he relocated there after being ousted from Venango by the French) and marched into the forest. Many historians think Braddock made a fatal mistake at this juncture by neglecting to send flanking parties to protect his advance. About one p.m. the advance guard under Lt. Col. Thomas Gage literally ran into a force of French and Native Americans that had rushed out from Fort Duquesne. The gallant commander of the French force, Capt. Daniel Beaujeu, was killed in the first volley, but the French and their allies recovered more quickly than the British from the shock. They fired upon Gage's men from behind rocks and trees; the advance force fell back only to jam into the main body of Braddock's army. Some historians think Gage could have saved the day if he had ordered an attack at the start to take a hill on the right. Instead, the British soldiers milled in confusion while the deadly firing continued. The Virginia troops fired back from behind cover, but many were shot by what today is called friendly fire.

Braddock rode to the front to encourage the British to form the firing formations typical of 18th century European warfare, but this proved futile with the now-panicky troops. Braddock had five horses shot out from under him before he was hit in the lung by a bullet. His Virginia aide George Washington also sought to rally the troops and his clothing became riddled with bullets. After two hours of slaughter, the surviving British broke and ran. Washington made sure the wounded Braddock was escorted safely off the field.

Of the 1,400 British in the battle, about 1,000 were killed or wounded. The French and Indian losses were minimal. Washington gave this assessment of the defeat in a letter written July 18 to Virginia Gov. Robert Dinwiddie:

The Virginian Companies behavd like Men, and died like Soldier's.... In short the dastardly behavior of the English Soldiers expos'd all those who were inclin'd to do their duty, to almost certain Death; and at length; in despight of every effort to the contrery broke and ran as Sheep before the Hounds....

The news of Braddock's defeat shocked those in the provincial capitals and border settlements. The myth of the invincibility of British arms was shattered. One Mrs. Browne, who was stationed at Fort Cumberland, wrote on July 11:

All of us greatly alarm'd; a Boy came from the Camp and said the General was kill'd 4 miles from the French Fort, and that allmost all Sr. Peter Hackets Regiment is cut off by a Party of French and Indians who were behind Trees. Dunbar's Regiment was in the rear so that they lost but few Men. It is not possible to describe the Distraction of the poor Women for their Husbands.

## COLONEL JAMES BURD AND THE BURD ROAD

James Burd was a Scottish emigrant who played a key role in the defense of Pennsylvania's frontier. One of his early endeavors was to build a road through the Pennsylvania wilderness to support the ill-fated Braddock expedition.

Burd (1726-93) married into the prominent Shippen family within several years after he arrived in Philadelphia in 1747 and got started as a merchant. The Shippen connections (Burd's father-in-law Edward had served as mayor) guided the young man's destiny. In 1752, he moved to Shippensburg, a town founded by his father-in-law in the Cumberland Valley, to engage in the Indian fur trade. He traveled to the various trading posts in the west and took on assignments for Pennsylvania provincial secretary Richard Peters. As preparations for Braddock's expedition were made in early 1755, Burd made the rounds of farms, purchasing food for the army.

Burd was named one of five commissioners in March 1755 to survey a wilderness road, to transport of supplies and food from Pennsylvania to Braddock's army. General Edward Braddock wanted the provincial leaders to build the road to the Youghiogheny River while his army marched westward from Fort Cumberland. Burd and the commissioners surveyed a road from McDowell's Mill near modern Markes, Pennsylvania, to the vicinity of the three forks of the Youghiogheny at a place called Turkeyfoot (modern Confluence, Pennsylvania).

Burd and his crew of road builders started work in early May, and although his crew encountered some resistance from unfriendly Indians, by early July they had reached the summit of Allegheny Mountain. When word of Braddock's defeat reached Burd on July 17, he stopped work immediately, buried the tools and led his men to safety at Fort Cumberland.

Three years later, the Forbes expedition cleared sections of Burd Road from Fort McDowell to Raystown (modern Bedford) for use in the successful campaign against Fort Duquesne. The road is better known today as Forbes Road.

The point where Burd Road diverges from Forbes Road is known as The Forks. Today this is the intersection of Routes 30 and 31 and the location of the 18th century Jean Bonnet Tavern. A stone monument at the intersection has this inscription: "The Forks. The Road cut by Col. James Burd 1755 and the Forbes Road diverge here. Forbes Road leaving southwest to Shawnee Cabins." The Burd Road veered southwest along Route 31 through an area known as the Glades, near the modern towns of Manns Choice, New Buena Vista and New Baltimore, Pa.

Despite the setback with Braddock's defeat, Burd's services to his adopted province were just beginning. He started to work building Fort Morris in Shippensburg and in April 1756 he was commissioned a major in the provincial forces. Burd was an officer with the Augusta regiment that built Fort Augusta at the forks of the Susquehanna River in the summer of 1756, and he took over command of Fort Augusta that fall. He was commissioned a lieutenant colonel in the provincial forces in January 1758 and took on oversight of the provincial forts in eastern Pennsylvania. He led Pennsylvania troops assigned with the 1758 Forbes expedition. Burd put his road-building expertise to use again on the stretch of new road being built west of The Forks. He helped to build Fort Ligonier and was the commanding officer there when it came under a French attack in October 1758.

After the conquest of the Forks of the Ohio, Burd was stationed in the west, opening up new supply routes along the Monongahela River to Fort Pitt. He built Fort Burd at modern Brownsville, Pa. By 1760, Burd was back in command at Fort Augusta, and he stayed at that post during Pontiac's War in 1763-64.

In 1764 at the age of thirty-eight, Burd left the provincial army and built a plantation called "Tinian" on the Susquehanna River near modern Middletown, Pennsylvania. The house, in private hands, still stands. A state historical marker for Col. James Burd is located on Route 230 in Highspire, Pennsylvania. The graves of Burd and his wife Sarah are located in the Middletown Cemetery on the west side of Route 441 just north of Middletown. The two flat weathered tombstones are nine rows back on the right side from the fieldstone columns at the cemetery entrance.

# Raids on the Conococheague Valley, 1755-1758

## INTRODUCTION

The Great Cove and the Conococheague Valley mark the western extent of the Pennsylvania frontier in the 1750s. Scots-Irish settlers moved into the area starting in the 1730s, and they did not always respect the boundaries of the land purchases that Pennsylvania negotiated with the Delaware and Iroquois. Those settlers who built cabins on Indian land were known as squatters, and were a major source of friction in relations between Pennsylvania and the Native Americans. At Burnt Cabins, Pennsylvania authorities sought to diffuse tensions by burning the cabins of squatters.

When Delaware and Shawnee warriors attacked the frontier in the fall of 1755 following General Braddock's defeat, the exposed settlements in this region were among the first to feel the blow. On November 1, 1755, 100 Delaware and Shawnee warriors under the leadership of the Delaware chief Shingas attacked the Great Cove and destroyed the settlement. The bodies of the slain victims are buried in the Big Spring Graveyard.

SITES AT A GLANCE—This map will give you a feel for the general locations of sites in this chapter. Some sites overlap and are not shown on this map.

Chambers Fort
Ft. Loudon     Shippensburg
Rev. Steel's Fort     Mary Jemison
                      birthplace
              Ft. McDowell

Shingas had become a Delaware chief in 1752. He owed his accession in part to British influence. But Shingas threw his lot in with the French when war broke out. His raiding activities earned him the title Shingas the Terrible.

The survivors of Great Cove fled east across Tuscarora Mountain and spread the alarm to the Conococheague settlers gathered at two makeshift defenses, Fort McDowell and the Rev. Steel's Fort. During the winter of 1756, settlers in the valley either fled east across the Susquehanna River or "forted up" at stockaded outposts when raiding parties were in the area. Fort Waddell was named for the landowner, Thomas Waddell. Fort McCord, marked today by a monument topped by a Celtic cross, fell to Shingas in April 1756.

Benjamin Chambers was one of the first settlers in the Conococheague Valley. He built a strong fort around the site of his mill. Fort Chambers was equipped with two small cannon and had a fireproof lead roof.

In 1756, provincial authorities built Fort Loudon at a strategic spot along an ancient Indian path. The British army used Fort Loudon during the 1758 Forbes expedition.

Despite the network of forts, Delaware raids on homesteads continued for several years. Whole families were taken captive and marched west to the Delaware village at Kittanning or to the French post, Fort Duquesne.

One of the most famous captives is Mary Jemison, known as the "White Woman of the Genesee." A statue marks the general vicinity of her capture in the spring of 1758. Other markers trace her route across the valley.

## BURNT CABINS
### EAST OF FORT LITTLETON, PENNSYLVANIA

The small town of Burnt Cabins on the west slope of Tuscarora Mountain is named for a haunting event in its past. This town began as a squatter's settlement in the 1740s. In 1750, provincial officials burned down the cluster of log cabins here, and drove out the squatters in order to keep the peace with the Iroquois who owned the land and regarded this area as prime hunting territory.

Situated in the shadow of Tuscarora Mountain, the settlement on a trader pack horse trail provided clear evidence that Scots-Irish and English settlers were ignoring the Blue Mountain boundary line between the Penns' land purchases and Iroquois territory. Iroquois complaints about this encroachment to Pennsylvania emissary Conrad Weiser prompted the provincial officials to take action.

They formed a posse to order the squatters to leave. The posse set out on May 22 to visit settlements from the Juniata River Valley to the Great Cove settlements. The provincial secretary Richard Peters and local magistrates George Croghan and Benjamin Chambers were members of the group. Several Iroquois delegates went along, including John Shikelamy and Saiuchtowano, two sons of the late Iroquois viceroy Shikellamy.

The posse started in the Juniata Valley and encountered some resistance with squatters fleeing into the woods. In one case, they faced a man with a loaded gun. Andrew Lycon was disarmed, and Shikellamy's sons demanded that Lycon's cabin be burned so he could not return. The cabin was set ablaze, but Lycon was allowed to remove his possessions first before being carted off to jail.

The posse arrived at the Burnt Cabins area in Path Valley on May 30 and found those settlers more willing to concede to authority. Still, the posse burned several cabins to dissuade them from returning. Accounts are sketchy, but apparently the posse burned a number of cabins in each squatters' settlement they visited to demonstrate their resolve.

Peters later made a report to the General Assembly. He described the burnt cabins as having little value, and spoke at length of his efforts to make sure the homeless families were resettled.

Burnt Cabins was resettled after the close of the French and Indian War. The new settlement prospered because of its location at the intersection of Forbes Road and the Three Mountain Road, an important route for drovers herding livestock to markets in New York and Philadelphia during the early 19th century.

Burnt Cabins was placed on the National Register of Historic Places in 1998. The town's buildings have an interesting architecture, a mix of renovated log houses and buildings that once served as inns and hotels for travelers passing by. The oldest buildings date to the 1790-1850 period.

## BIG SPRING GRAVEYARD
## SOUTH OF MCCONNELLSBURG, PENNSYLVANIA

*Directions: Head south on Route 522 from McConnellsburg for 2.8 miles, look for state historical marker for Big Spring Graveyard on east side of road. Follow dirt farm lane by marker east for 4/10 mile. Look for cemetery on hill at right.*

A cluster of crude headstones on a hillside marks the resting place of victims of the Great Cove massacre on November 1, 1755. The grave markers, cut from limestone and lacking names or dates, are testament to a hasty burial. The Great Cove massacre marked an end to decades of an uneasy peace on Pennsylvania's western frontier. The Great Cove is a sheltered valley west of Tuscarora Mountain that was settled in the 1730s and 1740s by English and Scots-Irish settlers.

In the wake of Gen. Braddock's defeat in July 1755, the 100 families living in the Great Cove and nearby Tonoloway settlement were among the settlers most vulnerable to attack by the French and their Native American allies. The attack on the Great Cove by a war party of 100 Delaware and Shawnee under the command of Shingas came on a late fall afternoon. About 50 settlers were killed or captured. The survivors fled east through a gap in Tuscarora Mountain to Rev. Steel's fort and Fort McDowell in the Conococheague Valley. They reported looking back from the mountain summit and seeing their houses in flames. Within a week, local militia returned to the Great Cove to bury the dead and round up wandering livestock.

The massacre prompted a mass flight of refugees eastward to Carlisle and the Susquehanna River. Those remaining converted their homes into stockaded forts. Pennsylvania Gov. Robert Hunter Morris ordered a chain of forts built.

The Big Spring Graveyard, as lonely and haunting a place today as it must have been in the 1750s, is on a hill facing east toward Tuscarora Mountain. The cemetery is maintained by the Fulton County Historical Society.

***Crude headstones mark the graves of victims of the Great Cove massacre of 1755.***

## SHINGAS AND CAPTAIN JACOBS

The massacre of the inhabitants of Pennsylvania's Great Cove in November 1755 by a war party of Delaware and Shawnee sent shock waves across the frontier. Terrified settlers quickly associated one name with the deed that ended decades of peace between the English and the Delaware. "We are informed that yesterday about 100 Indians were seen in the Great Cove, among whom was Shingas the Delaware King," wrote John Armstrong to Pennsylvania's governor.

Shingas personified the terror that swept the frontier during the next three years, as raiding parties fell on isolated settlements and crude forts. Shingas became Shingas the Terrible and a reward was offered for his head. Along with a Delaware warrior named Captain Jacobs, Shingas led attacks against a string of provincial forts during the early years of the French and Indian War.

Shingas sought to free the Delaware from both English and Iroquois influence. He had been part of the great migration of Delaware from eastern Pennsylvania to the Ohio Valley. He resented the English for encroaching on Delaware lands and the Iroquois for depriving the Delaware of the right to speak on their own.

Shingas emerged as the Delaware "king" or spokesman in 1752 following the death of his uncle, Sassoonan. Delaware leaders derived their legitimacy from the maternal side of the family. The notion of a king or leading chief was foreign to the Delaware, for whom local chiefs or patriarchs had traditionally governed affairs at the village level. But the English anointed Sassoonan as the Delaware "king" so they would only need to deal with one leader when it came to purchasing land. They elevated Sassoonan's status by inviting him to conferences and giving him gifts. The arrangement also suited the Iroquois. Sassoonan proved a pliable fellow.

The English and Iroquois made a mistake when they picked Shingas as the next king. Based in the Ohio valley, Shingas had access to French arms and trading goods, and was among the Indian delegation that met with British General Braddock during his stay at Fort Cumberland. Braddock's dismissal of Indian land rights dismayed Shingas and his Shawnee allies. Following Braddock's defeat, they sought to drive the English back to the sea. Shingas led the attack that overran Fort McCord in April 1756. Captain Jacobs captured Fort Granville that July.

Provincial troops under John Armstrong struck a heavy blow two months later when they raided Kittanning, the base of Shingas and Captain Jacobs on the Allegheny River. Captain Jacobs was killed during that raid. His log house was surrounded and torched. As the flames reached gunpowder stored inside, he fled the house and was shot down. Shingas escaped to fight again, but he was eventually replaced as leader of the Delawares by his brother King Beaver.

King Beaver negotiated a truce that paved the way for British soldiers to capture Fort Duquesne in 1758. Shingas died in 1764.

## SHIPPENSBURG, PENNSYLVANIA—ROUTE 11 (KING STREET)

Shippensburg was founded in the 1730s by Edward Shippen along an Indian path that later became the Great Wagon or Potomac Road. Shippen was a prominent Philadelphia and Lancaster merchant; his daughter Sarah married Colonel James Burd who built provincial forts here and at other locations.

The God's Acre Cemetery on land donated by Shippen has graves dating to 1733. A stone monument is dedicated "to the Patriots and Pioneers who Sleep in God's Acres." The cemetery is on North Prince Street behind the Vigilant Hose Co. at 129 East King Street. A bronze tablet on the front wall of the firehouse is dedicated to Shippen (1703-81), who was also a mayor of Philadelphia, paymaster of the 1758 Forbes expedition, and a founder of Princeton University.

Shippensburg prospered to the extent that it served briefly in 1750-51 as the Cumberland County seat and court was held in a tavern that still stands. This limestone building is located at 352 East King Street at the intersection with Queen Street. The building, erected in 1735, was known as the Widow Piper's Tavern. Proprietor Janette Piper allowed court to be held in the tavern. A state historical marker for "Old Court House" is located in front of the house.

As the 1755 Braddock expedition got underway, Shippensburg served as a supply depot, with provisions stored in a stone house owned by Shippen. After Braddock's defeat, the depot was moved west to McDowell's Mill at modern Markes, Pennsylvania.

Pennsylvania Gov. Robert Hunter Morris ordered that a provincial fort be built to defend Shippensburg. Delaware raiders struck frequently in this area in 1755-57; the town was a magnet for refugees fleeing the Conococheague Valley to the immediate west. Colonel James Burd built a log stockade called Fort Morris and apparently finished the work in late 1755. Provincial soldiers garrisoned Fort Morris until the end of 1759. The fort was reactivated in the 1763-64 Pontiac's War.

There has long been controversy in Shippensburg about where Fort Morris and Shippen's stronghouse were located. The issue has been clouded by the supposed existence of a Fort Franklin in the 1740s. The debate has led to questioning of traditional local histories and the removal of some state historical markers. Earlier historians thought Fort Morris was located on Burd Street on the north side of town, or at a limestone outcrop on West King Street north of Morris Street.

Hayes Eschenmann, a Shippensburg resident and author of a book called The Elusive Fort Morris believes the site of the provincial fort to be at Ridge Avenue and Walnut Street on the southwest side of town. This site is on an elevation overlooking the pathway of the old Potomac Road. A water well and buried logs have been found in the vicinity. Eschenmann's evidence is compelling, but the state of Pennsylvania has yet to erect a new historical marker for Fort Morris at the Ridge Avenue site. Meanwhile, a bronze tablet, a relic of a 1920 effort to mark the site of Fort Morris, is still embedded in the limestone outcrop on West King Street. The Pennsylvania Historical Commission and the Civic Club of Shippensburg purchased the site and put up the tablet.

The lesson to be learned from this story is that history is not fixed in stone, especially when oral tradition is passed down to succeeding generations. As new evidence comes to light, sometimes the certainties of the past have to be revised.

## CHAMBERS FORT
## CHAMBERSBURG, PENNSYLVANIA

*Directions to fort site: West on Route 30 in downtown Chambersburg. Turn right on North Franklin Street. Right on West King Street. Look for parking lot by the park.*

Benjamin Chambers led a wave of Scots-Irish immigrants into the Conococheague Valley in the 1730s. When the valley was raided by Delaware and Shawnee warriors twenty years later, Chambers built one of the strongest private forts along the Pennsylvania frontier.

Chambers (1708-88) came to America from Northern Ireland when in his twenties. He was one of four brothers who crossed the Susquehanna River and pushed beyond the settlements. The brothers settled by limestone springs which later developed into towns along the Great Wagon Road (modern Route 11).

Benjamin picked a spot that became known as Falling Spring for its eighteen-foot waterfall. There, he built a water-powered saw and grain mill. Chambers also donated land for a Presbyterian church, for that was the religion that the Scots-Irish firmly established in their settlements.

A prominent man, Chambers was among the local officials who evicted the squatters at Burnt Cabins in 1750. When war threatened in 1755, he built a stockade around his substantial two-story stone house and mill at Falling Spring. To deter firebombs, he put sheets of lead on the roof. Chambers guarded the fort with two four-pound swivel cannon. Provincial officials wanted the cannon removed for fear they would be captured if a raiding party overran the fort. They sent the county sheriff to seize the cannon, but Chambers refused to give them up. With local sentiment on his side, the authorities backed down. The fort did not come under attack, but raiders struck in the area several times.

*Benjamin Chambers tombstone.*

The site of Chambers Fort is located in a small park by the waters that still flow over Falling Spring. Near a footbridge by the waterfall is a small stone monument with the inscription: "Fort Chambers Southwest 150 feet. built 1755-56." A state historical marker for Fort Chambers is located on West King Street.

Benjamin Chambers is buried in the Falling Spring Presbyterian Church graveyard in Chambersburg. A log church was built here in 1737, and the existing stone church was built in 1808. Behind the church is the cemetery on a bluff overlooking Conococheague Creek. Chambers' white marble tombstone is in a plot enclosed by a brick wall. Its inscription reads: "In memory of Col. Benjamin Chambers First white settler of Franklin County in 1730. Founder of Chambersburg and donor of these grounds to the Presbyterian Church in 1768 who died in 1788 age 80." Tradition has it that some graves of Delaware tribe members are located in this cemetery.

*Directions to cemetery: Take North Main Street two blocks north of Chambersburg Town Square. Church on left side. State historical marker in front of church.*

## CAPTAIN JACK: A FRONTIER LEGEND

The frontier produced its share of heroes, heroines, and larger-than-life figures who actually may have existed, but more likely are part of legend. Captain Jack was such a legendary figure, a haunted individual who roamed the borderlands and was known as "the wild hunter of the Juniata" or "the black hunter."

Captain Jack's tale begins in the mid-1750s in the Juniata River Valley, where he was a land squatter and expert hunter. He returned to his cabin one day from a hunting trip to find his wife and children murdered by Indian raiders. From that day on, Captain Jack swore vengeance on the Indians and ambushed them on forest paths. He lived something of a hermit's existence, avoiding the white settlements. But Captain Jack appeared in times of peril, occasionally advising a backwoods family that he had saved them by waylaying the marauders at their cabin door.

Captain Jack is sometimes described as a swarthy fellow, perhaps half-Indian, and having superhuman strength. He commanded a group of rangers during the French and Indian War and supposedly offered his services to Gen. Edward Braddock only to be turned down. He is said to have gone west after the war ended.

Does the key to the legend of Captain Jack rest in a grave in the Chambersburg cemetery? Some 19th century writers thought so, but the evidence at hand contradicts the legend. Just a few feet west of Benjamin Chamber's grave in the Falling Spring Presbyterian Church Cemetery is the weathered tombstone of Colonel Patrick Jack. The inscription reads, "Col. Patrick Jack, an officer of the Colonial and Revolutionary Wars, died January 25, 1821, aged 91 years."

This Colonel Jack was no doubt a historical figure. Court records note his ownership of a mill along Jack's Road in Franklin County. He is believed to have served in Col. Henry Bouquet's 1763 expedition in Pontiac's War, and muster rolls from the Revolutionary War list Capt. Patrick Jack commanding a company of Cumberland County militia. Colonel Patrick Jack is buried with his wife and daughters who lived into the 19th century.

## FORT MCDOWELL — MARKES, PENNSYLVANIA

*Directions: From Route 30, take Route 416 southwest to town of Markes at intersection of Route 416 and SR 3007. The monument is on the northeast corner of intersection.*

John McDowell, a Scots-Irish emigrant from Northern Ireland, built a mill along the west branch of Conococheague Creek in 1740. In the spring of 1755, Col. James Burd started to build a supply road at McDowell's Mill to help the Braddock expedition. McDowell's stockaded mill became a shelter and early rallying point for settlers in the aftermath of the Great Cove massacre in November 1755. Cumberland County Sheriff John Potter called a meeting of local residents at the mill to plan a defense. The meeting had just started when someone spotted flames and clouds of smoke from the residence of Matthew Patton two miles away. Potter and about 40 men went to investigate, but encountered no Delaware or Shawnee raiders. The raid on Patton's house was the first of many in this area.

Throughout most of 1756, Fort McDowell served as a supply depot and assembly point for militia. When provincial officials decided to build a new fort in the area, they selected land where Patton's cabin had stood as a more defensible location than Fort McDowell. The new fort was named Fort Loudon. Supplies at Fort McDowell were transferred to this new fort by the end of 1756.

A stone monument marks the site of Fort McDowell. The inscription reads:

> This stone marks the site of the fort at McDowells Mill erected by John McDowell before 1754, it was used as a base of supplies and as a magazine until the erection of Fort Loudon in 1756. The military road from Pennsylvania connecting with the Braddock Road at Turkeyfoot was built from this point in 1755 under the supervision of Col. James Burd. Pennsylvania Historical Commission, Enoch Brown Association, Descendants of John McDowell 1910.

The monument is next to a state historical marker. The old mill race is visible in the vicinity.

## FORT WADDELL
### WEST OF ST. THOMAS, PENNSYLVANIA

The site of this private fort is on farmland at the southeast foot of Parnell's Knob. Thomas Waddell was one of many landowners in the area who built their own stockades to provide refuge from the frequent Indian raids. Provincial officials listed the fort as part of their defense plan for the region.

A stone monument on Route 30 is located south of the fort site. The inscription on the monument reads:

> Fort Waddell 1754—One of the forts for the defense of the Cumberland Valley from Fort Davis to Shippensburg, stood near this marker on the plantation then owned by Thomas Waddell. Marked by the Pennsylvania Historical Commission, and the Franklin County Chapter of the Daughters of the American Revolution, 1930.

The monument is on the north side of Route 30, near the junction with Route 416. A state historical marker for Fort Waddell is nearby.

*Fort Waddell marker.*

## Fort McCord
### NORTHEAST OF EDENVILLE, PENNSYLVANIA

*Directions to fort site: Westbound on Route 30 from St. Thomas, take St. Thomas-Edenville Road, aka Apple Way/SR 4008 north to Edenville and through town to intersection on northeast side with two stop signs. Go north on Fort McCord Road for 2.8 miles. Look for Fort McCord state historical marker. Turn right on Rumler Road (also TR 464). The memorial is nearby on left side of road across from fieldstone farmhouse.*

Fort McCord was the first of three forts in central Pennsylvania to fall to Delaware raiding parties during the first half of 1756. But the story of Fort McCord is somewhat unusual in frontier annals because a company of provincial soldiers pursued the raiders and fought them in a battle at Sideling Hill, a mountain range to the west.

Fort McCord, a private fort built by Scots-Irish settler William McCord, was located northeast of Parnell's Knob. In early spring 1756, Shingas led a war party from the Delaware village of Kittanning on the Allegheny River to attack the Pennsylvania settlements. The occupants of Fort McCord awoke on April 1 to find themselves surrounded by Shingas and his warriors. Shingas' force was strong enough to burn and overrun the fort, killing or capturing the 27 settlers who had taken shelter there.

The Delaware and nine captives headed west on an early traders' path that later became known as Three Mountain Road. The militia followed in pursuit, led by Captain Alexander Culbertson. Culbertson stopped at Fort Lyttelton to get reinforcements from provincial troops stationed there. The combined force, numbering about 50, met the Delaware at Sideling Hill in Fulton County near modern Maddensville, Pennsylvania. The two forces fought a pitched battle for about two hours, but the Delaware gained an advantage when reinforcements arrived. Twenty-one soldiers, including Culbertson, were killed in the battle. Delaware losses were similar.

Five of the Fort McCord captives escaped during the battle and reached Fort Lyttelton. Two other captives, Ann McCord and Martha Thorn, were rescued in September 1756 when Colonel John Armstrong led a retaliatory raid on Kittanning.

Today the site of Fort McCord is in a meadow near a small stream. A memorial here to Fort McCord, dedicated in 1914, pays a unique tribute to the Scots-Irish heritage of the fort's defendants. The white granite monument is topped by a Celtic cross with a Scottish thistle engraved in the middle of the cross. The monument's inscription is also somewhat unusual, for it lists the names of the soldiers killed or wounded in the Sideling Hill battle. The inscription reads:

> The site of Fort McCord, where twenty-seven pioneer settlers, men, women and children, were massacred by Indian savages or carried into captivity, April 1, 1756, was a few rods southeast of this spot.
>
> In the list of victims were Mary McCord, Mrs. John Thorn and babe, Mrs. Annie McCord, wife of John McCord, and two daughters, Martha, then a young mother with unborn babe, and a young girl.
>
> Names of Provincial soldiers killed in pursuit of the Indians on Sideling Hill: Killed Captain Alexander Culbertson. John Reynolds, Ensign. William Kerr. James Blair, John Layson. William Denny. Francis Scott. William Boyd. William Paynter. Jacob Jones. Robert Kerr. William Chambers. Daniel McCoy. James Robertson, "tailor." James Robertson, "weaver." James Peace. John Blair. Henry Jones. John McCarty. John Kelly. James Lowder.
>
> Wounded: Lieutenant Jamieson. Abram Jones. Francis Campbell. John McDonald. Isaac Miller. William Hunter. William Reynolds. John Barnet. Benjamin Blyth. Matthias Gaushorn. William Swails.
>
> Erected by joint action of Enoch Brown Association and Pennsylvania Historical Commission. 1914.

A state historical marker for Fort McCord is located on Route 30, two miles west of St. Thomas, about nine miles from the fort site.

*A distinctive Celtic cross tops the Fort McCord monumnet. Delaware raiders captured Fort McCord in 1756.*

## FORT LOUDON
### SOUTHEAST OF FORT LOUDON, PENNSYLVANIA

*Directions: West on Route 30 from St. Thomas. Look for brown and white sign, south side of Route 30. Left on North Brooklyn Road and go 1/2 mile to fort.*

Fort Loudon (or Fort Loudoun) occupied a strategic location at the gateway to invasion routes into the Conococheague Valley. Situated along the west branch of Conococheague Creek, about five miles east of Tuscarora Mountain, the fort was southwest of Parnell's Knob, the most distinctive landmark in the region, and southeast of Path Valley, a north-south pass between two mountain ranges that was part of the ancient Tuscarora Path.

Fort Loudon was located just south of the 1755 Burd Road that became Forbes Road several years later when Gen. John Forbes and his army passed by. Built in 1756 by Col. John Armstrong, it was one of the provincial forts erected to protect the settlers on Pennsylvania's frontier. This was the location of Matthew Patton's homestead, one of the targets of Delaware raiders in November 1755. The fort was built of wooden posts eight inches in diameter with shooting platforms on two of the corners.

Fort Loudon was an important supply and rendezvous point during the 1758 Forbes campaign against Fort Duquesne. Colonel Henry Bouquet spent weeks here arranging for supplies, meeting with Cherokee allies, and complaining about the poor roads. "It is almost im-

passable from Loudoun to Littleton," he wrote on June 11, 1758, to Forbes. "Of all the roads where it is possible for a wagon to go, this is the worst, and it cannot be repaired. It is of rock, partly solid, partly loose and sharp stones." Fort Loudon again served Bouquet during his 1763 and 1764 campaigns to the Ohio country during Pontiac's War.

With the end of that war, Fort Loudon was garrisoned by a detachment of the 42nd Royal Highland Regiment, the "Black Watch." Within a few months, a gang of settlers

*Fort Loudon was reconstructed in 1993.*

38

known as the Black Boys challenged the British Crown's authority. The Black Boys episode was an early spark of the colonial discontent that led to the American Revolution.

The Black Boys and their leader James Smith took issue with the Crown's policy of allowing Philadelphia-based merchants to trade guns, ammunition, and other goods with the western tribes in exchange for furs. The gang ransacked one traders' pack train on Sideling Hill. A platoon of soldiers from Fort Loudon captured several of the Black Boys; Smith retaliated by capturing some British soldiers. The confrontation peaked in 1765 when Smith and 300 followers fired on Fort Loudon and forced the garrison to evacuate. The British formally abandoned the fort in 1766.

John Smith's exploits are portrayed in The First Rebel, a novel by Neil Swanson, and in the 1939 movie, Allegheny Uprising.

The Fort Loudon site was the subject of an archaeological dig in 1982 by the Pennsylvania Historical and Museum Commission. Artifacts from the dig, including a bird's eye view of the reconstructed fort well, are on display at the Pennsylvania State Museum in Harrisburg. The findings established human occupation of this area at intervals dating to 8000 B.C.

The 207-acre fort site is owned by the state, but the Fort Loudon Historical Society administers it. In 1993, the society reconstructed the fort's palisade and shooting platforms on the spot where it stood almost 250 years ago. Colonial reenactments are held there. Several buildings are on the site, including a two-story log house built after the fort was abandoned, and a one-story house and stone springhouse on Conococheague Creek.

## REV. STEEL'S FORT
### NORTHEAST OF MERCERSBURG, PENNSYLVANIA

*Directions: From Route 75 in Mercersburg, take SR 3009 (Oregon Street) east 2.5 miles to three-way intersection with SR 3002 at Church Hill. State historical marker for Rev. Steel's Fort on Route 16, 2.3 miles southeast of Mercersburg.*

Reverend John Steel (or Steele), a Presbyterian pastor, came to the Conococheague Valley in 1752 to minister to the spiritual needs of its Scots-Irish inhabitants. He had previously been an ordained minister for eight years in eastern Pennsylvania. Steel traveled a circuit among churches in the Conococheague settlements. He showed a flair for military leadership. He built a stockade in the summer of 1755 around a church meeting house in an area now known as Church Hill. Steel's fort provided shelter for survivors of the Great Cove massacre that November.

Steel was active in planning the area's defense and he was entrusted with ammunition by the provincial government. He became a captain in the provincial forces in March 1756 and commanded a company of soldiers.

Accounts tell of an occasion in July 1756 when Steel was preaching a sermon at a church near modern Greencastle. Interrupted with news of a raid on a nearby farm, Steel abruptly ended the sermon and led the congregation in pursuit of the raiders.

Today the site of Steel's fortified meeting house is located in the crossroads village of Church Hill. A stone monument marking the fort site is located on a knoll in front of an 18th century stone-walled cemetery. The monument is beneath a cluster of pine trees. The inscription reads: "Site of Fort John Steel Built August 1755. Presbyterian Church built here in 1738. Only fort in Franklin County built to protect worshipers from Indians."

## PHILIP DAVIS FORT
### NEAR WELSH RUN, PENNSYLVANIA

*Directions to monument: From town of Welsh Run, take Route 995 south to Bain Road. Turn left on Bain Road for 1.3 miles to intersection with dirt farm lane. Monument is on right, red brick farmhouse and white barn is across Bain Road on left. The monument is on a ridge overlooking a small stream named Welsh Run.*

Philip Davis was a leader of the Welsh immigrants who settled along the West Branch of Conococheague Creek in the 1730s near the Maryland border. When the first Welsh Quakers came to Pennsylvania in the 1680s, they settled in the Welsh Barony, a tract of land along the Schuylkill River. But the effort to establish a separate enclave faded as the frontier beckoned, and Welshmen of different religious faiths came to Pennsylvania.

By 1741, enough Welshmen had settled along the Conococheague that they formed their own Presbyterian Church. Davis was a church leader and local tax collector. When war broke out in 1755, he built a stockade on his plantation near a small stream aptly named Welsh Run. Philip Davis' fort proved to be the southernmost fort in Pennsylvania along a northeast arc that extended to the Poconos.

Philip Davis' Fort escaped direct attack, but settlers in the area fell victim to Indian raids. The church was reportedly burned at one point, and on July 26, 1756, two young brothers, John and James McCullough, were captured near their home by a Delaware raiding party. The boys were taken while trying to warn their parents that raiders were nearby. Both brothers were taken to Fort Duquesne, but after that they were separated. James was taken to Canada and is lost to history, but John was adopted by the Delaware and lived happily with them for eight years until he

*Fort Philip Davis monument.*

was exchanged as a result of Col. Henry Bouquet's expedition to subdue the Delaware tribes in Ohio in 1764. John eventually returned home and lived to an old age.

Today in the tiny hamlet of Welsh Run, the memory of the Welsh settlement is kept alive at the Robert Kennedy Memorial Presbyterian Church, the successor to the church burned down during the French and Indian War. The white frame church, built in 1871, stands on a hill where Routes 995 and 416 intersect. This church is named in honor of a 19th century minister.

A limestone monument for Fort Philip Davis is located southwest of town of Welsh Run off Route 995. The monument's inscription reads: "Fort Davis was located near this marker on the plantation of Philip Davis — Welshman, patriot, collector of taxes, member of the Presbytery of New Castle who built the fort about 1754 as a protection against the Indians." The monument was erected in 1931 by the Pennsylvania Historical Commission and Franklin County Chapter of the Daughters of the American Revolution.

## MARY JEMISON BIRTHPLACE WEST OF CASHTOWN, PENNSYLVANIA

*Directions to statue: Westbound on Route 30 from Cashtown, turn right on Route 324. Take Route 324 east until Church Road. Turn right on Church Road until you reach the church.*

Hundreds of English captives were seized by the Delaware and Shawnee during the French and Indian War. Many were assimilated into tribal life, but only a few like Regina Leininger and Mary Jemison became well known. Jemison (1743-1833) is also known to history as the "White Woman of the Genesee." Her fame is due to her longevity and the acclaim that followed publication of her life story in 1824.

Mary Jemison was born aboard ship as her Scots-Irish parents immigrated to America from Ulster. Settling near the Marsh Creek settlement west of modern day Gettysburg, Pennsylvania, the family began farming. In April 1758, a party of six Indians and four Frenchmen raided the Jemison homestead. Two of her brothers escaped, but Mary, her parents, and three siblings were captured. They and several other captives were marched westward, but on the journey's second night Mary was given moccasins and separated from her family. Mary's mother took this as a sign that her child's life would be spared. The rest of the family was killed, and Mary learned their fate when she saw their scalps being dried. "Those scalps I knew at the time must have been taken from our family by the color of the hair," she recalled in The Life of Mary Jemison. "My mother's hair was red; and I could easily distinguish my father's and the children's from each other."

Jemison was taken to Fort Duquesne and then adopted by two Seneca women to replace a dead brother in the family circle. She spent the rest of her life living with the Seneca and Delaware in the Ohio Valley and Genesee River region of western New York. She outlived two husbands during her long life and had several children. Jemison refused to be part of a captives' exchange at Fort Niagara at the end of Pontiac's War in 1764.

As white settlers moved into the Genesee region in the early 19th century, word of Mary Jemison's story spread. In 1823 James E. Seaver interviewed her and wrote her story. By 19th century standards, the published book was a bestseller. Jemison's grave is located at the Indian Council Grounds, Letchworth State Park, Castile, New York.

In Pennsylvania, a small statue of Jemison as a young girl overlooks the Buchanan Valley, her frontier home. A state historical marker at the intersection of Routes 30 and 324 refers to this statue. The statue is located in front of the Church of St. Ignatius Loyola.

Another monument to Mary Jemison is northeast of Edenville, Franklin County, Pennsylvania. A small stone marker is near the spot where her parents were killed. The marker is located on Gilbert Road which leads to a gap through North Mountain known as Nancy's Saddle. The inscription reads:

In this mountain gorge, the child Mary Jemison — later the white squaw — rested with her captors on their way from Marsh Creek to the Ohio Country April 15,

*This statue of Mary Jemison in Indian garb overlooks Buchanan Valley.*

*Mary Jemison Gap marker.*

1758. Her parents were tomahawked near this spot. Erected by Fort McCord Chapter Pennsylvania Alpine Club. Sept. 25 1926.

*Directions to marker: Follow routes to Fort McCord monument. Westbound on Route 30 from St. Thomas, take St. Thomas-Edenville Road, aka Apple Way/SR 4008 north to Edenville and through town to intersection northeast of town with two stop signs. Go north on Fort McCord Road for 1.5 miles to Gilbert Road. Stone monument on left berm of road.*

## RICHARD BARD

*Directions to Bard's Mill site: Go eastbound on Route 116 to Fairfield, Pennsylvania. On east side of town, turn right onto Carroll's Tract Road. Head north on Carroll's Tract Road about one-half mile. Turn left onto Mount Hope Road. Head west on Mount Hope Road about one mile. Look for stone walls—the ruins of Bard's Mill—on the left side where the road bends. Pullover area for parking. Yellow split-level ranch house on right just past ruins. Middle Creek flows along left side of Mount Hope Road.*

"On a woeful day the heathen came,
    And did us captives make:
And, then the miseries commenced,
    Of which we did partake."

These are the opening lines of *The Ballad of Richard Bard*, an Indian captivity story set to verse. Richard Bard (1736-1799) and his family were abducted from their home at Bard's mill, at Virginia Mills, near modern Fairfield, Pennsylvania, on April 13, 1758 by a Delaware raiding party. Bard's father Archibald had built the grist mill, one of the first in the 18th century Marsh Creek settlement near Middle Creek. The ruins of the mill are still visible.

Richard Bard and his wife Catharine were married in 1756 and settled at the mill to start raising a family. When the raiding party of nineteen Delaware warriors launched their raid that spring morning two years later, Bard and his cousin Thomas Potter offered resistance at first, and the family barricaded themselves in their house. Feeling that they could not hold out for long given the size of the raiding party, they decided to surrender after getting a promise that they would not be harmed. As the Delaware escorted the group of nine captives westward, it became clear that the promise would not be kept. Potter was killed early on in the trek, then the Bards' one-year-old son was scalped and his body flung into the woods.

Bard and the other captives were subjected to beatings on the forced march. Bard resolved to escape on the trail after one side of his face was painted, a sign that he might

41

be put to death. He saw his chance on night when the Delaware were preoccupied with dressing up in Catharine's gown. Bard escaped, but faced an ordeal trying to get back to the English settlements. Beset with a sore foot, lack of food, and snowfall, he managed to walk across the rugged mountains.

But now although at liberty
Through mercy I am set,
Yet miserable is my life
For want of food to eat.

Meanwhile, the Delaware led the rest of the family westward to Fort Duquesne and the Ohio country, subjecting them to beatings and privations along the way. Bard eventually met some friendly Indians who took him to the provincial outpost at Fort Lyttelton.

But on the evening of this day
I met with Indians three;
Surprised I was, and really thought
Them enemies to be.

But they proved kind and brought me to
A place where English dwell,
Fort Littleton; the place by me
Was known, exceeding well.

And now, from bondage thought I'm freed,
Yet she that's my beloved,
Is to a land that's far remote,
By Indians removed.

Catharine Bard spent two years living in various Indian villages. Bard eventually learned that she was living in a village along the Susquehanna River, and obtained her release. They moved to the Conococheague settlement near modern Upton, Pennsylvania, and had more children. Bard later became a local magistrate, served in the American Revolution, and opposed ratification of the U. S. Constitution in 1788. He and Catharine are buried together in Church Hill cemetery near Mercersburg, Pennsylvania.

Visitors can stand by the ruins of Bard's grist mill on a hillside at the base of Culp Ridge near Fairfield, Pennsylvania, just above the tiny settlement of Virginia Mills, and hear the waters of Middle Creek running below. The stone walls are overgrown with vines and it is best to tread carefully, with snakes about. But the mill location gives an idea of how vulnerable Bard and his family were to Indian raiders, even at the relatively late date in the conflict of 1758.

---

*Directions to Richard Bard grave: From Route 75 in Mercersburg, Pennsylvania, take SR 3009 (Oregon Street) east 2.5 miles to three-way intersection with SR 3002 at Church Hill. The stone-walled Church Hill graveyard is on right side. Stone monument for Rev. Steel's Fort is in vicinity. Tombs of Richard Bard and his wife are in front of the cemetery.*

---

*A portion of Bard's Mill still can be seen along Mt. Hope Road.*

# 4 Attack and Counterattack in Central Pennsylvania, 1755–1756

## INTRODUCTION

In central Pennsylvania along the tributaries of the Susquehanna River some of the bloodiest fighting of the French and Indian War took place. A long-standing if uneasy peace between the English and Delaware and Shawnee tribes came to an end in October 1755. Two months after Gen. Braddock's disastrous defeat, Delaware warriors from the village of Kittanning struck the first blow against Pennsylvania's unguarded frontier at Penn's Creek. They raided the cabins of German and Swiss settlers who had settled in the area during the previous two years, killing fifteen residents and taking ten others prisoner.

The raid occurred about five miles from the important Delaware village of Shamokin at the Forks of the Susquehanna River. A relief party of militia under the leadership of John Harris Jr. headed north from Harris Ferry. Harris and his men went first to the massacre site and then to Shamokin where the reception was unfriendly. On their return trip, Harris' party was ambushed at the

mouth of Penn's Creek and a number of his men were killed. Fearing reprisal, many of Shamokin's residents fled to upriver Indian towns at Wyoming, Madame Montours, and Great Island. Shamokin was deserted and later burned. In early 1756, Pennsylvania authorities built a line of frontier defense posts at Fort Granville, Patterson's Fort, and Fort Shirley.

But the most important defense undertaking in 1756 was the building of Fort Augusta at the site of Shamokin at the Susquehanna forks. Fort Augusta was supplied along a river route guarded by Fort Halifax and Fort Hunter.

Fort Augusta proved too strong for either the French or Delaware to attempt assault, but in July 1756 Fort Granville fell to a Delaware force led by war chief Captain Jacobs. Two months later, Pennsylvania launched a retaliatory strike against Kittanning. Departing from Fort Shirley, Col. John Armstrong marched across the Allegheny Mountains with a force of 300 men and attacked the village at dawn. Captain Jacobs, his wife, and his son were killed as they attempted to flee their burning cabin.

## SHAMOKIN—SUNBURY, PENNSYLVANIA

The village of Shamokin at the Forks of the Susquehanna River was considered the largest and most important of the Indian villages in Pennsylvania during a 30-year period from the 1720s to 1750s. Here the Delaware established their capital after migrating from eastern Pennsylvania. The Delaware "King" Sassoonan or Allumapees lived here as did Shikellamy, the Iroquois regent who came in 1727 to oversee the subject Delaware and negotiate treaties with Pennsylvania officials. At its peak, Shamokin's population numbered several hundred from a mix of displaced tribes. The village consisted of 50 dwellings surrounded by a wooden palisade. Situated at the forks, Shamokin boasted a central location with major trails leading to the Wyoming Valley, Great Island on the west branch of the Susquehanna, Conrad Weiser's house in the Tulpehocken Valley and the Potomac River.

The Moravians established a mission at Shamokin in the 1740s, but the duty was considered hazardous because of

SITES AT A GLANCE—This map will give you a feel for the general locations of sites in this chapter. Some sites overlap and are not shown on this map.

Penn's Creek massacre
Kittanning
Ft. Augusta
Ft. Shirley
Ft. Hunter
Carlisle
Harris mansion

the village's reputation for debauchery. In 1747, honoring a request from Shikellamy, the Moravians established a blacksmith's shop at Shamokin so gun repairs could be made on the spot. The Moravian blacksmith Marx Kieffer and two missionaries on duty fled Shamokin in 1756 after the Penn's Creek massacre. The Delaware fled to other villages leaving the village deserted and Shamokin's days as an Indian capital came to an end.

## SHIKELLAMY

Think of a Roman proconsul of a border province or an English viceroy in India for an understanding of the role that Shikellamy played on the American frontier. A representative of the formidable Iroquois nation, for two decades starting in 1727 Shikellamy served as regent overseeing Iroquois dealings with such tributary tribes as the Delaware, Conoy, and Nanticoke, and with Pennsylvania officials. Working in league with provincial negotiator Conrad Weiser, Shikellamy is credited with keeping peace for two decades on the Pennsylvania frontier. But that peace only survived Shikellamy's death in 1748 by seven years.

During the long peace, Iroquois policy in Pennsylvania rested on two precepts: staying on good terms with the British, and encouraging migratory tribes to settle in the Susquehanna River Valley as a barrier against further white settlement.

Shikellamy's headquarters was the Indian village of Shamokin at modern day Sunbury, Pennsylvania. This town was a refugee center for tribes like the Delaware being pushed westward by white settlement in eastern Pennsylvania.

As vassals of the Iroquois, the Delaware were forbidden to make war and negotiate their own treaties. This put Shikellamy in the position of negotiating treaties for the sale of Delaware lands to Pennsylvania and settling disputes over the controversial "Walking Purchase" of 1737. Shikellamy also tried to limit the sale of alcohol among the tribes and keep a watchful eye on the Iroquois traditional enemies, the Cherokee and Catawba tribes in the south.

Reports of Shikellamy's early years are conflicting. Some accounts say his father was French and his mother was Cayuga; others say he was a French child, captured and adopted by the Cayuga when a young child. Whatever his roots, Shikellamy was considered a natural diplomat with a dignified and courteous manner.

Much is made of the friendship between Shikellamy and Weiser, an emigrant from the Palatinate region of Germany who had lived among the Mohawks. The well-worn trail between Shikellamy's home at Shamokin and Weiser's home at Womelsdorf was

known as the Tulpehocken Path. But there is an often-repeated story about the pair, that while perhaps fictional, illustrates the tensions between the white and red races on a rapidly changing frontier. It concerns the tradition of granting a wish from a dream.

Shikellamy told about a dream where Weiser gave him a rifle and Weiser obliged him, the story goes. Then Weiser said he had a dream that Shikellamy gave him an island in the Susquehanna River known as the Isle of Que. Shikellamy fulfilled Weiser's dream, but suggested that the two not dream together again.

## MADAME MONTOUR

An interpreter who became familiar with three cultures during a long adventurous life spent on the frontier, Madame Montour (1667-1753) was born in Quebec to a French father and Algonquian Indian mother. Some accounts say her father was a high-ranking Canadian official or nobleman.

Montour spent her early years with family members who traded goods at French posts at Detroit and Milchimackinac. Her life reached a turning point in 1709 with the death of her trader brother Louis at Albany. She blamed French officials for her brother's death and allied herself with the English. Her first important role was as an interpreter for New York's governor.

Montour married an Oneida chief named Carandowana and moved in 1727 to Shamokin where the Iroquois viceroy Shikellamy set up headquarters to negotiate with the English. She continued her duties as interpreter at important peace conferences with Pennsylvania officials. Carandowana was killed later during a war expedition against the Catawba tribe in the south. Madame Montour's homes at Shamokin and the village of French Margaret near modern-day Montoursville were regular stops for travelers.

Madame Montour's son Andrew was also prominent in frontier affairs, having undertaken diplomatic missions for Pennsylvania and Virginia. The family name lives on in Montoursville, Montour County, and Montour's Island near Pittsburgh.

## PENN'S CREEK MASSACRE NEAR NEW BERLIN, PENNSYLVANIA

*Directions: Follow Route 304 three miles west of New Berlin. Go right on Route 3016 or Ridge Road, continue for one mile. At intersection with Dice Road or TR 338, look for small stone monument on left. Landmarks in vicinity include a SR 3016 sign, a small traffic island of grass at intersection, and green farmhouse with red barn.*

For seventy-five years, the agreements reached by William Penn and the Delaware chiefs under the Treaty Elm at Shakamaxon kept peace on Pennsylvania's frontier. It was Penn's policy to expand Pennsylvania's boundaries by purchasing tracts of land from the Delaware. Penn's sons continued this policy even though they angered the Delaware with the infamous Walking Purchase of 1737 and later by negotiating land sales over the Delawares' heads with their overlords, the Iroquois. The Penns' final land purchase before the French and Indian War, opened lands drained by the Juniata River to white settlement. This purchase was negotiated in 1754 with the Iroquois at Albany, New York.

Within months of the Albany agreement, German and Swiss settlers started to build homesteads and till the rich soil along Penn's Creek at the northern boundary of the purchase. Many of these settlers had only recently made the transatlantic crossing from Europe and were attracted by the prospect of affordable land on the frontier.

When war threatened in 1755, the Delaware tribes along the Allegheny River sided with the French, and set out to drive the whites off their lost lands. The Penn's Creek settlers were isolated and vulnerable, and on Oct. 16, 1755, they were the first to feel the blow. A Delaware war party from Kittanning came over the mountains to the headwaters of the west branch of the Susquehanna River, crossed the plains known as the Clearfields and then followed the course of Penn's Creek to the settlements.

They attacked a number of homes along Penn's Creek without warning, killing fifteen settlers and taking ten others captive. The victims suffered a grisly death in some cases. The home of John Jacob LeRoy was attacked first. LeRoy, a French Huguenot from Switzerland, was killed and his children, Marie and Jacob, as well as another girl who lived in the house were taken prisoner. LeRoy's body was later found half-charred in the ashes of his home. Two tomahawks were embedded in his head.

The raiders moved on to the residence of Sebastian Leininger and demanded rum and tobacco. They then killed Leininger and his son and took his two daughters, Regina, 10, and Barbara, 12, captive. Mrs. Leininger was at a nearby mill and escaped the carnage. Survivors fled to the home of George Gabriel near where Penn's Creek flows into the Susquehanna River. Reports of the massacre soon reached Conrad Weiser at Tuplehocken, and John Harris Jr., downriver at Harris Ferry. On October 20, fourteen residents "living near the Mouth of Penn's Creek on the West Side of the Susquehannah" sent a petition for help to Pennsylvania Gov. Robert Hunter Morris:

> ...The Terror of which has drove away almost all these back Inhabitants except us, the Subscribers, with a few more who are willing to stay and endeavor to defend the Land; but as we are not able of ourselves to defend it for want of Guns and Ammunition, and but few in number, so that without assistance we must fly and leave the Country to the mercy of the Enemy.

William Penn's peace was broken.

Today, the site of the Penn's Creek Massacre remains a farming valley noted for its pastoral scenes of cornfields, rolled bundles of hay, and mountain ridges off to the west. The site of the LeRoy homestead is several miles north of Penn's Creek, marked by a small stone monument erected in 1919 by the Union County Historical Society. The plaque reads: "John Jacob LeRoy was killed by the Indians near this spot during the time of the Penn's Creek Massacre—Oct. 16, 1755." LeRoy chose this spot to settle because of a nearby spring. The spring still flows today and is called LeRoy Spring.

*John LeRoy was killed in 1755.*

## Regina Leininger

*Directions: Take Route 422 east of Reading, turn onto Main Street, Stouchsburg, go to west end of town. Before road connects with Route 422, turn left on lane toward imposing fieldstone church. Walled cemetery to right of church. The Leininger gravestone is in first row of graves to right of gate.*

45

Regina Leininger's captivity and reunion with her mother is one of the more remarkable stories in frontier annals. Regina was ten years old when captured by Delaware warriors on Oct. 16, 1755, during the Penn's Creek massacre. Her father and brother were killed defending the family home. Her mother was away at a mill when the raiders struck and thus spared death or captivity. Regina, her older sister Barbara, and Marie LeRoy were led west to the Delaware village of Kittanning under the care of a Delaware named Kalasquay.

Barbara made an escape attempt, but was quickly recaptured. After that, Regina was separated from the other two girls. When Col. John Armstrong attacked Kittanning in 1756, the captives there were moved to the west. Regina's trail fades at this point, but Barbara and Marie were taken first to Fort Duquesne and then to other villages in the Ohio Valley. In the spring of 1759, Barbara and Marie along with other captives made their escape from a village along the Muskingum River in Ohio and traveled 150 miles east to reach British-held Fort Pitt and eventually went to Philadelphia.

For Regina, recovery came five years later at the end of Pontiac's War. She was among hundreds of captives handed over by the Shawnee and Delaware. Colonel Henry Bouquet led an invading army into the Muskingum River region in the fall of 1764 and the tribes sued for peace. Bouquet demanded that all white captives be given up even in situations where the whites had become acclimated to Indian life and wanted to stay.

*Stouchsburg Church. Regina Leininger is buried here.*

In December, Bouquet brought many of the captives to the main square at Carlisle for reunions with their long-lost families. Mrs. Leininger came from Berks County, but failed to recognize her now-grown daughter among the former captives standing in line. She asked Bouquet for help and the colonel suggested she try to spark the girl's memory with something familiar from their life together.

Mrs. Leininger sang a verse in German, "Alone, yet not alone am I, in this my solitude," and Regina ran to her. Regina lived out her life in Berks County. She is buried in the graveyard of the 1786 Christ Evangelical Lutheran Church in Stouchsburg off Route 422. The modern gravestone was erected by the Berks County Cemetery Association. The engraving reads: "Regina Leininger in legend. Regina Hartman. As a small child held Indian captive 1755-1763. Identified by her mother's singing the hymn "Allein, und doch nicht ganz allein.""

## JOHN HARRIS AMBUSH
## SELINSGROVE, PENNSYLVANIA

*Directions: Route 11/15 south from Shamokin Dam. Take exit for Selinsgrove onto Susquehanna Trail. At first stoplight, turn left on Airport Road. Then take first right on Old Trail Road. Look for stone monument just right of "No Outlet" sign.*

The Penn's Creek massacre drew an immediate response from English settlers living south of the Blue Mountain range. John Harris Jr. and a party of 40 men left Paxton and rode on horseback to scout the burned cabins along Penn's Creek. They headed to the Delaware village of Shamokin to learn the identity of the attackers and stayed overnight, but the reception was strained. Harris was advised to return along the east shore of the Susquehanna River, but fearing a trap he led his party down the west shore.

The party was ambushed by a band of 20-30 hostile Indians near the mouth of Penn's or Mahantango Creek. Harris and his men headed into the woods and killed four Indians in the initial volley. The group retreated a half-mile through the woods losing three of their party and then crossed the Susquehanna River to make good their escape.

On a small bluff overlooking Penn's Creek stands a stone monument erected in 1915 to commemorate the massacre and ambush. Another monument marks the northern boundary line of the 1754 Albany land purchase. The inscription reads: "October 25, 1755, John Harris and a party of 40 who came up the river to investigate the massacre were ambushed near the mouth of the creek at the Isle of Que, one-third mile south of this spot."

*These monuments note the ambush of the John Harris party and the boundary of disputed land purchase.*

## Fort Augusta — Sunbury, Pennsylvania

*Directions: From Route 15 on west shore of Susquehanna River. Cross river on Veterans Memorial Bridge (Route 61) to Sunbury. Follow North Front Street north along east shore of river for several blocks. Fort signs and state historical markers are on right. Parking lot behind Hunter House.*

Fort Augusta was built in 1756 at the Forks of the Susquehanna River. One of the most strategic spots on the Pennsylvania frontier, this is where the north and west branches of the Susquehanna meet to form the main stem. It was a meeting place for several major Indian trails — the Warriors Path, Tulpehocken Path, and Tuscarora Path, to name a few. Because of its central location, the mixed-tribal village of Shamokin, known as the Indian Capital of Pennsylvania, was established here in the 1720s. The residents of Shamokin fled north after the initial Delaware raids into nearby Penn's Creek in the fall of 1755.

At the urging of Iroquois emissaries, Pennsylvania officials sent troops up the Susquehanna River to build Fort Augusta on the site of abandoned Shamokin in the summer of 1756. Iroquois leader, Scarouady, saw the fort as a means of protecting pro-British Indians in the region from both French intrigues and frontiersmen seeking revenge for raids. Governor Robert Hunter Morris desired a fort at this spot to guard against a French advance from the west. The fort's legal standing was tenuous, however, as it stood on land outside Pennsylvania's official boundary.

Colonel William Clapham, Major James Burd, and the "Augusta" regiment of 400 soldiers departed from Harris Ferry in May 1756 on the fort-building expedition. The soldiers first built Fort Halifax as a supply point on the east shore of the Susquehanna River. A fleet of bateaux carried supplies upriver from Harris Ferry. The construction of Fort Augusta started in July and was completed by September.

Fort Augusta was of substantial size on the river's east bank — a log structure measuring 200 x 200 feet, surrounded by a moat. The fort featured four bastions at the corners, and inside the walls were six buildings. With a garrison of 400 men and 12 mounted cannon, Fort Augusta boasted enough firepower to discourage a direct attack by the French or their Delaware and Shawnee allies.

Periodic rumors spread of a large French army marching south along the west branch of the Susquehanna, but the threat never materialized. At one point, a small French force probed Fort Augusta's defenses to see if an assault was feasible. Twice, companies from the fort went on expeditions up the Susquehanna's West Branch to attack pro-French Indian villages, but found the villages burnt and abandoned.

In early 1757, Col. James Burd took over command of the fort. The province established an Indian trading post there, also in 1757. In 1758, an underground brick powder magazine was built inside the fort. The magazine survives today as one of the best preserved military structures in Pennsylvania from the French and Indian War.

Fort Augusta was an important stopping point for emissaries of the Iroquois, and eastern and western Delaware involved in negotiations leading up to the Treaty of Easton in 1758. During the American Revolution, Fort Augusta served as a refuge for American settlers fleeing attacks by the pro-British Iroquois. The fort was a supply base for the 1779 Sullivan expedition that put Iroquois villages in New York's Genesee River region to the torch.

*The Hunter mansion houses the Fort Augusta museum.*

Today the fort is a state historical site managed by the Northumberland County Historical Society. Visitors to the site can walk down a stairway into the underground powder magazine. Exhibits dealing with the fort's history are in the 1852 Hunter House, built by the grandson of the fort's last commandant. Thanks to several archaeological digs, the exhibits feature many interesting items, including tools from the pre-fort Moravian blacksmith shop, pieces of stockade posts, and gun parts. Also on display is a four pounder cannon recovered from the river bottom and a striking opalescent trade bead necklace recovered from the grave of Shikellamy, Iroquois viceroy at Shamokin. The museum is open 1 p.m. to 4 p.m. Monday, Wednesday, Friday and Saturday. Call to check hours at 570-286-4083.

## PATTERSON'S FORT — MEXICO, PENNSYLVANIA

*Directions: Heading west on Route 322, take Route 75 exit south to Route 3001 (or old Route 322). Turn left on Route 3001 past Fort Bigham state historical marker. Drive east through Mexico to fork in road with sign for Fish Commission's Walker access area. Patterson monument and Staring highway marker on small plot of land at fork. Head east short distance on Route 3001 to reach Patterson's Fort highway marker. Note high ground in vicinity and Tuscarora Mountain looming in background.*

James Patterson is a good example of the Scots-Irish settlers who moved into the Juniata and Tuscarora Valleys in the 1740s and 1750s. These settlers took possession of land with the title sometimes in doubt, and within a few years were forced to defend their holdings. Patterson (1715-72) was born in Lancaster County, then moved west, settling in 1751 near Tuscarora Mountain and the ancient Tuscarora Path on land overlooking the Juniata River. Patterson built a mill and fortified house at the site and traded rum and tobacco with Indians for furs. He was known as "Big Shot" among the Delaware for his skill at hitting a shooting target that he kept in a prominent place.

Patterson settled on lands that once had been occupied by "squatters," immigrants who settled west of provincial boundary lines in defiance of official edicts to stay out of Indian territory. As early as 1741, Frederick Staring (also known as Star or Starns) and others from New York's Mohawk Valley had settled at this spot. He was among a number of squatters who were forcibly evicted from their cabins by provincial officials intent on keeping on friendly terms with the Delaware. After his eviction, Staring moved on to Virginia.

Patterson arrived after the last round of evictions in 1750 and always maintained he held clear title to his land. With the outbreak of the French and Indian War in 1755, he played an important role in the region's defense. Patterson and his son William maintained two fortified houses for use as refuges and supply depots and led scouting parties in search of enemy raiders. In the fall of 1755, Patterson successfully defended his fort from attack. In March 1756, Patterson and a party engaged in a skirmish with Indians in the Middle Creek area. Both Pattersons held important commands with provincial forces throughout the war.

At the eastern edge of the small village of Mexico, a stone monument to James Patterson stands. It was erected in 1920 by Patterson family descendants. In the same vicinity is a highway marker commemorating the first white settlement in Juniata County. This relates the story of Frederick Staring and his eviction. A state highway marker for Patterson's Fort is located on Route 3001, 1/10 mile east of Mexico.

## FORT BIGHAM
### SOUTH OF PORT ROYAL, PENNSYLVANIA

*Directions: Heading south on Route 75, Fort Bigham monument is on west side of road in small grove of hemlock trees. The monument is at intersection of Route 75 and SR 3006 that veers off here at northeast angle. An unpaved farm lane extends to west. State highway sign next to monument reads "Fort Loudon 43 Port Royal 12."*

Fort Bigham was a private stockade built by Samuel Bigham. This fort was situated in a valley just west of Tuscarora Mountain and thus it was in an exposed position when Delaware warriors raided the Juniata Valley. A war party overran Fort Bigham on June 11, 1756, and killed or captured all 23 settlers who had gathered there for protection. The Delaware had apparently set out to attack Fort Shirley, but found that too heavily defended and settled on Fort Bigham as a substitute target. The fall of Fort Bigham and of Fort Granville a month later showed the Juniata Valley to be one of the weakest links in a line of English forts running from the Delaware River to the Shenandoah Valley.

***Fort Bigham monument.***

Today, the drive along Route 75 from Port Royal to Fort Loudon at Route 30 is one of the most scenic in Pennsylvania. Route 75 follows the Tuscarora Path, an ancient Indian path associated with the northern migration of the Tuscarora tribe from North Carolina to New York State.

A stone monument for Fort Bigham is located on Route 75 twelve miles south of Port Royal. The inscription reads:

> 58 Rods (one rod equals 16.5 feet) northwest is the marked site of Fort Bigham. Erected 1754 by pioneer settlers: captured and burned by Indians June 11, 1756. The twenty or more persons in the fort were massacred or carried away. Rebuilt 1760. Destroyed by Indians 1766. The Inhabitants were warned by a friendly Indian and escaped. Erected and dedicated by the Historical Society of Juniata County June 12, 1934.

## FORT GRANVILLE—LEWISTOWN, PENNSYLVANIA

*Directions: Take Route 522 south to boundary for city of Lewistown. Look for red brick PennDOT building on left. Stone monument next to state historical marker.*

The fall of Fort Granville in July 1756 to a force of French, Delaware, and Shawnee came as a profound shock to Pennsylvania officials and led to a rethinking of their war strategy. Fort Granville was built in January 1756, one of three provincial forts intended to guard settlers living west of the Susquehanna River. The two other forts in this defensive line were Fort Shirley and Fort Lyttelton. Fort Granville was built in the vicinity of scattered settlements in the Juniata River valley, but it also held strategic value. "This Fort commands a narrow pass where the Juniata falls through the mountains which is so circumscribed that a few men can maintain it against a much greater number," wrote Gov. Robert Hunter Morris.

Built under the direction of Captain George Croghan, the fort consisted of a wooden stockade with bastions at the corners and barracks to house a garrison of 75 men. During its brief existence, the garrison was plagued by supply problems that at times left gunpowder scarce. In the spring of 1756, Delaware and Shawnee war parties skirted Fort Granville and ranged through the Juniata and Tuscarora Valleys, falling upon isolated cabins and killing the inhabitants. Fort Bigham, a private stockade fifteen miles southeast of Fort Granville, fell to the enemy on June 11. On July 22, a force of 60 Delaware and Shawnee warriors and French soldiers attacked Fort Granville, but they were driven back after a five-hour battle with the help of the fort's swivel guns. Then in a fateful move, the commander Captain Edward Ward and a large portion of the garrison departed the fort to guard farmers gathering hay in Sherman's Valley.

The weakened garrison of 24 men remaining at Fort Granville found itself under attack on July 30 by a larger force under the command of French Capt. Louis Coulon de Villiers, the victor at Fort Necessity, and the Delaware Captain Jacobs. The garrison was short of ammunition, and to compound its problems, the attackers crawled through a natural ravine and got close enough to the fort's stockade to set it afire. The ranking officer, Lt. Edward Armstrong, was killed after a wall was breached and the attackers called upon the garrison to surrender. John Turner opened the fort gates and twenty-two men, three women, and a half-dozen children were captured. Many of the captives were taken to the Delaware town of Kittanning, and Turner was burned at the stake there.

With the loss of Fort Granville, Pennsylvania officials decided to retrench farther to the east and the remaining settlers fled the Juniata Valley. Pennsylvania soon launched a retaliatory raid on Kittanning. This raid was led by Col. John Armstrong, the brother of Fort Granville's fallen commander.

The Fort Granville site was destroyed by construction of the Pennsylvania Canal in 1829. However, a stone monument to the fort was erected in 1916 on Route 522 in the southwest section of Lewistown. The monument stands in front of the state transportation department's District 2-3 maintenance building. A plaque reads: "About 650 yards south of this spot on the high bank of the Juniata River was the site of Fort Granville, erected 1755-56." Public access to the river is limited in this area by commercial development, yet one can stand at the spot and see how the fort was ringed by hills. The nearest riverfront access is at the Klinger boat launching area north of this spot.

## Fort Halifax—North of Halifax, Pennsylvania

*Directions: Take Route 147 north of Halifax for 1/2 mile. Monument is on left side of road near fort site. State historical marker nearby.*

Fort Halifax stood along a bend on the east bank of the Susquehanna River. This log stockade served as a supply depot and communications post, and was situated near the mouth of Armstrong's Creek. The creek was named for Robert Armstrong who operated a mill in the vicinity prior to the French and Indian War.

Fort Halifax was too far north of the Blue Mountains to offer any real protection to frontier settlements, but it served as a key supply link to Pennsylvania's stronghold in the region, Fort Augusta at the Forks of the Susquehanna. In fact, Colonel William Clapham and the "Augusta" regiment built Fort Halifax quickly in June

1756 so they could get on with the main task of constructing Fort Augusta. The provincial troops built a log stockade and four bastions here.

Named after a British earl, Fort Halifax was at its busiest while supplies were shipped upriver to Fort Augusta. Provincial officials abandoned Fort Halifax in October 1757. They felt that the location was not the best for defense due to the surrounding hills and a large island in the Susquehanna River that obscured the view of the west shore.

Today the fort site is in a cornfield on an elevation overlooking the Susquehanna. This site is on private property, but a tall stone monument on Route 147 marks the location. The inscription reads:

One of the chain of frontier defenses of the Province of Pennsylvania in the French and Indian Wars stood 500 feet to the west. Built 1756 by its commander, Colonel William Clapham. Marked by the Pennsylvania Historical Commission and the Society of Pennsylvania Women in New York. 1926.

*View of Susquehanna River from area of Fort Halifax.*

## Fort Hunter Park—Rockville, Pennsylvania

*Directions: From I-81 eastbound to Harrisburg, take Front Street north exit. Follow Front Street for two miles until signs for Fort Hunter Park. Parking lots on both sides of road.*

Fort Hunter occupied a strategic position on a bluff overlooking the point where Fishing Creek enters the Susquehanna River. Fort Hunter was situated on the east shore of the river at the southern end of Blue Mountain.

Benjamin Chambers and his three brothers settled at this spot in the 1720s before moving on to the Conococheague Valley. Samuel Hunter, a son-in-law of one of the Chambers brothers, inherited the property and ran the grist and saw mills located here.

In October 1755 after the Penn's Creek Massacre, local militia gathered here to await the rumored approach of 1,500 French troops down the Susquehanna. After matters calmed a bit, Hunter's Mill continued to be guarded by militia. During the winter, a log stockade was built around the mill here. Thomas McKee, an Indian trader, commanded troops here in early 1756.

Fort Hunter was one of the stopping places for ranger companies patrolling the Blue Mountain passes. Captain Adam Reed was responsible for patrolling an area between Indiantown Gap and Fort Hunter with his 50 rangers. Despite the activities of the rangers, Delaware raiders killed settlers in the fort's vicinity during the next two years. One attack occurred in October 1757 while four local men were harvesting corn. Two escaped, but two were killed and scalped.

In the spring of 1756, Fort Hunter played a role in the march of the "Augusta" regiment to the Forks of the Susquehanna. A contingent from the regiment was stationed here to facilitate the movement of supplies upriver while Fort Augusta was built.

Provincial officials had planned to abandon Fort Hunter in 1757 so they could station their forces more effectively, but they relented after Paxton Township residents sent a petition saying such a move would expose them to danger. Thus, soldiers were stationed here at least through 1758. During Pontiac's War in 1763-64, troops were again stationed here.

Today this picturesque spot is the site of Fort Hunter Park, owned by Dauphin County. The Federal-style mansion on the fort site was built in three sections starting in 1786 by Captain Archibald McAllister. This mansion on the west side of North Front Street is maintained as a museum open to the public. A stone monument to Fort Hunter is located on North Front Street near the steps leading to the rear of the mansion. The inscription reads:

> A short distance west of this stone stood Fort Hunter, otherwise known as the fort at Hunter's Mill. This fort, consisting of a blockhouse, surrounded by a stockade, was built during the winter of 1755-56. It was used as a base of supplies and as a rendezvous for troops during the period of the Indian Wars. All traces of this fort were removed when the present building was erected in 1814. Erected by the Pennsylvania Historical Commission 1916.

A state historical marker is nearby.

Fort Hunter Park consists of a number of distinctive 19th century farm buildings. A stone tavern built in 1800 by McAllister has been recently restored. A nearby trail follows the course of a preserved, but waterless, section of the Pennsylvania Canal on the east side of the park.

## JOHN HARRIS MANSION AND HARRIS FERRY
## HARRISBURG, PENNSYLVANIA

Harris Ferry was a major crossing point on the Susquehanna River for generations of westbound settlers. John Harris Sr. (1673-1748), a licensed Indian trader, established himself in the vicinity about 1712. His son John Harris Jr., (1727-1791) helped to organize the region's defenses at his fortified house here after the outbreak of the French and Indian War in 1755.

Harris Sr., an English emigrant, built a trading post at this natural ford and dealt in furs with the Shawnee and Delaware living along the Susquehanna. In 1733, he was granted the right to operate a ferry here by the Penn brothers. Harris Ferry served as a funnel for Scots-Irish and German settlers headed into the Cumberland Valley.

There is a famous legend about John Harris, Sr. He operated an inn where liquor was sold, and according to the story, a group of Indians arrived at the inn one day in 1720 and demanded to buy rum. Harris would not sell them any alcohol, so they tied him to a mulberry tree and prepared to burn him. Harris was saved by the actions of his black servant Hercules who recruited some friendly Indians to intervene on his behalf. Or so the legend goes.

John Harris Jr. took over the trading and ferry operation established by his father. He went on numerous trading trips via the pack trails to the Ohio Valley. On one westward trip, Harris kept an account of the mileage between major landmarks on the Frankstown Path. In 1754, after the French expelled the British from the Ohio Valley, the Iroquois viceroy Tanacharison who was pro-British ended up as an exile at Harris Ferry. Tanacharison died here and is buried in an unknown location.

Harris played a key role in defending the Susquehanna Valley after the Penn's Creek massacre in October 1755. He led a party of 40 men north to investigate the attack, but this group was ambushed at the mouth of Penn's Creek. He furnished Pennsylvania Governor Robert Hunter Morris with information about conditions on the frontier in the aftermath of the Delaware and Shawnee raids. Tension ran high during this time, and gave birth to a widely-circulated but false rumor that a force of 1,500 French and Indians were marching toward the Forks of the Susquehanna at Shamokin.

Harris turned his house into a fortified stronghold by cutting firing loopholes in the walls of his house, and putting a stockade around it. Harris Ferry occupied a strategic location on the war front. The provincial government sent ammunition to Harris and groups of militia gathered here. War councils were also held here.

In the spring of 1756, Harris Ferry served as the staging point for the provincial army's expedition to build Fort

Augusta at the Forks of the Susquehanna. Governor Robert Hunter Morris went there to oversee operations. The "Augusta" regiment of 400 soldiers left Harris Ferry on May 31 to start the expedition that built Fort Halifax and Fort Augusta. A fleet of boats was built to carry supplies upriver.

After the war ended, Harris in 1764-66 built the limestone mansion that stands today at 219 South Front St. He laid out the town of Harrisburg in 1785. The mansion is the home of the Dauphin County Historical Society. John Harris, Sr., is buried in a plot surrounded by an iron fence in Riverfront Park across from the mansion. Harris Jr. is buried in the graveyard of Paxton Church on Wilhelm Street in Harrisburg. A stone monument in the park on the west side of South Front Street has this inscription:

Harris Ferry. On the river bank, a short distance west of this stone, was the landing place of Harris' Ferry, the most historic crossing place on the Susquehanna. A great part of the early migration into western Pennsylvania and the Ohio Valley passed this way. The ferry-right was first granted to John Harris Sr., father of the founder of Harrisburg in December 1733. For over half a century the site of Harrisburg was known as Harris' Ferry. Erected by the Pennsylvania Historical Commission September 24, 1915.

## State Museum of Pennsylvania
### Harrisburg, Pennsylvania

The state museum features four floors of exhibits on Pennsylvania's human and natural history. The circular-shaped building next to the state capitol building is operated by the Pennsylvania Historical and Museum Commission.

The museum contains artifacts and exhibits relating to the colonial period. The archaeology rooms include artifacts recovered from digs at Fort Augusta and Fort Loudon. The exhibits feature the reconstructed water well at Fort Loudon. The well is positioned to give visitors a worm's eye view of the objects thrown down into it by British soldiers, settlers, and farmers.

Nearby are impressive displays of artifacts from 10,000 years of prehistoric occupation of Pennsylvania. The displays feature choice examples of dugout canoes, projectile points, clay pots, stone tools, and trading beads. Life-size dioramas depict Susquehannock and Delaware habitations in the forests and riverbanks. The technology rooms include exhibits on log-cabin construction, grain mills, and iron furnaces.

The museum is open 9 a.m. to 5 p.m., Tuesday through Saturday and noon to 5 p.m. Sunday. Admission is free.

## Carlisle Public Square
### Carlisle, Pennsylvania

*Directions: Follow Route 34 (Hanover Street) or Route 641 (High Street) to their intersection at the center of Carlisle.*

The intersection in the center of Carlisle was once the junction of several Indian paths. The square was laid out in 1751, the year of Carlisle's founding, on land donated by Thomas Penn for public use. During the French and Indian War, Carlisle was the largest British town west of the Susquehanna River. It boasted more than 60 houses, a shelter for refugees, and a starting point for military expeditions to the west.

In July 1755, Pennsylvania Gov. Robert Hunter Morris was in Carlisle at the time of General Braddock's defeat. He ordered the building of a provincial fort on the west side of the square (West High Street) and commissioned militia companies. A makeshift stockade was constructed, and in 1756 work began on a larger log fort. Provincial troops under Col. John Armstrong were stationed here.

In 1757, troops from the Royal American regiment under General John Stanwix arrived in Carlisle and built earthworks on the northeast side of town where the modern Carlisle Barracks, a U.S. Army post, is located. These troops helped to build the stone First Presbyterian Church that today, still stands on the northwest corner of the public square. Then, in 1758, Gen. John Forbes used Carlisle as the starting point for his expedition to drive the French from the Forks of the Ohio. And Carlisle was again flooded with refugees during Pontiac's War in 1763-64.

Near the public square a gunsmith shop built in 1764 still stands. The shop of gunsmith Thomas Butler is on Dickinson Alley off West Pitt Street.

In 1764, a poignant reunion occurred at the square. Some 200 white captives taken by the Shawnee and Delaware during a decade of warfare accompanied Col. Henry Bouquet's army back to the east after the successful Muskingum River campaign. They gathered at the square where long-separated parents and children, siblings and spouses found each other again. Here Regina Leininger, a captive taken in the 1755 Penn's Creek massacre, was reunited with her mother. The mother and daughter recognized each other only after the mother sang a verse of a German song.

A stone monument and site map of historic sites is located on the square's southwest corner near the old courthouse.

## FORT ROBINSON
### WEST OF LOYSVILLE, PENNSYLVANIA

*Directions: From Carlisle, take Route 34 across "Croghan's Gap" to Route 850. Follow Route 850 west which parallels the old traders path to Loysville. Two miles west of Loysville is intersection of Routes 850 and 274. A state historical marker for Fort Robinson is near intersection. Bear right on Route 850 for 8/10 mile. Look for stone monument in cul-de-sac on right curve by a 30 m.p.h sign.*

Fort Robinson was a private stockade built in 1755 by George Robinson and his brothers. They were among the first white settlers in the Shermans Creek Valley, and may have squatted on the land before they secured title. The fort was situated along the New Path, one of the key routes for Indian traders headed to the Ohio country. The New Path linked trader George Croghan's house in East Pennsboro Township along the Conodoguinet Creek with his trading post at Aughwick.

Fort Robinson was located north of the Blue Mountain range near Sherman Creek. Delaware raiders struck the area in December 1755, and in July 1756, Delaware warriors attacked the fort. They killed several women, and took others prisoner, including Hugh Gibson, a fifteen-year-old boy who years later gave an account of his captivity.

*Fort Robinson monument.*

Gibson was first taken to Kittanning where he was adopted as a member of the tribe. After Kittanning was burned by Col. John Armstrong's troops, Gibson lived at Kuskuski and King Beaver's Town in the Ohio Valley and later at a village along the Muskingum River. In 1759, Gibson and fellow captives Barbara Leininger and Marie Le Roy made a successful escape to British Fort Pitt.

The site of Fort Robinson is farmland today and marked by a stone monument. The inscription reads:

> On the elevation 130 feet east of this marker the pioneer settlers erected a stockade known as Fort Robinson in 1755, the very year of the opening of these lands to settlement. In an attack on the fort during harvest time in 1756, the Indians killed a daughter of Robert Miller, Mrs. James Wilson and took Hugh Gibson and Betty Henry prisoner. Perry County Historical Society 1927.

The monument is located in a natural cul-de-sac on north side of Route 850 at base of the elevation. A small stream, Bixler's Run, is on the south side of the road.

## FORT SHIRLEY — SHIRLEYSBURG, PENNSYLVANIA

The story of Fort Shirley and George Croghan, the roguish Indian trader who gained and lost several fortunes, are inextricably linked. Croghan came to America from Ireland in 1741 and within several years was licensed as an Indian trader. Croghan's trading activities extended into the Ohio Valley and he was a frequent visitor to Logstown, the capital of the Iroquois living in that region. Croghan first lived in East Pennsboro Township just west of the Susquehanna River, but by 1751 he established his main trading post at Aughwick west of Tuscarora Mountain and within territory claimed by the Delaware. Croghan was deep in debt to Philadelphia merchants; he moved west to escape being imprisoned for debt, a common punishment at the time.

Croghan often represented Pennsylvania authorities in dealings with the Iroquois and Delaware. When the British position in the Ohio Valley was jeopardized after the surrender of Fort Necessity in 1754, Queen Aliquippa, Tanacharison, and other pro-British Indians sought safety at Aughwick. Croghan lost several storehouses and inventories of trading goods when French forces occupied the Ohio region.

Crogan fortified his trading post at Aughwick in 1755; after Braddock's defeat he was commissioned a captain of provincial forces. He raised a force of several hundred men and built Fort Granville, and also erected a stockade around his trading post. The post was named Fort Shirley in honor of Massachusetts Gov. William Shirley.

Meanwhile, Croghan's creditors took note of his service to Pennsylvania and persuaded the General Assembly to pass legislation giving him a 10-year moratorium on paying his debts. King George II repealed that law in 1758. Financial matters continued to trouble Croghan. By March 1757, Croghan had resigned his captain's commission following a dispute with authorities over bills he submitted to cover pay and supplies for his men. Croghan became deputy superintendent of Indian affairs under Sir William Johnson and continued to play a major role in the war.

Captain Hugh Mercer took command of Fort Shirley. Like the officers at Fort Granville, Mercer struggled with supply problems, warning at one point that his guns were unfit for use and his men lacked cartridge boxes and pouches to store powder and lead. With the fall of Fort Granville in July 1756, Fort Shirley was considered too vulnerable. The fort served as a rendezvous for Col. John Armstrong's raid on Kittanning, and after that it was abandoned.

The site of Fort Shirley is marked by stone monument and state highway marker at the northern edge of Shirleysburg on the left side of Route 522. The monument is located on a knoll near a highway bridge that crosses a stream named Fort Run.

*Monument to Fort Shirley.*
**Built in 1755 by Indian trader George Croghan.**

# KITTANNING—KITTANNING RIVERFRONT PARK, KITTANNING, PENNSYLVANIA

*Directions: From Route 422 east, follow signs to Kittanning. (Avoid West Kittanning). Take Water Street exit north along riverfront park. Monument at Water and Market Streets by river bridge.*

For thirty years, Kittanning, or Attique, was the principal village of the Delaware who had migrated west in the 1720s from eastern Pennsylvania. This village along the Allegheny River was at the juncture of important trading paths. The main village was on the bottomland by the east shore of the river, but there were settlements on the west shore as well. The village consisted of log cabins, cornfields, and a longhouse where ceremonies were held.

With the start of the French and Indian War in 1755, Kittanning became the base from which the Delaware war chiefs Shingas and Captain Jacobs launched raids on English settlements in the Susquehanna and Potomac River valleys. One of the war paths used was the Great Shamokin Path leading from Kittanning to Shamokin at the Forks of the Susquehanna. Many of the white prisoners captured in those raids were taken to Kittanning.

In the summer of 1756, the provincial defense system in the Juniata River valley was in tatters. Fort Bigham and Fort Granville had been captured and burned down by Delaware raiders. Lieutenant Edward Armstrong, the commander of Fort Granville, was killed in the defense of the fort. Pennsylvania officials decided a retaliatory attack was necessary. Colonel John Armstrong, brother of the slain lieutenant, was picked to lead an attack on Kittanning. Armstrong gathered a force of several hundred men from garrisons at Fort Lyttelton, Fort Shirley, Fort McDowell, and Patterson's Fort.

The troops set out from Fort Shirley on August 30. Following Indian trader paths, they arrived undetected at Kittanning in the early morning hours of September 8. Armstrong's troops attacked the village at daylight and the Delaware emerged from their cabins yelling that the white men had attacked. Many villagers fled, taking their white captives with them, but others fired back at the attackers. The fighting was most intense around Captain Jacobs' cabin. Armstrong was wounded in the shoulder by a shot fired from that cabin.

His soldiers began setting the cabins on fire. Captain Jacobs was killed in the battle; some accounts say Captain Jacobs, his wife and son were shot down when they fled their burning cabin. The fighting lasted until noon. Armstrong decided to withdraw after receiving word that reinforcements for the Delaware had been spotted on the west shore of the river.

*Kittanning monument.*
*Delaware village on the Allegheny River was attacked by Pennsylvania troops in 1756.*

About 100 white prisoners were at Kittanning. Eleven prisoners escaped in the confusion of the fighting, but the rest were spirited away and eventually taken to Delaware villages along the Ohio River. Barbara Leininger and Marie Le Roy, two girls seized during the Penn's Creek massacre in October 1755, later reported that a woman captive who was recaptured after a brief escape met a horrible end. This captive was burned at the stake in the ruins of Kittanning. Hugh Gibson, a teenage boy captured at Fort Robinson in Shermans Creek Valley earlier that year, was taken from Kittanning to Kuskuski and then King Beaver's Town.

Armstrong's men made a hurried journey home arriving back at Fort Lytellton on September 12. Some of his command became separated in the wilderness and arrived days later at places as distant as Fort Cumberland and Fort Augusta. Armstrong lost about 20 men altogether; Delaware casualties are harder to determine. Armstrong's raid

provided a psychological boost to the British, but provincial authorities decided to evacuate Fort Shirley and concentrate on a defense line further east. The Delaware war leaders abandoned Kittanning for towns along the Ohio.

The modern town of Kittanning occupies the site of the Delaware village. The town's Riverfront Park, which includes part of the village site, provides a scenic greenway and public access to the river. A large stone monument at Water and Market Streets in the park carries this inscription:

Kittanning or Attique Indian Town was located on this river flat. The chief settlement as early as 1727 of the Lenni-Lenape or Delaware Indians in their early westward movement from the Susquehanna River. Became the most important Indian center west of Allegheny Mountains. Destroyed September 8, 1756 by Col. John Armstrong and his 300 frontier troops from the Cumberland Valley. Pennsylvania Historical Commission and Armstrong County Historical Society—1926.

# 5

# Moravian Missions Attacked—
# Benjamin Franklin Organizes Defense,
# 1755-1757

## INTRODUCTION

The land bounded by the Delaware and Lehigh Rivers was prized by two races. The fighting in the region covering the Forks of the Delaware in 1755-57 determined that European settlers—the Moravians and Scots-Irish—would hold this land and leave it to their descendants. The Delaware claimed they were cheated of ownership in a controversial 1737 land transaction with the sons of William Penn. They made one last attempt to reclaim their birthright, sending raiding parties over the Blue Mountains in the fall of 1755. But the British victory over the French in western Pennsylvania in 1758 ended any Delaware hopes of returning to the Forks of the Delaware.

The Delawares' specific grievance dealt with the Walking Purchase, a trick used by Thomas and John Penn to extend the boundaries of a land tract they purchased from the tribe as far as possible. Instead of having men measure the boundaries in a leisurely walk over a day-and-a-half as was customary, the Penns hired runners who covered 65 miles to a point north of the Blue Mountains. On their

SITES AT A GLANCE—This map will give you a feel for the general locations of sites in this chapter. Some sites overlap and are not shown on this map.

journey, the runners camped at night near the Delaware village of Hockendauqua and heard the residents howling with rage at the scam.

The Delaware protested, but they were subordinate to the more powerful Iroquois based in central New York State. The Iroquois ordered the Delaware to relocate to the Wyoming Valley and Shamokin, and with their departure, the territory was open for settlement.

The Moravians, a group of German pietists escaping persecution in the Old World, arrived in 1741 and founded Bethlehem, the center of a novel spiritual and economic experiment. Moravians also settled at Nazareth, the breadbasket for their colony. Over the next forty years, Moravians established settlements and Indian missions extending into Ohio. The Scots-Irish settled at a location that became known as the Irish Settlement. In 1752, the Penns created the county of Northampton and built a courthouse seat from scratch at Easton.

When the French and their Indian allies crushed General Braddock's expedition in 1755, the Delaware under their self-proclaimed king Teedyuscung saw their opportunity. From their villages in the Wyoming Valley, the Delaware destroyed the Moravian mission at Gnadenhuetten, north of Lehigh Gap, in November 1755. The following month the Delaware attacked the Dansbury Mission in the Minisink country or Poconos.

The frontier raids forced a political upheaval in Philadelphia where the pacifistic Quakers were in control of the provincial assembly and refused to appropriate money for defense. Frontiersmen took mangled bodies of scalp victims to the doorstep of the assembly to demand action. The assembly then voted money for defense; another vexing political dispute was resolved when the Penns agreed to contribute some of their own money toward the effort.

Pennsylvania's governor named Benjamin Franklin, an assembly leader and one of the province's most famous men, to organize a defense along the Blue Mountains. Franklin went first to Bethlehem, where the Moravians were already building stockades around that town and Nazareth. Franklin then headed north and built Fort Allen at Lehigh Gap, and he dispatched soldiers to build Fort Norris and Fort Franklin.

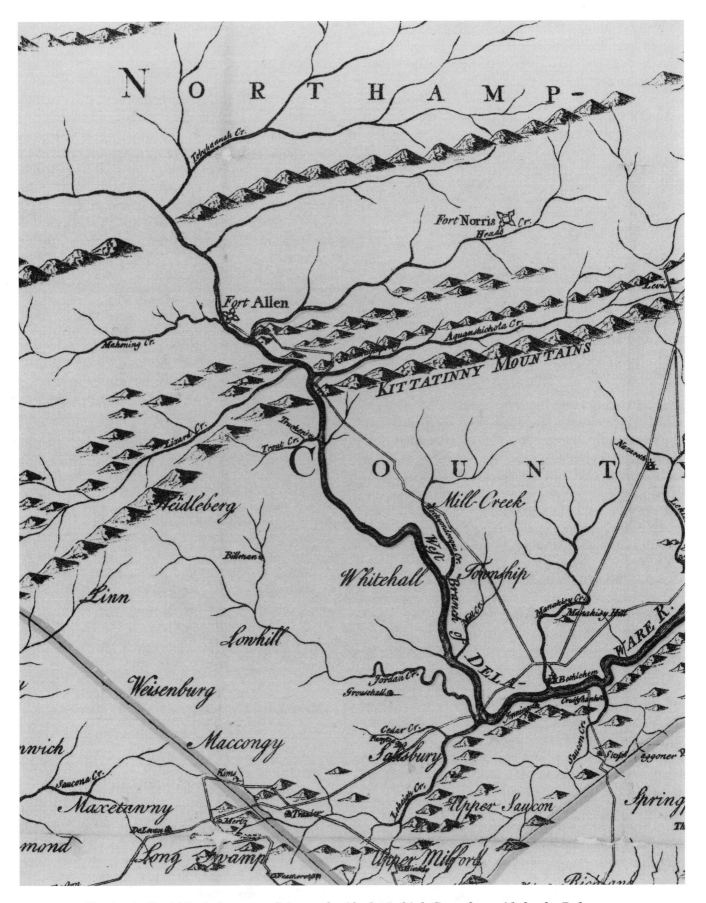

*Benjamin Franklin led an expedition to fortify the Lehigh Gap after raids by the Delaware.*

During 1756 and 1757, Delaware raiding parties fell on isolated homesteads and settlements, killing scattered victims here and there and taking others captive. Meanwhile, provincial authorities engaged in a series of peace conferences with Teedyuscung at Easton in efforts to persuade him and his followers to quit the warpath. Teedyuscung proved to be a wily adversary and reminded the English of the Walking Purchase fraud. But in the end, it was Iroquois diplomacy and the success of British arms at the Forks of the Ohio that brought peace to the Forks of the Delaware.

## HOCKENDAUQUA
### EAST OF NORTHAMPTON, PENNSYLVANIA

*Directions: Stone monument marking the site of Hockendauqua is located just east of the borough of Northampton on Route 329. The monument is on the south side of Route 329 by the Hockendauqua Creek Bridge.*

Hockendauqua was a Delaware village in the 1730s located on the east bank of the Lehigh River. The village and its two chiefs, Lappawinzoe and Tishcohan (or Teeschacomin) played an important role in the Walking Purchase. This was a controversial land transaction in 1737 between the Delaware and the sons of William Penn. The purpose of the deal was to settle questions over the land included in a 1686 deed and to extend Pennsylvania control over squatters settling along the upper Delaware River.

The Walking Purchase led to the removal of Delaware tribes from the Forks of the Delaware region. Resentment over their loss of land was one reason the Delaware took to the warpath against English settlements almost twenty years later in 1755.

The Walking Purchase takes its name from the manner in which the Penns measured the land they were purchasing from the Delaware. The customary approach was to measure distances in a leisurely walk. The Penns hired three runners who covered 65 miles over a day-and-a-half to a point north of the Blue Mountains. Only one of the three runners, Edward Marshall, covered the whole distance, but that was enough to establish boundaries for a land tract extending far beyond what the Delaware anticipated.

On the night of September 19, 1737, Marshall and James Yeates, the two runners still in the race, camped near Hockendauqua, the village of Lappawinzoe and Tishcohan, two of the four Delaware chiefs who signed a deed ceding the land a month before. Marshall and Yeates were close enough to hear the residents of Hockendauqua howling with rage at the scam pulled by the Penn brothers. The two continued the run the next morning with only Marshall in shape to finish at midday.

The Delaware moved west to villages along the Susquehanna River, but the loss of the Forks lands remained a sore point. The Quakers also used the Walking Purchase as an issue to score political points against the Penn brothers. When Delaware raids began along the Blue Mountains in 1755, their leader Teedyuscung charged the Pennsylvania leaders with land fraud. The British promised an investigation into Teedyuscung's charges at the Easton treaties, but Teedyuscung withdrew the complaint in 1762 before any findings were made.

Lappawinzoe and Tishcohan's portraits were painted by the artist Gustavus Hesselius and are frequently reproduced in publications today. A 1925 monument to the village reads:

Hockendauqua Indian town of the noted chiefs Lappawinzoe and Tishcohan who treated with the Penn Proprietors of Pennsylvania in the famous Walking Purchase was located in the present Northampton on the east bank of the Lehigh River. Three fourths of a mile to the northwest of this marker the fleet-footed youth Edward Marshall and his associates of the walk of a day and a half, September 19-20, 1737, crossed Hockendauqua Creek a half mile below this point on the stream and slept the first night in the woods a half mile from the Indian town. The survey line of the purchase was run later in 1737, 1 3/10 miles to the east. Marked by the Pennsylvania Historical Commission and Northampton County Historical and Genealogical Society 1925.

Near the town of Kreidersville is a similar 1925 stone monument marking the spot where the runners passed by the next morning. Kreidersville is located north of the borough of Northampton. This monument also by Hockendauqua Creek is reached by taking Kreidersville Road through the center of town to Indian Trail Road. Follow Indian Trail Road west to junction with Kohls Road at Hockendauqua Creek. Monument in front of ranch house.

## BENJAMIN FRANKLIN—IN WAR AND PEACE

Benjamin Franklin (1706-90) was the best known American of his day in his varied roles as publisher, scientist, inventor, philosopher and politician. He is thought of as an urbane man, at home in the port of Philadelphia, the imperial center of London, and later, the courts of Paris. But Franklin also helped to shape the history of America's frontier—as a negotiator with Native Americans, formulator of a plan of union for the colonies, and as a militia commander building several forts in the hinterlands.

Franklin's involvement in political affairs began when he was named clerk of the Pennsylvania Assembly in 1736. Eventually elected to the Assembly, he emerged as one of its key leaders in the 1750s. He also wielded influence beyond Pennsylvania's borders once he assumed the post of deputy postmaster for the colonies in 1753.

With the prospect of another war with the French, Franklin joined representatives of the thirteen colonies at a meeting in Albany, New York in 1754 to consider common action. Franklin lobbied there for a plan to unify the colonies. He was aware that due to a confederacy, the Six Nations in upstate New York had strength beyond their numbers. He thought a similar structure would benefit the diverse and parochial-minded colonies.

With his suggestions for a legislative body to sign Indian treaties and oversee new settlements, Franklin's proposal was a forerunner to the federal form of government adopted by the United States some thirty years later. Although the Albany delegates endorsed the plan, the assemblies of the various colonies, including Pennsylvania, rejected it. A year later, war with the French was a reality and the colonies had no joint plan for defense.

Through his postmaster's post, Franklin proved helpful in supplying wagons and supplies for the 1755 Braddock expedition. At a meeting in Frederick, Maryland, he warned Braddock about the dangers of Indian ambush in the wilderness. The general dismissed his concerns.

When Braddock's defeat left Pennsylvania's frontiers exposed, Franklin played a key role in organizing the province's defense. His first task was to steer a course between an Assembly dominated by pacifistic Quakers and a proprietary governor seeking money to wage an offensive war. Franklin secured passage of a compromise militia law that authorized defensive measures. As the head of a seven-member defense committee, Franklin prepared to undertake that defense. The raid on the Moravian mission of Gnadenhuetten north of Lehigh Gap spurred him to action.

In December 1755, at age 50, Franklin led a military expedition to build forts to protect Reading, Bethlehem, Easton, and the Minisink area. He built Fort Allen at modern Weissport, and sent troops to build Fort Norris at modern Kresgeville and Fort Franklin at modern Snyders.

Even as Franklin attended to military matters, he could not resist making scientific calculations. One such opportunity came as Franklin watched his soldiers cut trees for Fort Allen. "Seeing the trees fall so fast, I had the curiosity to look at my watch when two men began to cut at a pine; in six minutes they had it upon the ground and I found it of fourteen inches diameter," wrote Franklin in his Autobiography.

Shortly after his return from the front, Franklin went to London as a colonial agent to represent the interests of Pennsylvania. He was back in Philadelphia when Pontiac's War erupted in 1763.

The reappearance of raiding parties on the frontier spelled danger for those tribes living at peace with the whites and the Christianized Indians living in Moravian missions. When a vigilante group known as the Paxton Boys massacred the remnants of the peaceful Conestoga tribe in December 1763, tensions between the residents of the frontier and Philadelphia mounted. City residents were appalled at the killing of peaceful Indians; frontiersmen felt that the city-dominated Assembly ignored their plight. Franklin, for one, published a pamphlet condemning the massacre of the Conestogas.

The situation deteriorated to the point where a mob of frontiersmen marched on Philadelphia to attack the Moravian Indians taking shelter there. Franklin helped to organize the city's defense. Then he met with the mob at the city gates and persuaded them to return home.

## TEEDYUSCUNG

If his efforts had succeeded, Teedyuscung might be remembered today as the father of the Delaware Nation. Instead, his efforts to secure autonomy and an eastern homeland for the Delaware were thwarted by the three-sided rivalry among the British, French and Iroquois. Throughout his life, Teedyuscung (1705-63) tried to meet the expectations of both the Native American and European worlds. But his violent death shows just how difficult bridging the gap could be.

Born in the Trenton area, Teedyuscung migrated with his family across the Delaware River to eastern Pennsylvania when New Jersey became crowded with white settlers. Living on the periphery of white settlement, he sold brooms and baskets and earned the nickname "Honest John."

He was among the Delaware dispossessed by the controversial "Walking Purchase" in 1737 that gave control of the land surrounding the Forks of the Delaware at modern Easton to the Penn family. The Delaware claimed that agents for the Penns unfairly expanded the size of the purchase by using runners to mark the boundaries, rather than taking a more diplomatic walking pace. Teedyuscung appears first in history as a member of Delaware delegations that went to Philadelphia to negotiate the issue.

By 1750 Teedyuscung decided to join the Moravians, a German pietist group that lived communally and had established missions among the Delaware. His baptized name was Gideon. Teedyuscung moved to the Moravian mission at Gnadenhuetten at the Lehigh Gap, but left after only four years.

He went to the Wyoming Valley area and had emerged as a prominent Delaware leader when the French and Indian War broke out in 1755. Teedyuscung initially cast his lot with the French and led a raid on English settlements in the Poconos. He still nursed a grudge over the loss of the Walking Purchase lands. But Teedyuscung also incurred the displeasure of the Iroquois, the Delawares' over-lords, who wished to remain neutral in the conflict between the Europeans.

Within months of that raid, Teedyuscung became involved in complicated peace negotiations with the British. At a 1756 conference in Easton, he declared the Delawares' independence from the Iroquois, and sought British assurances for a permanent Delaware homeland in the Wyoming Valley.

Teedyuscung was sometimes referred to as the "King of the Delawares," but his leadership was not recognized by the tribes who had migrated westward to the Ohio Valley. It took another conference in Easton in 1758 to win all the scattered Delaware tribes over to the English side. The switch in alliance was a fatal blow to the French cause in the Ohio.

To reward his efforts, Pennsylvania officials built a house for Teedyuscung in the Wyoming Valley. But on April 19, 1763, he was murdered when the house was set afire while he was inside. The homes of his followers were set ablaze as well. Some historians pin the blame for Teedyuscung's murder on the Iroquois, but the destruction of the Delaware village opened up the Wyoming Valley to settlement by emigrants from Connecticut. Teedyuscung's son, Captain Bull, led a raiding party that massacred the Connecticut settlers in the fall of 1763 during Pontiac's War.

## GNADENHUETTEN — LEHIGHTON CEMETERY
## LEHIGHTON, PENNSYLVANIA

*Directions: Take Route 443 west across Lehigh River from Weissport. At traffic light, turn right. Take Mahoning Mountain Road or East Penn Street, cross bridge, then right on Bridge Street. Take first left on 4th Street. See historical sign. Enter main gate of Lehighton Cemetery. Take outer road to south side. Look for white monument bordered by railing and white post stones.*

The Moravian Brethren were eating a communal supper in the Pilgerhaus at the Gnadenhuetten mission on the late fall evening of Nov. 24, 1755. Suddenly they were interrupted by the barking of dogs. When Brother Joachim Sensemann opened a back door to check on the commotion, a Delaware war party started firing their guns inside. Brother Martin Nitschmann was shot dead. His wife Sister Susanna Nitschmann and several others fled upstairs and barricaded themselves in the garret. Some escaped by jumping out back windows. The raiders then set fire to the building and waited for the trapped inhabitants to flee. Sister Anna Catherine Sensemann was last seen engulfed in flames and calling out, "Tis all well, dear Savior, I expected this." Sister Nitschmann was taken into captivity. She died a year later at the Delaware village of Tioga.

All told, ten Moravians were killed that night in one of the most chilling and well-documented massacres during the French and Indian War. The Gnadenhuetten massacre was a shock to the nearby Moravian communities in Bethlehem and Nazareth. It was also the first sign of the troubles ahead for the Moravians' ambitious experiment to convert native Americans to Christianity.

Gnadenhuetten or "Huts of Grace," the first Moravian mission town for Indians in Pennsylvania, was established in 1746. The Moravians selected a site north of Lehigh Gap where Delaware converts, as well as Mohican and Wampanoag converts, could gather. Members of the latter two tribes were refugees from Moravian missions at Shekomeko, Wechquadnach, and Pachgatgoch in New York and Connecticut. The missions ended there because of white settlers' uneasiness with having Indian converts living nearby during King George's War from 1744-48. This war was largely fought along the northern frontier. New Yorkers threatened to destroy the missions and the exodus to Gnadenhuetten began. It was a pattern repeated at successive Moravian missions in Pennsylvania and Ohio for the next forty years.

The mission at Gnadenhuetten grew to several hundred persons by 1749. The Moravians operated a saw mill which cut logs that were shipped down the Lehigh River to Bethlehem. The Indian converts and Moravian missionaries also kept busy farming, hunting, and participating in worship services at the chapel. The converts generally adopted European manners and lived in wooden huts. The original mission was on the west shore of the Lehigh River at modern Lehighton, but within several years most of the converts moved to the east shore at modern Weissport in search of productive farmland.

One of the most famous converts was Teedyuscung, the Delaware chief baptized as Gideon in 1750. Teedyuscung and his family lived there for four years, but by 1754 he had rejected the Moravians. He led a party of 65 residents to the Delaware towns in the Wyoming Valley. As war tensions mounted in 1754 and 1755, the missionaries and converts at Gnadenhuetten found themselves caught between two worlds. White settlers outside the Moravian faith regarded the mission with suspicion and considered the converts a pro-French fifth column. The Delaware in the Wyoming repeatedly asked the converts to leave Gnadenhuetten and join them in their villages. Teedyuscung's departure revealed the extent of the divide among the converts.

The attack on the Pilgerhaus on Nov. 24, 1755, spelled an end to Gnadenhuetten. The converts living on the east shore of the river saw the burning buildings and fled to Bethlehem. They eventually relocated to the new mission town of Nain, situated several miles away from Bethlehem. The missionaries who escaped from the burn-

*Gnadenhuetten Martyrs Grave.*

ing Pilgerhaus spread the alarm at Bethlehem and residents there prepared for war. Within two months, an army of provincial militia led by Benjamin Franklin had marched through Lehigh Gap and built Fort Allen on the burnt ruins of Gnadenhuetten at Weissport.

Today you can stand at the windswept cemetery that occupies the site of Gnadenhuetten's Pilgerhaus. The site is ringed by hills that overlook the Lehigh River to the east. A monument to the Moravian martyrs was erected in 1788. The bones of the murdered missionaries are buried in a common grave. These words are inscribed face-up in the Moravian style on a white marble slab:

> To the memory of Gottlieb and Christina Anders, with their children, Johanna, Martin and Susanna Nitschman; Ann Catharina Senseman, Leonhard Gattermyer, Christian Fabricus, clerk, George Schweigert, John Frederick Lesly, and Martin Presser; Who lived at Gnaden Huetten unto the Lord and lost their lives in a surprise from Indian warriors November the 24th, 1755. Precious in the sight of the Lord, is the death of his saints—Psalms cxvi.15.

## Fort Allen—Weissport, Pennsylvania

*Directions: Take Route 248 north through Lehigh Gap to intersection with Route 209 in Weissport. Go to Franklin Street on west side of Weissport town square. State historical markers for Fort Allen on Route 209 and on Franklin Street.*

The Delaware raids in late 1755 on the Moravian missions at Gnadenhuetten and Dansbury alarmed Pennsylvania Gov. Robert Hunter Morris and the provincial assembly at Philadelphia. They feared a French army would fortify the Lehigh Gap in the Blue Mountains and march south to attack their city. Meanwhile, Pennsylva-

nia was shedding its defensive posture. The political hold that the pacifist Quakers held over the assembly eroded. A crowd of angry German settlers from Berks and Northampton Counties marched on Philadelphia after the first wave of attacks in early November. They carried the scalped corpses of their relatives and neighbors in carts to graphically make the case for action to protect the frontier. The group went first to the governor's residence and then to the State House (now Independence Hall) where Benjamin Franklin, chairman of assembly's defense committee spoke to them.

Morris later appointed Franklin to organize a defense along the Blue Mountain barrier. Franklin, his son William, and a detachment of militia journeyed north in December to Bethlehem, Easton, and Reading. Franklin soon got word that a company of provincial troops camped at the ruins of Gnadenhuetten had been attacked by Delaware warriors and forced to retreat. This set the course for his next move. On Jan. 15, 1756, Franklin and a force of 100 soldiers left Bethlehem bound for Lehigh Gap, an imposing gap where the Lehigh River flows through the mountains. In his autobiography written twenty years later, Franklin recalls the army's passage through the gap as a miserable affair:

> We had not marched many miles before it began to rain and it continued raining all day; there were no habitations on the road to shelter us till we arrived near night at the house of a German, where, and in his barn, we were all huddled together, as wet as water could make us. It was well we were not attacked in our march for our arms were of the most ordinary sort and our men could not keep their gun locks dry.

Reaching the section of Gnadenhuetten where the Indian converts had lived on the east shore of the Lehigh River, Franklin built Fort Allen, the first of several defense posts erected in the region. In his autobiography, Franklin described the post:

> We had one swivel gun, which we mounted to one of the angles, and fired it as soon as fixed, to let the Indians know if any were within hearing, that we had such pieces; and thus our fort (if that name may be given so miserable a stockade) was finished in a week, though it rained so hard every other day that the men could not well work.

Franklin left in late January to return to Philadelphia, leaving garrisons at Fort Allen. The fort consisted of three buildings and a well, surrounded by a stockade with bastions. Because it guarded the approaches to Lehigh Gap, Fort Allen was considered one of the most important of the Blue Mountain posts. Provincial troops were stationed there until 1761; they returned briefly during Pontiac's War in 1763. The Delaware chief Teedyuscung stopped at Fort Allen on his journeys to peace conferences at Easton in 1756 and 1757.

A statue of Franklin stands today on Franklin Street in the Weissport town square. Fort Allen's well can be seen today in an alley behind a store on the west side of the square. The well is near a flood protection levee for the Lehigh River. But the well looks little like it would have been in Franklin's day, having been built up with bricks and covered with a gabled roof. Colonial wells were usually lined with paving stones.

## MENIOLAGOMEKA
## SOUTH OF KUNKLETOWN, PENNSYLVANIA

*Directions: From Route 209 at Kresgeville, turn left onto Kunkletown Road or SR 2003, just west of Fort Norris monument and elementary school. Follow Kunkletown Road five miles south bearing left at fork in road and continuing past Eldred Elementary School in Kunkletown. On east side of Kunkletown, turn right onto Chestnut Ridge Road. Follow the winding Chestnut Ridge Road two miles. Monument is on right side of road by a two-story brown house. Park along the widened stretch of road by bridge over Aquashicola Creek. Look north to see monument. Chestnut Ridge Road leads into Upper Smith Gap Road at bridge.*

This is a Delaware word meaning "fat land in the midst of barrens." The Delaware had a village here along the banks of Aquashicola Creek near what today is called Smith Gap. In 1742, the Moravian leader Count Nicholas Von Zinzendorf stayed here during a journey north to meet with the Iroquois.

Moravian missionaries made periodic stops at Meniolagomeka during the next few years, and finally in 1752 a permanent minister, Brother Bernhard Adam Grube, was assigned to live here. Grube was one of a select group of missionaries who received rigorous training before being sent to establish mission stations among the Indians. Grube translated the Bible into the Delaware language.

Zinzendorf made missionary work among the Indians a top priority of the Moravian Church in America. The missionaries were trained in Indian languages and customs and survival in the wilderness before being sent on their assignments. The Delaware continued their traditional pursuits of hunting and farming. But under the Moravian influence, an evening religious service with hymns sung in the German and Delaware languages became part of the daily routine. Once a month, the inhabitants of Meniolagomeka journeyed to Gnadenhuetten to partake in the Lord's Supper.

When Grube's tour was over, he presided over a traditional Moravian love feast, sharing cups of hot chocolate and buttered bread with the villagers. Brothers John Jo-

*This stone marks the site of a Moravian mission.*

*Delaware Indians lived along the banks of the Aquashicola Creek.*

seph Bull, Abraham Buhninger, and John Joseph Schmick also had tours of duty at Meniolagomeka during the next half-dozen years.

But Meniolagomeka's days were numbered. The village was located on land sold by the Delaware chieftains to the sons of William Penn in the 1737 Walking Purchase. The Moravians tried to buy the land from the Penns, but to no avail. In May 1755, provincial officials evicted the residents of Meniolagomeka, and the homeless converts moved to Gnadenhuetten.

In 1901, the Moravian Historical Society erected a stone monument at the site of this mission station. This was a festive occasion with excursion trains coming from Bethlehem and crowds gathering to hear speakers and brass bands. The monument inscription reads: "The site of Meniolagomeka. A Moravian Indian mission station. 1749-1755." The monument is located on a hillside in a beautiful spot. The waters of Aquashicola Creek flow at the base of the hill. Looming to the south is Blue Mountain.

## FORT NORRIS—KRESGEVILLE, PENNSYLVANIA

*The monument is located on left side of Route 209 just east of intersection with Route 534. A state historical marker is nearby.*

Fort Norris, named for Assembly Speaker Isaac Norris, was one of several defense posts along the Blue Mountains built during the winter of 1755-57 on orders from Benjamin Franklin. The fort was garrisoned for less than two years, but during that period the commanders had to deal with a mutiny, rotting food, and danger from Delaware raiders in the neighborhood.

Fort Norris resulted from the military expedition that Franklin led through the Lehigh Gap in January 1756. After he built Fort Allen in modern-day Weissport, Franklin wanted to protect his right flank. He dispatched Capt. Jacob Orndt (or Arndt) to build Fort Norris about fifteen miles east of Fort Allen. Franklin never visited Fort Norris, for his mission was ending and he soon returned to Philadelphia. By early February, Orndt commanded a post garrisoned by 50 soldiers. A log stockade with half bastions equipped with swivel guns, inside were barracks, a guard room, storehouse and well.

Orndt had his share of problems at Fort Norris. He once informed a superior that some of the fort's provisions of beef spoiled for want of salt, used as a preservative. In August 1756, a mutiny broke out when a man refused to do sentry duty and his comrades supported him. The garrison also sent a petition to provincial commanders complaining about their food and pay.

The commanders dealt with the problem by ordering the garrisons of Fort Norris and Fort Allen to trade places. Captain George Reynolds took over command at Fort Norris. Troops from Fort Norris were later sent to Easton during treaty negotiations with the Delaware chiefs in 1756 and 1757. Following the 1757 Easton conference, Fort Norris was evacuated and its soldiers were relocated to Adam Dietz's blockhouse near Wind Gap.

Today a stone monument marks the site of Fort Norris about 230 yards north of Big or Pohopoco Creek on an elevation. The inscription reads, "Fort Norris Built 1756 one mile southeast across Pohopoco Creek by James Hamilton and Benjamin Franklin." An 1893 map of the area in Frontier Forts of Pennsylvania shows a spring and graveyard in the vicinity.

## KRESGE MEMORIAL—GILBERT, PENNSYLVANIA

*Directions: From Stroudsburg, take Route 209 south to Gilbert. Turn right at stoplight by Turkey Hill food market onto SR 3005. Make first left to cemetery of redstone Salem United Church of Christ. Stone Kresge memorial with bas-relief is visible from road.*

A bas-relief memorial in the Salem churchyard here gives testament to the terror wrought by Delaware raiders in the vicinity of Fort Norris. The memorial depicts a sudden death in the forest. A father swings an axe toward a tree stump. His son sits on a fallen log watching him. Both are unaware of the Indian lurking behind a tree and aiming a bow and arrow at them.

Conrad Kresge and his twelve-year-old son John were killed in 1757. The Kresges were among families who cleared and settled the land along Pohopoco Creek in Minisink Country. The location of the two Kresge graves is unknown. This memorial was erected in 1916 by Kresge family descendants. The descendants shared a misconception about the frontier, however. By the mid-18th century, the Delaware and other tribes had long forsaken bows and arrows for guns.

***Family memorial to victims of the 1757 attack.***

## DANSBURY GRAVEYARD
## STROUDSBURG, PENNSYLVANIA

*Directions: To reach cemetery, go eastbound on I-80. Take Broad Street Exit. Right on Main Street toward boundary of Stroudsburg and East Stroudsburg. The cemetery is on right side in grove of trees. Look for state historical marker for Dansbury mission. The site of Fort Hamilton is on the west side of Stroudsburg at the intersection of Ninth and Main Streets (or Routes 209 and 611). Look for state historical marker for Fort Hamilton. See plaque on Jacob Stroud Mansion at northwest corner of intersection, now the home of the Monroe County Historical Society.*

The graves of the Moravian Brethren who founded the Dansbury mission in the 1740s are located in this tree-shaded walled cemetery overlooking Brodhead Creek on the east side of modern-day Stroudsburg. But historians are not sure where the estimated 40 to 50 Moravian burials are located in the graveyard.

The Dansbury mission came under attack on December 10, 1755, when Delaware warriors burned the chapel and homes of the Moravians. On the same day raiding parties destroyed the Hoeth's Creek settlement near modern-day Kresgeville. Raids in the Minisink region north of the Delaware Water Gap took the lives of an estimated 89 settlers in late 1755.

Dansbury fell under Moravian influence after a visit by Count Nicholas Von Zinendorf in 1741 to the Delaware Valley. Daniel Brodhead, a former Indian trader, invited Moravian missionaries to Dansbury where he had established a plantation. From their base at Dansbury, the missionaries visited mission stations in New York and New Jersey. By 1755, Dansbury had become a prosperous settlement with a grist mill, saw mill, chapel, and school where the missionaries taught. Then the Delaware attacked on December 10, and the Moravians fled south to Bethlehem; Brodhead repulsed an attack on his fortified home.

In early 1756, provincial soldiers built Fort Hamilton, a building enclosed by a stockade with four half-bastions, just west of the Dansbury settlement. The fort was garrisoned until 1757.

Today the Dansbury cemetery is the only reminder of the Moravian mission here. A stone monument there memorializes Colonel Jacob Stroud (1735-1806), the founder of Stroudsburg, and the Moravian mission with this inscription:

> Colonel Jacob Stroud is buried in this graveyard, originally the cemetery of the mission of Dansbury, begun by the Moravian Brethren in 1743. The chapel destroyed in the Indian uprising of 1755, was erected in 1753 under the leadership of Daniel Brodhead, who settled one-half mile

to the east in 1736. The members of the mission in 1747 were Daniel and Esther Brodhead, John and Catharine Hillman, Joseph and Helen Haines, Francis and Rebecca Jones, William and Mary Clark, Edward and Catherine Holley, John and Hannah McMichael, George and Mary Salathe, Daniel Roberts, John Baker.

The Monroe County Historical Society recently published the diaries of Rev. Sven Roseen and other Moravian missionaries stationed at Dansbury from 1748-1755.

## NAZARETH—NAZARETH, PENNSYLVANIA

This collection of settlements was known as "The Upper Places" to the Moravians in Bethlehem. Nazareth was considered the breadbasket of the Moravian colony in Pennsylvania, but during the French and Indian War it was in an exposed position. Residents erected stockades around some of the main buildings and sent their children to Bethlehem for safety. The Nazareth settlements never came under attack, but Delaware raiders were spotted in the vicinity. The diary of the Nazareth Moravian congregation records this entry for Dec. 15, 1755, several days after the raid at Dansbury:

> Towards evening about 30 soldiers arrived, and were billeted here. They consider Nazareth and the other places of the brethren as a pass for the whole region. They say that if this pass is lost, all is lost. They will therefore take good care to protect this place.

Nazareth got its start through the vision of a prominent English Methodist missionary, George Whitefield, who bought a 5,000-acre tract from the Penn family in 1740 as a site to settle immigrants and build a school for black children. Whitefield recruited Moravian settlers from a failing colony in Georgia to come to Nazareth and build the school building, still standing today and known as the Whitefield House. But Whitefield had a falling out with the Moravians. The Moravians moved to the Forks of the

***Grey Cottage. First building in Nazareth.***

Delaware and acquired the land for Bethlehem. By 1741, Whitefield found himself in dire financial straits and sold the Nazareth tract to the Moravians.

## Nazareth historic sites:

**The Whitefield House** (1743) is a three-story stone house in Nazareth which has served at various times as a home for married couples, a boarding school for girls, a home for children of missionaries, and a home for retired missionaries. Today it is the headquarters and museum for the Moravian Historical Society. Next door is the 1740 Grey Cottage, the first building completed in Nazareth. It has been used as a schoolhouse and a home for retired ministers.

The Whitefield House is at 214 East Center Street. Follow Route 191 east to corner of Center and New Streets. The museum is open 1 p.m. to 4 p.m. daily. Call 610-759-5070 for more information. The museum displays paintings by Moravian artist John Valentine Haidt, and hand-made musical instruments including violins, horns, and a rare pipe organ, and household items.

**Nazareth Hall Square**, Center and Green Streets. The first building here was Manor House, intended as a future residence for Count Nicholas Von Zinzendorf. Other church and residence buildings were added to form the square. A Moravian cemetery dating back to 1756 is located west of the square on Center Street.

*The 1743 Whitefield House is home to the Moravian Historical Society.*

**The Indian Tower** and Monument northwest of town was erected by the Moravian Historical Society in 1918 in memory of those Moravians, both white and Indian converts, who lost their lives in the French and Indian War. This hilltop location served as Nazareth's first cemetery, in use from 1744 to 1762.

An obelisk erected in 1867 marks the graves of 67 persons, including four Indian converts. Two of the converts were Delaware children who died in a small-pox epidemic in 1746. The obelisk also lists the name of Johann Bauman who was "murdered by Indians" in 1757. This spot offers a superb view of the Blue Mountains to the north and Lehigh Valley to the south.

---

*To reach the monument, take High Street west to the top of the hill. Pass the boundary marker for Upper Nazareth Township. On left, look for unmarked road with sign for Holy Family Cemetery. Turn onto road and look for tower on right side.*

---

*The Indian Tower.*

## Surrounding settlements:

**Gnadenthal** (Dale of Grace), established in 1745 as a farming community for married Brethren two miles west of Nazareth. The harvest from the farm was so plentiful in 1746 that it is known as the "Great Harvest." Stockaded in 1756-58. Site occupied by Northampton County home.

**Christian's Spring** (1748), a settlement southwest of Nazareth for young men, served as a vocational school where young men were apprenticed to learn trades such as carpentry. Indian raiders were spotted in this area in 1756. A palisade was erected around the buildings. To reach Christian's Spring site, take Route. 248 west of Nazareth. Go right on Christian's Spring Road. Follow to stop sign. Look for stream by red building with stone foundation. Sign says Christian's Spring (1740-1790).

**Friedenstahl** (1749). Moravians built a mill here about two miles east of Nazareth on Bushkill Creek. Stockaded in 1756-58. Site occupied by cement plant on Friedenstahl Road on right side of Route 191 east of Nazareth.

**Rose Inn** (1752). A Moravian hotel one and one-half mile northeast of Nazareth. Site occupied by housing development on Rose Inn Drive off Route 191 northeast of Nazareth.

## HISTORIC BETHLEHEM PENNSYLVANIA

In 1755, Bethlehem was a thriving community of 1,000 residents who followed the teachings of the Moravian Church. The Moravian faith originated in central Europe, emphasizing personal piety and reverence for God. Rather than establishing a formal denomination, the Moravians created the unitas fratrum, United Brethren, a group of men and women seeking religious renewal. Successive congregations of Moravians migrated from Saxony where they had lived on the estate of Count Nicholas Ludwig Von Zinzendorf (1700-60).

Establishing Bethlehem on the banks of the Lehigh River in 1741, the Moravians adopted a communal system known as the General Economy, where residents labored in trades for the good of the Church and received food and shelter in return. The Moravians lived segregated in buildings by social status. Single sisters lived together as did widowers, for example. The Economy system helped make Bethlehem self-sufficient and supported the work of Moravian missionaries at Indian missions like Gnadenhuetten and communities of Brethren at Emmaus, Hebron, Lititz, Oley, and elsewhere. Delaware and Mahican converts also lived at Bethlehem and were baptized in the Old Chapel. With residents engaged in 32 different trades, Bethlehem grew into something unique: an 18th century industrial community on the very edge of the Blue Mountain frontier.

When Delaware raiders burned the mission at Gnadenhuetten in November 1755, the residents of Bethlehem could spot the glow of fire in the mountains to the north. The Indian converts at Gnadenhuetten took refuge at Bethlehem as did non-Moravian settlers. The English and Scots-Irish had previously been suspicious of the Moravians as a potential pro-French fifth column, but now Bethlehem was the main bulwark between a French invasion force and the provincial capital at Philadelphia.

The Moravians had pacifist leanings, but when danger threatened they banded together for self-defense. They built a palisade around Bethlehem and posted watchmen. Bishop August Gottfield Spangenberg suggested that a fort be built on the Gnadenhuetten ruins. Arriving in Bethlehem in December 1755 on his expedition to defend Pennsylvania's frontier, Benjamin Franklin noted approvingly the Moravians' efforts. As he would write later in his Autobiography:

> The principal buildings were defended by a stockade; they had purchased a quantity of arms and ammunition from New York and had even placed quantities of small paving stones between the windows of their high stone houses for their women to throw down upon the heads of any Indians that should attempt to force into them.

The Moravians under the direction of Spangenberg and Timothy Horsfield, an Englishman who served as justice of the peace, cooperated with provincial authorities in the war effort. Bethlehem itself never came under attack, but it served as an important supply center.

The Moravians received financial aid from provincial officials for feeding and sheltering friendly Indians. In return, they provided important intelligence about movements of hostile tribes and prospects for peace with them. During the winter of 1758, the eastern Delaware leader Teedyuscung, a former convert, took lodging in a Bethlehem inn. Later that year, Moravian missionary Christian Frederick Post served as the key intermediary in three-way peace negotiations among Pennsylvania and the eastern and western tribes.

The Moravians were particularly concerned about the welfare of the Indian converts, caught in a no man's land between settlers thirsting for revenge and the tribes they had left. With overcrowded conditions in Bethlehem, the Moravians built a village called Nain west of town for the converts.

With the war's end, Bethlehem went through more growing pains, shedding its communal system in the 1760s for a more privatized economy. But the Moravian Church remained in control of the town until 1845.

## Key sites:

Bethlehem offers modern visitors a collection of 18th century buildings with a distinctive style of German architecture. A dozen such buildings stand today in the Moravian Church enclave in the area bounded by Main (west), Market (north), New (east), and Church (south), Streets. Some buildings are still used as private church residences. Bethlehem has a visitor center at 509 Main Street, where walking tours of the historic district begin. At the Moravian Museum housed in the Gemeinhaus on Church Street, visitors can make an appointment to tour several of the church buildings.

Along the banks of Monocacy Creek is a scenic ten-acre, 18th century industrial quarter operated by Historic Bethlehem Inc.

**Gemeinhaus**, a five-story log building built during 1741-43. This was an early place of worship. It now houses the Moravian Museum with artifacts about Bethlehem's history.

**Old Chapel** 1751, borders the Gemeinhaus. This was the place where Indian converts were baptized during the 1750s.

**Central Moravian Church**, Church and Main Streets. This federal-style church was built in 1803.

Brethren's House 1748, across from Central Moravian Church. The building housed young men who worked in the town's various trades, and served as a hospital for the American army during the Revolution.

**Apothecary** 1752, Main Street. Open by appointment. This contains artifacts of the druggist's trade.

**God's Acre**, Market Street. One of the most interesting and poignant places in Bethlehem. The flat stones in this cemetery include some of the Moravians' most notable religious leaders as well as Indian converts and blacks. The deceased were buried according to their marital status, age, and sex rather than by family. In the cemetery's northwest corner is the grave of Tschoop, a Mohican Indian who was the model for Uncas in James Fenimore Cooper's novel, *Last of the Mohicans*.

The inscription on Tschoop's headstone reads:

In memory of Tschoop, a Mohican Indian who in holy baptism April 16th 1742 received the name of John. One of the first fruits of the mission at Shekomeko, and a remarkable instance of the power of divine grace, whereby he became a distinguished teacher among his nation. He departed this life in full assurance of grace at Bethlehem August 27th 1746. There shall be one fold and one shepherd John X:16.

*Gemeinhaus. Early place of worship in Bethlehem.*

*Grave of an Indian convert from the Mohican tribe.*

**Sun Inn** 1758, 564 Main Street, north of enclave. This served as the Moravians' official guest house for colonial dignitaries and Indian chiefs. The Penn brothers stayed here as well as Sir William Johnson, the British commissioner of Indian Affairs. Restored today as a restaurant.

The 18th century industrial area is located to the west of the Moravian enclave. The area can be reached by walking downhill on Ohio Road off Main Street. Motorists can take Main Street to Union Boulevard. Go west on Union Boulevard. Make left turn on Old York Road to area.

The area includes five restored buildings. By 1747, Moravian craftsmen had developed 32 industries along the banks of the Monocacy. By the 1950s, the area was a junkyard. Restoration efforts got underway a decade later. Buildings include the Tannery (1761), Waterworks (1762), Luckenbach Mill (1869), and log springhouse (1741).

Living history guides demonstrate the process of making leather out of animal skins at the Tannery. The waterworks housed a system for pumping spring water up the hill to Bethlehem's church buildings. Interpretive exhibits are housed in the Luckenbach Mill.

## NAIN HOUSE—BETHLEHEM, PENNSYLVANIA

The Nain House in Bethlehem's Moravian enclave is the remnant of a grand 18th century idea—that Christianized Indians could follow the ways of the Gospel, live in their own European-style villages and coexist peacefully with white settlers. For forty years from the 1740s to 1780s, Moravian missionaries pursued this goal by establishing missions and villages first in New York and eastern Pennsylvania and later in western Pennsylvania and

*The Tannery at the 18th century industrial area in Bethlehem.*

***The Nain House. Remnant of a village for Indian
converts brought to Bethlehem from Nain.***

Ohio. But the Moravians' dream died in the ashes of three
continental wars. And the Delawares and Mahicans who
converted to the Moravian religion endured numerous trials of faith and fire.

The first missions were established in the 1740s at
Shekomeko, Wechquadach, and Pachgatgoch in New York
and Connecticut through the efforts of Brother Christian
Henry Rauch. The missions flourished, but the outbreak
of King George's War in 1744 in the northern colonies
fueled suspicions about the loyalty of the missionaries and
converts to the British cause. The missionaries opposed

taking loyalty oaths on principle and they were attacked
as papists for it.

The New York Assembly passed a law in 1746 ordering the eviction of the missionaries. This ended the mission at Shekomeko; the Indians living there resettled at
Gnadenhuetten north of Lehigh Gap on land purchased by
the Moravians. Gnadenhuetten was a thriving settlement;
logs from Gnadenhuetten's saw mill were floated down the
Lehigh River and used in Bethlehem's buildings.

But the Gnadenhuetten experiment ended in 1755 with the
Delaware attack on the mission house. Gnadenhuetten refugees crowded into Bethlehem and by 1757 the Moravian ad-
ministrators decided to establish a new village for the
converts, at Nain west of Bethlehem near the plantation of
missionary James Burnside. The Moravians secured the support of Pennsylvania officials for this venture. Nain developed into a town of 15 buildings, including log houses for the
converts, a meetinghouse, school, orchards, and cemetery.
When the French and Indian War ended, Nain residents
earned the goodwill of their neighbors by using their contacts
to assist the return of white captives to their families.

With the outbreak of Pontiac's War in 1763, however,
the residents of Nain were once again caught between two
worlds. Delaware raiders attacked the Irish Settlement in
western Northampton County in October 1763 and killed
settlers. The survivors of these attacks suspected Nain
residents of aiding the raiders. One Nain resident, Renatus,
was seized on charges of murder and jailed in Philadelphia.

He was later acquitted. Some accounts place blame for the mistrust on followers of the murdered Delaware chief Teedyuscung. This faction may have fled to Nain from the Wyoming Valley.

In any event, Pennsylvania officials sought to remove Nain's residents to Philadelphia, partly to protect them and partly to neutralize any fifth column on the frontier. The vast majority of Nain residents prepared for their journey with Christian stoicism. They attended a farewell sermon in Bethlehem. More than one hundred converts were escorted to Philadelphia by the county sheriff and Brother Adam Grube. But trouble awaited them in the "City of Brotherly Love." The converts were in continual jeopardy first from city mobs and later from the Paxton Boys, the posse of frontiersman who had wiped out the peaceful Conestoga Indians in December 1763.

The initial plan was to lodge the converts in the army barracks, but the soldiers refused them entrance. The converts were then taken to Province Island, where the city's medical quarantine houses were located.

Governor John Penn planned to send the converts to New York and place them under the protection of Sir William Johnson, the British Indian commissioner. Escorted by British troops, the converts got as far as New Jersey, but New York officials barred them entry. The Indians returned to Province Island and the next threat came when the Paxton Boys marched on Philadelphia in early 1764. This time, the Indians were allowed in the barracks for safety.

Provincial officials mounted a defense and negotiators met the Paxton Boys at the city outskirts. Tensions were diffused when several of the frontiersmen were allowed to visit the Indians at the barracks to see if they could identify anyone who had participated in the frontier raids. They could identify none.

During sixteen months of confinement in Philadelphia, a smallpox epidemic and other forms of sickness claimed the lives of 56 Indians. With the defeat of Pontiac's uprising in 1764, those surviving Indians returned to Nain briefly and then in 1765, set out once again for the North accompanied by two Moravian missionaries and a guard of provincial troops. They found the charred ruins of the old Wechquetank mission and camped there for a month. But Wechquetank could not serve as a permanent home since the Iroquois had sold the land to the province of Pennsylvania. The Indians went next to a new Moravian mission at Wyalusing or Friedenshutten (Huts of Peace) on the Susquehanna River for several years and then in 1772 embarked on a longer journey to new missions in the Ohio Valley.

During the American Revolution, the Moravian Indians in Ohio were caught between two sides once more—the Americans and the British and their Indian allies. In 1782, American troops burned the Moravian mission at New Gnadenhuetten and killed many of the residents.

After 1765, the buildings of Nain were sold at auction. Six of the buildings were dismantled and rebuilt in Bethlehem. This stucco house with green shutters at Heckewelder Place is the only one that survives. The stucco covers a log frame bound with unique dovetail joints. The House is located on the west side of Heckewelder Place near the intersection with Market Street. A plaque says: "Last house of the Nain Mission. Built 1758. Moved to Bethlehem 1765." Across the street is the house of Moravian missionary John Heckewelder.

## WECHQUETANK — GILBERT, PENNSYLVANIA

_Directions: Take Route 209 fourteen miles west of Stroudsburg to Gilbert. At Gilbert by traffic light, turn left onto Gilbert Road. Travel short distance south on Gilbert Road. Turn right onto Mill Pond Road for 1/4 mile. Monument on right side of road._

Wechquetank was an effort to reestablish Moravian Indian missions north of the Blue Mountains at the end of the French and Indian War. Founded in 1760, its success was short-lived for it was abandoned in the fall of 1763 with Pontiac's uprising. The Moravians established Wechquetank on the site of Hoeth's Creek, a Brethren settlement that was destroyed at the start of the war in 1755. Frederick Hoeth, the settlement leader, was killed in that raid.

In 1760, the Moravian Church purchased a tract of 1,400 acres from the estates of Hoeth and family members for a new mission for Indian converts. They picked this site because of its distance from the white settlements. The Indians could still hunt and trap and not run afoul of property lines. On April 25, 1760, 60 Indian converts from Nazareth and Bethlehem arrived at Wechquetank, and in a short time a meeting house and cabins were built. During Wechquetank's brief idyll, Brother Bernhard Adam Grube translated portions of the Bible from German into the Delaware language.

In the autumn of 1763, however, hostile Delawares had raided the Irish Settlement in western Northampton County. On October 10, church leaders ordered Grube and the converts to abandon Wechquetank and go to Bethlehem for safety. The converts were in jeopardy from Pontiac's allies and white settlers seeking revenge. Shortly after the converts left Wechquetank, the deserted buildings were torched. Contemporary accounts are vague about which group is to blame.

The Wechquetank converts were destined for the same trials as their brothers at Nain. They, too, were taken to Philadelphia, virtually confined for sixteen months while mobs and ruffians demanded their blood, and were finally allowed to return to Bethlehem with the end of Pontiac's

*The Wechquetank mission lasted for several years.*

uprising. The converts headed north to the mountains once again in 1765 and camped for months at the ruins of Wechquetank. Their stay was short and the exiles went west to Wyalusing.

The Moravian Historical Society erected a granite monument at the site of Wechquetank in 1907. The inscription reads, "The site of Wechquetank A Moravian Indian Mission Station 1760-1763." The monument stands in a pastoral spot on a country road near Hoeth's or Head's Creek, surrounded by a wrought iron fence topped with red spikes. Near the creek are the ruins of a stone mill.

## WILLIAM PARSONS HOUSE
### EASTON, PENNSYLVANIA

*Directions: Eastbound on Route 22, take right exit for Route 611 or Fourth Street (last exit in Pennsylvania before Delaware River and New Jersey border). Head toward downtown Easton on Fourth Street. Go several blocks to intersection of Fourth and Ferry Streets.*

William Parsons played an important role in the defense of eastern Pennsylvania during the years it lay vulnerable to attack. As a young man, Parsons (1701-1757) left England and came to Philadelphia to practice the shoemaker's trade. He had an intellectual bent and became an associate of Benjamin Franklin and a founding member of the American Philosophical Society. The ambitious Parsons was appointed Surveyor-General of Pennsylvania in 1741.

Parsons' career took a turn, however, when he separated from his German Pietist wife Johanna over religious differences. The breakup split the family and left Parsons an embittered man. Parsons moved westward, first to a remote plantation on Swatara Creek north of Reading in 1745, and then to Lancaster. He gave up the surveyor-general post in 1748, but continued to undertake government assignments such as plotting the streets of Reading.

When the Penn family decided in 1752 to plan the town of Easton as the courthouse seat for newly formed Northampton County, they chose Parsons as the man for the job. He held several county offices, and when the Delaware raids began in late 1755, Parsons oversaw the care of refugees and helped Franklin coordinate the defense of Northampton County.

Parsons was named a major of the county militia and made periodic trips to the provincial forts along the Blue Mountains. He was also charged with keeping order during the numerous peace conferences with the Delaware and other tribes at Easton during 1756-57. The strain of these duties broke his health and he died before the war's end.

In the last year of his life, Parsons built a two-story fieldstone house in Easton to replace the log cabin he occupied. The house was later owned by George Taylor, one of the signers of the Declaration of Independence. This house is currently maintained by Northampton County, and a state historical marker for George Taylor is in front of the house. The Northampton County Historical and Genealogical Society is across the street at 101 S. Fourth St., Easton.

## EASTON GREAT SQUARE — EASTON, PENNSYLVANIA

Some historians think that Fort Duquesne's fall was determined as much by peace conferences at the Forks of the Delaware as by British force of arms at the Forks of the Ohio. On four occasions between 1756-1758, the Great Square at Easton was the scene of peace negotiations between various Indian tribes and provincial officials.

The conferences held in 1756 and 1757 were dominated by Teedyuscung, the leader of the eastern Delaware tribes who wanted to regain the lands lost as part of the 1737 Walking Purchase. Those conferences led to a curtailment of the bloody raids along the Blue Mountain frontier, but it was an uneasy peace and the eastern Delaware still harbored deep resentment of the British. By the fall of 1758 the diplomatic focus had shifted. General John Forbes' army was at Fort Ligonier preparing to renew its methodical march on Fort Duquesne.

In October, arrangements were made for another conference at Easton to involve not only the Delaware and Shawnee, but also Iroquois leaders from New York and representatives of smaller tribes in Pennsylvania and New Jersey. The goal of the British at this conference was to woo the western Delaware and Shawnee away from the French and leave Fort Duquesne ripe for the taking. During the summer, Moravian missionary Christian Frederick Post had traveled to western Pennsylvania to personally deliver a peace message from Pennsylvania Gov. William Denny to the western tribes. Post was favorably received, and Pisquetomen, one of the Delaware accompanying him, served as an intermediary between the council at Easton and the western tribes. The powerful Iroquois acted as chief negotiators this time and agreed to support the British. The western Delaware and Shawnee declined to assist the French when Forbes' army made its final approach in November. The outnumbered French blew up the fort and retreated north to Fort Machault.

The 1758 Easton conference ratified the Walking Purchase, but provincial officials agreed to return lands taken northwest of the Susquehanna River under the 1754 Albany Purchase. The Iroquois also undercut the position of Teedyuscung and moved to reassert their hegemony over the eastern Delaware. The conference in the tree-lined Great Square was a colorful assemblage with some 500 Indians from various tribes, the governors of Pennsylvania and New Jersey, Conrad Weiser, the diplomat and military leader, and a large delegation of Philadelphia Quakers who sought to protect the Indians' interests. Indian conferences were also held at Easton in 1761 and 1762.

The square today at Third and Northampton Streets is a traffic circle dominated by a Civil War monument and fountain. However, there is enough space for park benches, shrubs, and a stone marker to the Indian Peace Treaties. The inscription reads:

> With one exception all the Indian peace treaties during the French and Indian War were held in this square between 1756 and 1762. These councils were attended by the governors of Pennsylvania and New Jersey and as many as 500 Indians at a time from 18 tribes in Pennsylvania and New Jersey.

## Moravian God's Acre — Emmaus, Pennsylvania

*Directions: On Route 22 east of Allentown. Go south on Northeast Extension of Pennsylvania Turnpike. At Emmaus, take exit east on Route 29 or Chestnut Street through town center to east side. Go south on Third Street to Adrian Street. Look for graveyard sign.*

Many of the frontier townships along the Blue Mountains were abandoned and refugees fled to Bethlehem and Easton during the opening years of the French and Indian War. But this did not stop the advancement of settlement in the region. Such is the case with the Moravian town of Emmaus, originally known as Macungie, a Delaware term for "feeding place of the bears."

German immigrants from the Rhineland started farming the area in the 1730s, and Moravian missionaries followed a decade later. As with settlements at Hebron and Oley farther west, these farmers were nominal members of the Lutheran or German Reformed Church who eventually coalesced into a Moravian congregation. This process started in the late 1740s when local leaders sought ties with Bethlehem. Moravian leaders decided in 1758 to make Emmaus a closed or congregational community, barred to those outside the Moravian faith. Land was surveyed and lots laid out even as the Moravians kept an eye out for Indian attacks. They planned for the town's defense and safeguarding of children and refugees in the event of an attack.

Emmaus was formally established in 1760 as a congregational village; this arrangement lasted on paper at least into the mid-19th century. One local leader who joined the Moravians was Jacob Ehrenhardt (1716-1760). He visited Bethlehem in 1742 and invited the Moravians to preach in his neighborhood. The first missionaries held a service in Ehrenhardt's log house; he donated the land for the first log church. Ehrenhardt was selected as a church warden when a Moravian congregation was formally organized in 1747. He donated land for the graveyard, or God's Acre, and is buried there. The headstones lie flat facing the heavens in the Moravian style. Ehrenhardt's inscription reads: "One of the founders and builders of the First Church at Emmaus. Born in Marstadt, Germany 1716 died 1760."

Today the graveyard is ringed by pine trees and is in the middle of a residential neighborhood. A sign reads, "Site of First Moravian Church and First Burial Ground of the Moravian Brethren of Emmaus 1742-1856."

***Emmaus Moravian Cemetery.***

## Wilson Block House
## Northampton, Pennsylvania

*Directions: Take Route 329 (or 21st Street) in Northampton to Laubach Avenue, turn right (south) and follow Laubach Avenue to Northampton Municipal Park. The Northampton Municipal Building is located at 14th Street and Laubach Avenue.*

Hugh Wilson was a prominent member of Northampton County's Irish Settlement, an enclave of Scots-Irish immigrants who settled along Hockendauqua Creek starting about 1729. He built an octagonal block house in 1756 as protection against Delaware raids. Wilson's block house survives in good condition today.

Wilson (1689-1773) emigrated from northern Ireland in 1727. He was related by marriage to the settlement's leader, Thomas Craig. Soon after the Penn family's controversial Walking Purchase in 1737, Wilson purchased about 1,250 acres of land on the west shore of Hockendauqua Creek from land speculator William Allen. Wilson built a grist mill to supply flour for the settlement. Mill operators played a key role in the economic life of frontier communities, and in time, Wilson became influential in political affairs. He petitioned the court in 1748 to create Allen Township, and four years later he became one of the first justices and trustees of newly created Northampton County.

With the outbreak of war after the burning of the Moravian mission at Gnadenhuetten in November 1755, the Irish Settlement as well as the German settlements in Northampton County were vulnerable to Delaware raids. Many settlers from the Irish Settlement fled to Bethlehem and Easton for protection. Wilson was among the local leaders who met provincial commander Benjamin Franklin on his journey to organize a defense among the Blue Mountains. Franklin urged Wilson and others to fortify their settlements instead of abandoning them.

Wilson and his son Thomas built the stone blockhouse near the mill. An eight-sided structure with a slanted roof, it has firing loopholes, one entrance, and walls two feet thick. There is no record of the block house coming under attack. In peacetime the building was used as a smokehouse and survived while log buildings rotted away. The block house remained at its original site, nestled by a small ridge on property owned by Universal Atlas Cement Co., until 1976. But vandalism posed a threat to the structure. In 1976, the borough of Northampton moved the block house to the municipal park. The well-maintained block house is located between the municipal building and the swimming pool.

***Hugh Wilson built this octagonal blockhouse in 1756.***

## TIOGA OR TEAOGA—ATHENS, PENNSYLVANIA

Tioga was a gateway from the Susquehanna Valley to the Iroquois or Six Nations territory in New York State. Because of its strategic position at a canoe portage connecting the Susquehanna and Chemung Rivers, Tioga was settled by a succession of tribes from prehistoric times to the Revolutionary War. Situated on the neck of a narrow peninsula between the Susquehanna and Chemung Rivers, it is today the town of Athens. Directly to the north is Spanish Hill, a 230-foot high palisaded stronghold of the Carantouan Indians visited by French explorer Etienne Brule in 1615. To the south is Queen Esther's Flats, a Delaware town along the bottom lands of the Chemung that was destroyed by the Sullivan expedition during the Revolutionary War. Tioga was also at the junction of the Warriors Path and Sheshequin Path, adding to its strategic importance.

During 1756-58, Tioga was a stronghold of pro-French Delaware headed by Teedyuscung. Many captives seized in raids south of the Blue Mountains were brought here. Among them was Susanna Nitschmann, a member of the Moravian Brethren living at Gnadehuetten during the attack in November 1755. Nitschmann was taken to Tioga and died there in captivity in May 1756.

Archaeological excavations in the 1890s unearthed the graves of the Andaste, a Native American tribe that had migrated from the south. The Andaste were conquered by the Iroquois in the 17th century.

Tioga became a watch town for the Iroquois Confederacy. A Cayuga viceroy was stationed there to keep watch on subject tribes living along the Susquehanna River. During the 1720s, the Palatinate Germans passed by Tioga on their migration from the Mohawk Valley to Tulpehocken Creek. In 1743, Pennsylvania diplomat Conrad Weiser and naturalist John Bartram stopped at Tioga enroute to the Iroquois capital at Onondaga. Bartram wrote, "...this town is called Tohicon, and lies in a rich neck between the branch and main river: the Indians welcomed us by beating their drum."

In early 1756, after hostilities began between the Delaware and the British, the Delaware chief Teedyuscung and his followers set up camp at Tioga. They staged raids on the British settlements from here and brought back captives and scalps. Teedyuscung's assemblage included Delaware, Shawnees, Mahican, Nanticokes and a few Iroquois. Tioga offered better protection from British attack than the vulnerable Delaware towns in the Wyoming Valley.

After the Easton peace treaty of 1758, Teedyuscung and his followers abandoned Tioga to settle in the Wyoming Valley. Other Delaware tribes established new villages in the area, but their occupancy was relatively short-lived. After Queen Esther's town was destroyed in 1779, the American army built Fort Sullivan on the site of Tioga.

The region's rich history is interpreted at Tioga Point Museum, 724 South Main St., Athens. Hours are Tuesday and Thursday 1-8 p.m., Saturday 10-1. Phone: 570-888-7225.

A plaque and state historical marker for the Carrying Path is located at the Chemung River Bridge on Route 199 leading into Athens. At this spot, Indian voyagers carried their canoes 190 yards across the neck to the Susquehanna. On Route 220, 2 1/2 miles south of Athens is a large stone tablet with a bronze marker. The monument was erected in 1928 by the Pennsylvania Historical Commission and Tioga Point Chapter of the Daughters of the American Revolution. The inscription reads:

> Teoga A Watch Town. The South Door of the Iroquois long house was situated at the meeting of the rivers 200 roads to the northeast. Queen Esther's Town of the Delaware Indians was 100 rods to the east along the Chemung River banks. Both towns were destroyed by Colonel Thomas Hartley and his troops Sept. 27, 1778. These flats for 5 miles known as Queen Esther's flats were grazing ground for their herds.

# 6 Pennsylvania Germans Defend Blue Mountain Region, 1756-1757

## INTRODUCTION

The Blue Mountain range of eastern Pennsylvania was a physical barrier that marked the frontier in the 1750s. South of the range, German farmers tilled rich farmland in the Tulpehocken and Oley Valleys. To the north Delaware and Shawnee villages were situated along the Susquehanna River. On a journey through the region in 1743, naturalist John Bartram described the Tulpehocken as "this fine limestone vale, many hundred miles long, and from 10 to 20 miles broad to the northern boundary formed by the Great Blue Mountains."

The first migration of Europeans into this region came in the 1720s when Palatinate Germans left their settlements on New York's frontier. They traveled by flatboat and canoe down the Susquehanna River to Swatara Creek and then journeyed east along that waterway until they came to Tulpehocken (land of turtles) Creek. Fort Zeller was one of the early defenses built by the Palatinates.

The Palatinates found a natural leader in Conrad Weiser, the Indian diplomat, judge, and soldier, whose home is preserved as a state historic site. Weiser's homestead was the southern terminus of the Tulpehocken Path, an Indian trail that led through a gap in the Blue Mountain to the village of Shamokin, home of the Iroquois regent Shikellamy.

Farther east, the family of Squire Boone was among the Welsh, English and Swedes who settled in the Oley Valley. Their son Daniel, born in 1734, is one of the most famous American frontiersmen and his birthplace is preserved as a state historic site. The pastoral countryside below the Blue Mountain attracted not only farmers, but also pietistic religious groups such as the Moravians and the communal society known as Ephrata Cloister, whose German-style buildings are also preserved by the state of Pennsylvania.

In the fall of 1755, Delaware and Shawnee warriors came through the ancient water gaps in the Blue Mountains from Nescopeck and other villages to attack German homesteads. About 150 settlers were killed during hit-and-run raids during the next several years. The Bethel Moravian Meetinghouse near Swatara Gap was fortified. A surviving cemetery contains the graves of murdered settlers. The Hebron Moravian Cemetery in Lebanon contains the graves of two Indian raiders and Johannes Spittler, killed and scalped in 1757 by "von den Wilden," a German phrase for the wild Indians.

In response to the raids, Pennsylvania built ranger stations and forts at the Blue Mountain passes. The string of defenses included Fort Swatara, Fort Dietrich Snyder, Fort Henry which guarded the Tulpehocken Path, Fort Northkill, and Fort Lebanon. These outposts were manned first by German-speaking militia and later by a battalion of provincial troops organized by Weiser. With the eastern Delaware Indians agreeing to peace at Easton in 1758, the raids subsided.

SITES AT A GLANCE — This map will give you a feel for the general locations of sites in this chapter. Some sites overlap and are not shown on this map.

Ft. Lebanon
Ft. Henry
Ft. Swatara
Ephrata Cloister
Weiser homestead
Boone homestead

## TULPEHOCKEN PATH

*Directions: To drive the Tulpehocken Path, from Sunbury take Route 147 south past 18th century inn at Fishers Ferry and Herndon to junction with Route 225. Take Route 225 east, watch for signs for the town of Urban. Because of confusing numbers for LR49008 and LR49007, the historian Paul Wallace recommends following road signs*

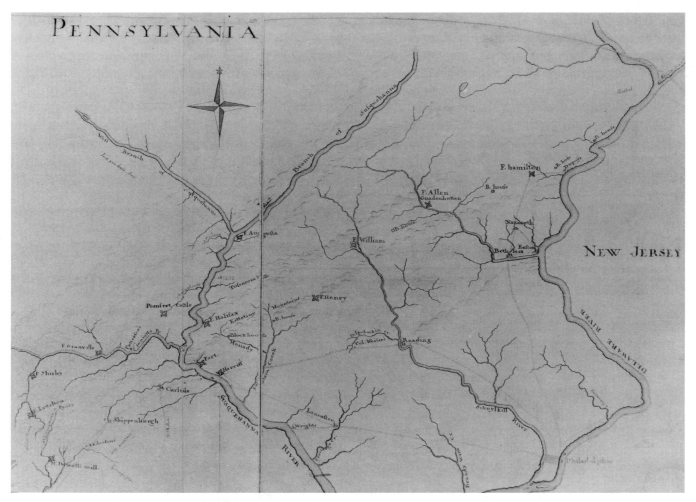

*Map of Pennsylvania showing frontier defenses.*

*for the towns of Klingerstown, Erdman, and Sacramento. At Sacramento, take Route 25 east to Hegins. At Hegins, follow signs for Goodspring, Jolliet, Lincoln Colliery, Ravine, and Pine Grove. At Pine Grove, take Route 501 across Blue Mountain to Bethel. Nearby is Fort Henry site. On Route 501 follow signs to Rehrersburg, then Route 419 south to Womelsdorf, where Conrad Weiser's home is maintained as a state historic site.*

This 70-mile trail connected Conrad Weiser's home on Tulpehocken Creek with the important Delaware village of Shamokin, at the Forks of the Susquehanna River. The trail crosses picturesque valleys and imposing mountains, and also takes advantage of the easy access offered through gaps in these mountains. The Tulpehocken Path was one of the most important of the many Indian paths that traversed Pennsylvania. It was the route that Conrad Weiser, Pennsylvania's Indian ambassador, and the Iroquois viceroy Shikellamy used on countless diplomatic missions to keep the peace from the 1720s to 1740s. Emissaries from the Iroquois capital at Onondaga in New York's Mohawk Valley went to Shamokin, then took the Tulpehocken Path to Weiser's enroute to meet with provincial officials in Philadelphia.

Weiser headed north along the path on several memorable journeys to Onondaga, accompanied by naturalist John Bartram on one such journey in 1743. Bartram described one stretch of the trail with, "Thence we traveled 7 miles over several hollows, swamps and small ridges, full of scrubby bushes, and still poor and stoney to the last great ridge."

When war broke out in the fall of 1755, scattered settlers living north of the Blue Mountains fled south along the path and roving bands of Delaware on the warpath followed in their wake. Fort Henry was situated south of where the Tulpehocken path crossed Blue Mountain near a small summit called Round Top.

Today, travelers can follow the route of the Tulpehocken Path both by heeding natural landmarks and driving along roughly parallel roads. The late historian Paul Wallace provides directions in his excellent *Indian Paths of Pennsylvania*, published by the Pennsylvania Historical and Museum Commission. The path started south at the Forks of the Susquehanna River, crossed Shamokin Creek and Shamokin Hill, skirted Mahanoy Mountain, crossed Mahantango Creek, passed through a gap in Mahantango Mountain, ran through

75

Pine Creek Valley, crossed Broad Mountain, passed through a gap in Second Mountain and crossed Blue Mountain to the farmlands below.

## PILGRIM'S REST (PILGER RUH) NORTH OF BETHEL, PENNSYLVANIA

*Directions: Head north on Route 501 from I-78. Look for state historical marker on right side 4.2 miles north of Bethel. Look for pulloff near Appalachian Trail. Sign says Pilgrim's Rest Ludwigs Brunne spring 150 feet. Follow dirt road. Low stone monument and spring to left of road.*

Thirsty travelers along the Tulpehocken Path welcomed the occasional resting stop and Pilger Ruh gained a reputation early on for its spring-fed water. The spring water still flows at Pilger Ruh on the summit of Blue Mountain today, but in a sad testament to environmental pollution, a posted sign says the water should be considered unsafe to drink.

Pilger Ruh was given its distinctive name by Count Nicholas Ludwig von Zinzendorf, the Moravian missionary who traveled along the Tulpehocken Path to visit Shamokin and Wyoming in 1742. Zinzendorf named many landmarks along the path for individuals or spiritual effect, but Pilger Ruh is one of the few names still used today.

*Pilger Ruh marker and spring.*

The spring is located near where the Appalachian Trail crosses Route 501 and is marked by a state highway marker. At the hillside site, water flows out of a pipe. A stone monument put up by the Blue Mountain Eagle Climbing Club and Berks County Historical Society reads: "1742 Pilger Ruh named by Count Zinzendorf who with Conrad Weiser and Moravian missionaries rested here besides this spring (Ludwigs Brunne) on their way to visit Shawnee Indians in Wyoming Valley."

## FORT HENRY—NORTH OF BETHEL, PENNSYLVANIA

*Directions: Take I-78 to Bethel. Exit Route 501 and go north for two miles. Look for state historical marker. At road fork, turn left (look for smaller Fort Henry sign) and go 3/4 mile. Look for stone monument on right side of road in front of white barn with stone foundation.*

Fort Henry was a key post in the chain of provincial forts along the Blue Mountains east of the Susquehanna River. The fort guarded the area where the Tulpehocken Path exited the mountainous no-man's land that sheltered Delaware war parties. Fort Henry was built on orders of Pennsylvania Gov. Robert Hunter Morris who drew up plans for the region's defense during a visit in January 1756 to Reading.

The fort was typical of the log stockades built by the province, but accounts describe it as having room for houses and a parade ground. Captain Christian Busse, a Reading doctor, was the fort's first commander. He oversaw a garrison of 50 men. Fort Henry's defenders were often dispatched on duty to other parts of Pennsylvania even though their own region needed protection. Busse led a detachment to Fort Augusta in October 1756 when rumors of a French attack on the Forks of the Susquehanna were widespread. In the winter of 1757, troops from Fort Henry went to Cumberland County.

And in October 1757, Fort Henry had the distinction of taking a young French soldier into custody. Michel La Chauvignerie, son of the commander of Fort Machault, had been part of a raiding party from western Pennsylvania. On the return journey, La Chauvignerie became separated from the party when he double-backed along the trail to look for a piece of bread that he had accidentally dropped. He wandered lost in the forests, then decided to make his way back to the English settlements rather than starve alone. La Chauvignerie approached Fort Henry and was spotted by a sentry. He was eventually taken to Philadelphia and then released under a prisoner exchange.

Today a stone monument erected by the Berks County Historical Society marks the site of Fort Henry. The fort was located about 25 yards northeast of the monument in what is now a second-growth pine forest.

*Fort Henry was built in 1756.*

## CONRAD WEISER HOMESTEAD
### EAST OF WOMELSDORF, PENNSYLVANIA

*Directions: Take Route 422 east of Womelsdorf several miles. Look for brown and white historical signs. Park is on right side of road.*

Conrad Weiser did as much as anyone to keep the peace on Pennsylvania's frontier for two decades. But when the peace faded, Weiser put on a different hat and commanded provincial troops defending the Blue Mountain settlements. Weiser (1696-1760) is an interesting figure even not counting his missions on behalf of war and peace. He was a family patriarch, farmer, linguist, judge, and founder of Reading. Yet Weiser also dropped out of society for a time to join Ephrata Cloister, the religious communal society not too far from his home that preached a regimen of self-discipline and simple living.

Weiser and his family emigrated in 1710 from the Palatinate Rhine region in Germany to New York. The Palatinates were a Protestant group who came to America to escape the continual warfare in their homeland. As a young man, Weiser gained a valuable knowledge of the Iroquois language and customs living as the adopted son of a chief in the Mohawk Valley. With land growing scarce and the title to their property in question, the Palatinates began another emigration to Pennsylvania's Tulpehocken Valley in 1723. Weiser arrived in the Tulpehocken Valley six years later in 1729.

About the same time, the Iroquois sent Shikellamy to Shamokin at the Forks of the Susquehanna River to oversee tribal affairs in the region. Weiser and Shikellamy reportedly met on a hunting expedition in New York. They formed a diplomatic team that worked effectively to settle frontier disputes. When Pennsylvania officials and the Iroquois began to edge closer together in the face of a growing French presence in the Ohio Valley, it was only natural that this pair would midwife the effort. Pennsylvania sought to bolster the Iroquois' political influence so they, in turn, could exert more control over the Delaware and Shawnee migrating westward into the Ohio Valley.

Weiser's first diplomatic foray came in 1732 when he served as an interpreter at a conference that paved the way for more Indian land cessions. Weiser later went on numerous missions to Onondaga, the Iroquois political seat in New York, and to Logstown, the Iroquois center in the Ohio Valley. Shikellamy often accompanied Weiser on these journeys until the former's death in 1748.

When war broke out in 1755, Weiser was put in charge of provincial troops stationed at the Blue Mountain forts. He advised British Gen. John Forbes and played a key role in the 1758 Easton conference that swung the Delaware away from the French orbit.

Weiser's home at the southern end of the Tulpehocken Trail is preserved as a 26-acre state historic park by the Pennsylvania Historical and Museum Commission. At one time, Weiser's holdings covered 1,000 acres and included a tannery operation. Delegations of Iroquois and other tribal leaders enroute to Philadelphia often camped here.

*Conrad Weiser House.*

Weiser's simple limestone house dates to 1730. The house consists of a large downstairs room with a fireplace and bake oven and sleeping quarters under the roof. The house is open to the public and furnished with period pieces.

Nearby are the graves of Weiser, his wife Ann Eve, and several of their fourteen children. Two of Weiser's grandsons rose to national prominence—Revolutionary War General John Peter Gabriel Muhlenberg and House Speaker Frederick Muhlenberg. Also on the grounds of the beautifully landscaped park is a springhouse built in the 1730s by Weiser and a statue of Weiser's ally, Shikellamy.

The park is open 9 a.m. to 5 p.m. Wednesday through Saturday and noon to 5 p.m. Sunday. Admission is charged. Special events, including French and Indian War reenactments, are held here.

## FORT ZELLER
### SOUTH OF NEWMANSTOWN, PENNSYLVANIA

*Directions: Take Route 419 south of Newmanstown. Turn right on Fort Zeller Road by state historical marker for Fort Zeller. Monument is on right side of road by farm entrance.*

This whitewashed stone house in a pastoral setting is a relic of the Palatinate migration to the Tulpehocken Valley. Fort Zeller was built as a defense against Indian raids. The Palatinates were a Protestant group fleeing from persecution in the war-torn Rhineland region of Germany. They were joined by French Huguenots or Protestants who fled France after a policy of religious toleration was revoked.

These exiles were given protection by the British crown and encouraged to settle in America. They arrived in New York in 1710 and settled on land provided by one of the semi-feudal landlords along the Hudson River. But the Palatinates found the economic conditions harsh and just a step above serfdom. They fled to the Schoharie Valley on New York's frontier and lived there for a decade, but their title to the land was in doubt.

Pennsylvania Gov. William Keith invited the Palatinates to move to Pennsylvania and selected land for them along Tulpehocken Creek. In the spring of 1723, sixteen families floated in canoes and rafts down the Susquehanna River to Swatara Creek and then followed Swatara Creek eastward to a point close to Tulpehocken Creek.

Other emigrants came by land routes. The Zellers were Huguenots who joined this migration. Clothide de Valois Zeller (1660-1749) was the family matriarch. Arriving in New York in 1710 recently widowed, with her grown sons she persevered through the trials facing the exiles and came to Pennsylvania. The Zellers built a blockhouse here

***Fort Zeller was built as a defense against Indian raids.***

in 1723, and in 1745, when Indian raiding parties were in the area, Heinrich Zeller built the existing stronghold. This structure is distinctive for its pitched roof, dormer windows and enclosed spring. Fort Zeller is on private property, but within clear view of the road.

The Zeller family erected a unique memorial in 1941 on the roadside by the property. The stone monument is graced by a carved silhouette of Clothide Zeller and two turtles symbolizing Tulpehocken or land of turtles. The inscription reads:

Lady Clothide de Valois Zeller, widow of Jacques Zeller, and her sons Jean Henri and Jean Zeller, settled here June 14, 1723 and built a blockhouse for protection of settlers on this frontier. Zeller Family Association and Fort Zeller Association 1941.

## EPHRATA CLOISTER—EPHRATA, PENNSYLVANIA

*Directions: Take Exit 21 off Pennsylvania Turnpike. Take Route 272 south to intersection with Route 322. Take Route 322 east to Ephrata. Watch for brown and white direction signs to Ephrata Cloister on Main Street, Ephrata.*

Many Germans who came to Pennsylvania were drawn by William Penn's promise of religious toleration. To this day, Pennsylvania is known for the German religious groups that continue to practice their faiths here—Amish, Mennonites, and Schwenkfelder, to name a few.

The Ephrata Cloister was an early communal society founded in 1732 on the banks of Cocalico Creek in Lancaster County, about thirteen miles south of the German settlements in the Tulpehocken Valley. The members of this society devoted themselves to a lifestyle that emphasized attainment of spiritual goals, rather than material success. By 1750 Ephrata Cloister was at its zenith, numbering 300 members who printed books, farmed the land, sang in choirs, made furniture, and perfected a distinctive type of hand-lettered designs called Fraktur.

With the outbreak of the French and Indian War, Ephrata Cloister became a place of refuge for settlers fleeing homesteads along the Blue Mountains. The members of the society provided food and lodging to these outside refugees. A company of provincial soldiers was sent to guard the Cloister, but it never came under attack.

The guiding spiritual light at Ephrata Cloister was Conrad Beissel (1691-1768), a mystic from the Rhineland who came to Pennsylvania in 1720 and moved to the frontier in search of spiritual solitude. With his charismatic personality, however, he attracted followers even when he sought seclusion. In 1732, Beissel moved to Cocalico Creek and his followers were not far behind.

The members of Ephrata Cloister practiced a life of worldly denial in order to get closer to spiritual union with God. They were industrious and ate a largely meat-free diet. The society was divided into an order of celibates who lived in separate buildings for men and women, married householders who lived on nearby farms, and even some who lived a solitary life. Society members devoted time to daily meditation and were noted for their choral singing and hymn-writing.

Conrad Weiser, the region's famous Indian diplomat, became a member of the Cloister for a time in the 1730s. But Weiser never became a whole-hearted follower of Beissel, and eventually he returned to his Tulpehocken farm.

During the Revolutionary War, the Cloister provided care for some 500 wounded American soldiers, but thereafter it entered into a slow decline. The last members of

*Sister's House at Ephrata Cloister.*

the celibate orders died by 1800. The Seventh Day German Baptist Church administered the Cloister from 1814 until the 1930s. In 1941, the Pennsylvania Historical and Museum Commission acquired the site, a fortunate thing for those interested in the 18th century.

The Cloister contains a collection of well-preserved buildings that reflect a distinctive style of medieval German architecture with slanting roofs and numerous dormer windows. Eleven of the original buildings, including the meetinghouse, Solitary House, Sister's House, Academy, and Almonry, can be visited. In some buildings, museum employees dressed in the white monk's habits of the celibate order provide interpretation. A visitor center contains exhibits of Fraktur and books printed at Ephrata.

Ephrata Cloister is open Mon-Sat. 9 a.m. to 5 p.m., and Sunday noon to 5 p.m. Admission charged. Closed holidays except Memorial Day, July 4 and Labor Day. 717-733-6600.

## DANIEL BOONE HOMESTEAD
## BIRDSBORO, PENNSYLVANIA

*Directions: Take Route 422 east of Reading to Baumstown. Turn left onto Daniel Boone Road (Route 2041) and go north one mile. Look for brown and white state signs at entrance.*

The advance of the American frontier in the 18th century can be marked by tracing the footsteps of Daniel Boone to Missouri. And Boone's westward journey began in a small log house in Berks County, then on the edge of Pennsylvania's frontier.

Born into a large Quaker family in 1734, Boone helped his father with farming chores. But he also showed a restless spirit. The boy found time to master the hunting and woodland skills that won him fame later as a frontiersman. He was given a rifle for his tenth birthday and shot his first bear at age thirteen. When Boone was sixteen, he and his family left Berks County and migrated south along the Great Wagon Road to western North Carolina. The move was prompted in part by Squire Boone's falling out with the local Quaker establishment.

Boone was a wagon driver on the 1755 Braddock expedition and the 1758 Forbes expedition to the Forks of the Ohio. After that, Boone's journeys took him into the country where he made his name—the dark and bloody ground of Kentucky. Boone died near St. Louis, Missouri in 1820.

Today Boone's Pennsylvania roots can be explored at a state historical park near Reading. Scattered about the 579 pastoral acres of the Daniel Boone homestead are 18th century buildings. The centerpiece is the Boone House, a two story fieldstone structure located on the site of the

*Daniel Boone was born in a log cabin at this site.*

Boone family cabin. This house is mainly the work of later property owners. But the original cellar of Boone's log house is accessible from an entrance on the left side. The stone cellar walls served as a foundation for the log cabin. The bottom of the Boone chimney is visible as well as spring waters flowing through a trough in the floor.

The park, administered by the Pennsylvania Historical and Museum Commission, is open Tuesday through Saturday 9 a.m. to 5 p.m. and Sunday noon to 5 p.m. The park features a number of events, including flintlock musket shoots.

## FORT LEBANON—EAST OF AUBURN, PENNSYLVANIA

*Directions: Take I-78 to Route 61 exit, then Route 61 north through the Schuylkill River gap at Port Clinton. Turn left or west on Route 895 toward Auburn. Go past Borough of Deer Lake Water Authority and then continue about three miles. Make left turn on Fort Lebanon Road. Continue west on Fort Lebanon Road about 9/10 mile. Look for stone monument for fort on left side in field. State historical marker for Fort Lebanon on Route 895 east of Auburn.*

Fort Lebanon was a crowded place in 1756. Located northwest of the gap where the Schuylkill River flows through the Blue Mountains, a number of families took shelter in this log stockade one hundred feet square. The fort contained a barracks, storehouse, cabins to shelter the settlers, and a spring to provide drinking water.

The settlers had good reason to seek the fort's safety because of continual attacks by Delaware raiders on the isolated homesteads in this area. The dispatches of Captain Jacob Morgan are filled with accounts of soldiers heading out from the fort to the scene of a raid or to check out fires spotted in the distance. November 1756 was particularly bloody with Delawares killing the wife, daughter, and son-in-law of Philip Culmor during a raid about one mile from the fort. The home of Martin Fell was raided about the same time. Fell was killed and his wife and children were reported missing.

Morgan (1716-92) was the provincial solder who built Fort Lebanon in December 1755 and served as its only commander. Morgan was a Welsh emigrant who came to Pennsylvania with his family while in his teens. The family settled in an area of Berks County around the headwaters of Conestoga Creek. The town of Morgantown is named for the family. In later life, Morgan represented Berks County at important conventions during the Revolutionary War and served as a county judge.

In 1757, troops from Fort Lebanon were sent to aid Fort Augusta. At some point in 1757, the fort was renamed Fort William. By spring 1758, Fort Lebanon or William was evacuated as the British prepared for the attack on Fort Duquesne.

Today, visitors can stand at the site of Fort Lebanon and get a good feel for the terror felt by settlers who took shelter here in 1756. The fort was due north of a ridge along the base of which runs Pine Creek. The Mahantango chapter of the Daughters of American Revolution of Pottsville erected a stone monument here in 1913 with this inscription: "On this site stands Fort Lebanon. Built in 1755 by Col. Jacob Morgan for the protection of the early settlers against the Indians." Nearby a brick springhouse covers the water supply that nourished those settlers.

*Marker for Fort Lebanon.*

# FORT NORTHKILL
## NORTHEAST OF STRAUSSTOWN, PENNSYLVANIA

*Directions: Take I-78 to Route 183 (Strausstown exit). Go south on Route 183 to intersection with old Route 22, then left on Old Route 22 to Power Road. Look for blue sign (Fort Northkill one mile) at intersection. Take Power Road across interstate. Go left on dirt gravel road called Bloody Spring Road. At nearby fork, go right on unnamed dirt road for about 1 1/2 miles past cornfields toward mountain range. Look for blue sign at edge of woods (Fort Northkill 500 feet northwest). Surrounded by private property, fort site is on a slight elevation through bramble-filled woods on north side of private road.*

Fort Northkill was built in the spring of 1756 near Northkill Creek at the base of the Blue Mountains. This fort was located midway between Fort Henry and Fort Lebanon.

In January 1756, Capt. Jacob Morgan of Fort Lebanon received orders from Gov. Robert Hunter Morris to lead a detachment and build Fort Northkill. Morris advised the captain to pick a site with a good elevation and where a spring or run of water was within firing range. The construction job was evidently not of highest caliber. Provincial commissary general James Young inspected the fort that June, and found that the stockade posts were not set well in the ground and the log house inside the fort lacked a chimney.

In the summer of 1756, soldiers from Fort Northkill were sent out to guard farmers harvesting crops. Indian raids were frequent in the area and the garrison saw its share of conflict. In November 1756, fort commander Lt. Samuel Humphreys reported an encounter in which one of his men was wounded and his own coat was pierced with bullet holes in four places.

By the fall of 1757, provincial officials considered abandoning Fort Northkill. They thought it poorly built and in a bad location. In October 1757 a raiding party captured four people living near Northkill Creek. In this instance, troops from the Royal American Regiment were dispatched from Reading to the area. By the early spring of 1758, Fort Northkill had apparently been abandoned even through Bern Township residents had petitioned provincial Gov. William Denny to keep troops in the area.

Today, the site of Fort Northkill is on an elevation and marked by a small stone monument placed by the Historical Society of Berks County. The fort's cellar is still visible as a depression in the ground, as it was in 1893 when described in "Frontier Forts of Pennsylvania," an official state survey of fort sites. Locating Fort Northkill poses a challenge to an intrepid visitor. The area around the fort has become more wooded since the society put up its monument in the 1910s. The road leading to the fort is

*A Fort Northkill marker leading to the fort site.*

marked with blue signs, but the site is on private property and posted with no trespassing signs. It is advisable to contact the landowner before venturing through the brush to the fort site or taking a private road that runs by it. Still, approaching the fort site no farther than the public road gives a feeling for a garrison of soldiers huddling in a poorly built fort in the shadow of the Blue Mountains.

# FORT DIETRICH SNYDER
## NORTH OF STRAUSSTOWN, PENNSYLVANIA

*Directions: Hikers can walk the Appalachian Trail 1/3 of a mile from Route 183 to reach the monument. A sense of the Blue Mountain terrain can be gained by walking a stretch of this public use trail. The Appalachian Trail Guide to Pennsylvania mentions the monument in its mile-by-mile-log.*

*To reach the monument from I-78, go north on Route 183 at Strausstown for several miles until near the summit. A public parking lot in a state gameland is located 1/3 mile south of the summit on the east side of Route 183. Cross to west side of Route 183 and walk up hill to a yellow gate marking the west entrance to the Appalachian Trail. A brown Appalachian Trail sign and Schuylkill County sign are in the vicinity. Go past the gate and look for white paint slashes that serve as trail markers. Bear left and follow a wide stone/gravel path across a field to some woods. Stay on the main trail and avoid the two forks to the right. The stone fort monument is visible in a clearing in the woods on the right.*

*Fort marker along the Appalachian Trail.*

Fort Dietrich Snyder was a log cabin used as a fortified lookout post. This fort was located on the summit of Blue Mountain in an area known as Schuberts Gap. From this spot, lookouts had a commanding view of the landscape. Smoke plumes were often a tell-tale sign that enemy raiding parties were in the area, and lookouts relayed word to soldiers at nearby Fort Northkill, located at the southern slope of Blue Mountain.

A stone monument marking the site of Fort Dietrich Snyder is located in a clearing along the Appalachian Trail. The inscription reads:

"1755 Site of Fort Dietrich Snyder. A lookout post to warn of the approach of enemies in the French and Indian War. The Historical Society of Berks County 1915. Relocated 1946."

## LIGHT'S FORT—LEBANON, PENNSYLVANIA

*Directions: Take Route 72 south into Lebanon on northwest side of town. Light's Fort is at corner of Maple and 11th Street. In 1999, Mangano's Pizza Restaurant occupied a red brick building next door.*

At first glance, this boarded-up, fieldstone building in an older neighborhood on Lebanon's west side may not seem like much. But the structure was built by Mennonite John Light (or Johannes Leicht) in 1742 and served as a place of refuge for 60 families during the French and Indian War.

Light's Fort has served many uses over the past 250 years—as a residence, Mennonite meetinghouse, private fort, distillery, and rental dwelling. The original structure

was a two-story saltbox, but it has been altered many times over the years. The building once had a running spring in the cellar, but that dried up sometime in the 19th century. The Tulpehocken chapter of the Daughters of the American Revolution put a bronze plaque on the building in 1974. It reads: "Home and refuge of Johannes Leicht (John Light) d. 1759 Light's Fort Built 1742."

*Light's Fort was once a Mennonite refuge, now its history is all but forgotten.*

## HEBRON MORAVIAN CEMETERY
## LEBANON, PENNSYLVANIA

*Directions: Take East Walnut Street, a one-way eastbound main thoroughfare through Lebanon to east edge of city. Turn left on Cloister Street. Look for small sign, "Lebanon Moravian Cemetery 1748." Cemetery gate is at end of Cloister Street.*

This old Moravian cemetery on the east end of Lebanon contains graves of victims on both sides of the French and Indian War. The hand-carved German script on the flat headstone of Johannes Spittler Jr., provides a clue to his gruesome fate: "Johannes Spittler Gebd. 24 Sept. 1718 Ermondt. Von den Wilden d. 16 May 1757 at 37 Jahres 9 Mo 3 Tag."

Spittler, a native of Ermondt, Germany, was doing chores on his farm south of Swatara Gap on a spring day when "den Wilden"—the German name for the wild Indians—attacked. Spittler, 37, was shot and scalped within sight of his wife and children. His mangled body was brought here for internment in Grave No. 28. Within five months the body of Spittler's 67-year-old father, said to have died of heartbreak, was buried in Grave No. 33.

Nearby is the grave of Christian Binnen. His home was raided and burned in the winter of 1757. Binnen's wife was taken into captivity, and Binnen died of his injuries a short time later.

*A Moravian killed "von der wilden."*

Moravian graves in Hebron Cemetery are numbered and laid out in neat rows. The graveyard also contains a common grave of two unknown Indian raiders killed in a skirmish two miles east of Hebron in the fall of 1756. A small stone marks this grave near a Civil War cannon.

Hebron was the main Moravian settlement in the Quittapahilla or Lebanon Valley. The first Moravian missionary to come from Bethlehem to the area was Johann Herzen in the late 1740s. He built a Moravian congregation among the German settlers living there. The congregation flourished until the Revolutionary War, but then it went into a long decline. The last member of the congregation died in 1901.

The Hebron cemetery dates to 1748. A monument in the cemetery says: "This Gotte's Acre of the Unitas Fratrum was hallowed March 1748 by Rev. John Philip Muerer." Today the cemetery occupies a tree-shaded knoll surrounded by a stone wall.

## BETHEL MORAVIAN MEETINGHOUSE
### EAST OF LICKDALE, PENNSYLVANIA

*Directions: From I-81 north, take Exit 30 (Lebanon Route 72). Turn left at exit. Head east through traffic light at Lickdale. Take Lickdale Road past state historical marker for Union Forge and cross blue bridge over Swatara Creek. Take immediate left on Darkes Road. Where road forks, turn left onto Mountain Road, then left on Cemetery Road. Across from intersection of Mountain Road and Werner Road, look for line of cedar trees on right to mark location of Moravian cemetery. Park on roadside. Moravian graves in rear of cemetery.*

On a hillside just south of the Blue Mountain range is a graveyard with about 30 headstones inscribed with German script. This is the remnant of a Moravian community that was putting down roots when the French and Indian War broke out. Moravians living in this area south of Swatara Gap inhabited what was then called "The Hole." The settlement resulted from missionary work by Johannes Brandmueller who came in 1743 and converted Germans living here who were either Lutheran or Reformed Church members. The Moravians named their settlement Bethel and built a meetinghouse.

The meetinghouse was a refuge in the time of "The Wilden," as Moravians called the Delaware. Those working in the fields were vulnerable to ambush. In July 1757, four young men of the Bethel congregation were killed while plowing fields. That same month, provincial soldiers from Fort Swatara were sent to the meetinghouse to guard those harvesting crops.

Today the meetinghouse is long gone, but the cemetery that the Moravians called "God's Acre" remains, and is believed to hold remains of massacred settlers. The Moravians' distinctive flat tombstones are here, as well as upright stones of Revolutionary War veterans.

*Bethel Moravian Cemetery.*

# Fort Swatara—near Lickdale, Pennsylvania

*Directions: From I-81 north, Exit 30 (Route 72 Lebanon). Turn left after exit, then left at traffic light at Lickdale. Head north on Route 72. Turn left on Bohn's Lane. Turn right on Fort Swatara Drive. Follow road to bend.*

*Look for first Fort Swatara stone monument on left side of road next to white farmhouse. Yellow barn is on right. Turn left at monument on unmarked farm lane and go 500 feet to second reddish stone monument at fort site. Drive through Swatara Gap on either Route 72 or I-81 north. State historical marker for Swatara Gap is on Route 72. Swatara State Park is accessible off Route 72. The park is partially developed, but there are ruins of old canal locks on Old State Road.*

Fort Swatara occupied a strategic position just southeast of Swatara Gap, a prominent water gap in the Blue Mountains. The waters of Swatara Creek eroded layers of sandstone and quartzite over eons to form a pass through the mountains. Delaware warriors came through this gap in the fall of 1755 attacking German and Moravian settlers in the region.

Local settlers put up a stockade around the home of Peter Hedrick. Governor Robert Hunter Morris designated this makeshift structure as Fort Swatara. It was garrisoned by provincial troops from January 1756 until the spring of 1758 when the theater of war shifted to western Pennsylvania. Captain Frederick Smith (or Friedreich Schmitt) and 50 men were dispatched to the area and made improvements to Hedrick's stockade.

The troops went out on ranging patrols and on occasion were sent to guard the nearby Bethel Moravian Meetinghouse, a place of refuge for settlers. The fort is described in 1756 as being well-built, clean, and supplied with water from a nearby spring. But officers worried that a straw-covered barn inside the fort could be set on fire by attackers. Delaware war parties were active in the area, killing settlers in isolated incidents through 1757.

A journal kept by Lt. Philip Marzloff, a German-speaking officer who commanded the fort in 1757, gives a glimpse of what the war was like. A portion of the journal was translated and published by the Lebanon County Historical Society in 1964. The following entry is dated August 6, 1757:

> This morning when I set out with my men to scout, I heard several shots at Kramer's place, and shrieks. I ran up with my men, supposing that the Indians were trying to seize the people in the house. When I came up, however, I heard that Winkelsblech's two sons, with one of Hetterich's soldiers who was put under my command, had gone out to fetch home the cows, when seven shots were fired at them. The younger of Winkelsblech's sons remained at the spot and was scalped, the larger was shot through the body and died in a few hours, the soldier was wounded in the left hand. I set out at once on their trail and tried to intercept them at the pass, but it appears they became aware of this, and retired across the mountain by another path.

Today, standing on the Fort Swatara site, it is easy to understand its strategic importance. Swatara Gap is clearly visible to the northeast. The fort site is on elevated ground directly north of a run of water. The Lebanon County Historical Society has erected two stone monuments, one on Fort Swatara Drive and another nearby at the site of the fort down a farm lane.

***Fort Swatara once guarded an important mountain gap.***

# 7 George Washington Defends the Virginia Frontier, 1755-1758

## INTRODUCTION

The assignment given to the young colonel was formidable. Fortify and defend several hundred miles of Virginia frontier. Protect scattered villages and homesteads of the German and Scots-Irish settlers in the Shenandoah Valley who were left vulnerable to French and Indian raiding parties.

George Washington accepted this assignment from Virginia's Gov. Robert Dinwiddie in October 1755. The veteran of several Ohio Valley campaigns proceeded to raise an army and oversee the construction of forts extending from the Potomac River watershed to the North Carolina border. From his headquarters at Fort Loudoun in Winchester, Virginia, Washington wrestled with supply problems, rival commanders, homeless refugees and the imposing task of maintaining communications with the far-flung garrisons under his command.

One of Washington's chief rivals was Killbuck, a Delaware chief from the Ohio Valley town of Sawcunk who led many of the raiding parties across the Alleghenies and into the Potomac and Shenandoah Valleys. Killbuck typically led groups of 50 to 100 warriors on these forays. French officers often accompanied the war parties. Killbuck scored some major victories, capturing and burning Fort Seybert and Fort Upper Tract along the Potomac's South Branch in the spring of 1758. Later that year, Killbuck was among the Delaware chieftains offering an olive branch to the British as French power crumbled.

Other forts along Virginia's long frontier saw plenty of action as well. A young Daniel Morgan was ambushed near Fort Edwards along the Cacapon River. Captain John Ashby narrowly escaped pursuing Indians at the fort that bears his name. Fort Ashby survives today as a museum. Fort Pleasant was situated near The Trough, a rugged canyon along the South Branch. The Trough was the scene of a fierce battle between the Shawnee and local militia. Fort Pearsall at Romney, West Virginia, was a stopover for Cherokee and Catawba warriors headed north to help the British.

While many Shenandoah Valley inhabitants fled eastward after the first wave of attacks, others stayed put and built their own private forts. Abram's Delight at Winchester was built with protection in mind. The Hite family, part of the original migration into the valley, built their own fort south of Winchester. Hupp Homestead was a private fort near Strasburg that stands today. Fort Harrison near Dayton served as a refuge and is maintained as a museum today. North of Staunton, the Augusta Stone Church is an architectural landmark. This limestone church doubled as a fort during the troubled times of the 1750s.

## WASHINGTON COMMANDS VIRGINIA'S ARMY

George Washington was only 23 when he was named commander-in-chief of Virginia's forces in October 1755. When the royal governor, Robert Dinwiddie, named the surveyor to defend Virginia's western frontier, he was well aware of Washington's youth. But Dinwiddie also knew that few other officers in Virginia could match Washington's familiarity with wilderness warfare. Washington had delivered Dinwiddie's warn-

SITES AT A GLANCE—This map will give you a feel for the general locations of sites in this chapter. Some sites overlap and are not shown on this map.

Ft. Ashby

Adam Stephen House

The Trough

Winchester

Ft. Harrison

Augusta stone church

ing to the French forces occupying the upper Ohio Valley two years earlier. He engaged French forces in an uneven fight at Fort Necessity, and, he managed to survive Braddock's defeat physically unscathed and with his military reputation intact.

Still, these experiences did not fully prepare Washington for the frustrations of defending several hundred miles of frontier for three years until the tide of war turned in the British favor in 1758. The young colonel had to cope with ill-trained militia, challenges to his authority, lack of equipment and supplies, inter-colonial rivalry, terrified refugees and a serious bout with illness.

Washington commanded an army authorized at 2,000 soldiers, but with far fewer actually available for duty. The Virginia House of Burgesses authorized Dinwiddie to build a chain of forts from the Cacapon River in the Potomac watershed to the south branch of the Mayo River near the North Carolina border. Dinwiddie gave Washington authority to locate the forts where he saw fit. Washington sought to build each fort fifteen miles, or a day's journey, apart with a garrison of at least 80 soldiers. But some garrisons fell below that strength.

From his headquarters at Winchester, Virginia, Washington oversaw the construction of Fort Loudoun, Virginia's main defense post. He journeyed to Boston in the winter of 1756 to settle a vexing dispute over whether he or a Maryland captain could exercise command at Fort Cumberland on the Virginia-Maryland border. In the fall of 1756, Washington undertook another long journey to inspect the forts in the Roanoke region. During the winter of 1757 he was sidelined at Mount Vernon with dysentery.

By 1758 Washington commanded the Virginia troops on the Forbes expedition to capture the Forks of the Ohio. He showed determination when he lobbied the British command incessantly to have the army take Braddock's old route from Fort Cumberland to reach French Fort Duquesne at the forks. Virginia's leaders believed that use of that road would buttress their claims to the Ohio land and open up trade. But Gen. John Forbes decided to build a new road across Pennsylvania.

Washington was elected to the House of Burgesses from the Winchester area during the Forbes campaign. This was the start of an auspicious political career.

### GEORGE WASHINGTON'S OFFICE
### WINCHESTER, VIRGINIA

*Directions: From I-81, take Exit 313 west on Routes 50/ 522. Right on Pleasant Valley Road. At first stoplight, turn left on Cork Street to Braddock Street and look for dark log building.*

This log building in the heart of modern Winchester served as the command post for Colonel Washington during his defense of the Virginia frontier. From here, Washington raised an army and built Fort Loudoun, the main defensive post in Virginia. The building is now a museum maintained by the Winchester-Frederick County Historical Society. Nothing remains of Fort Loudoun except for an old well in a private backyard. So the story of the fort is told at the museum.

Virginia's General Assembly passed a law authorizing construction of Fort Loudoun in March 1756. Washington drew up the fort's plans, and work continued on it for the next two years. The fort was considered a formidable one even though it was never completed. The fort stockade enclosed a half-acre of land just north of the small village of Winchester.

Washington owned a plot of land in the vicinity of Fort Loudoun at the corner of Braddock Street and Fairfax Lane. Here he established a blacksmith shop to do iron work for the fort. Two of Washington's slaves from his plantation at Mount Vernon came to make iron fittings. A historical marker is on the site.

Fort Loudoun did not come under direct attack, but it was an important supply depot and launching point for expeditions to the Ohio country. Cherokee and Catawba warriors loyal to the British stopped here on the way north to join the 1758 Forbes expedition. In 1757, French officers reportedly had scouted the fort, but concluded it was strong enough to withstand an attack. Raiding parties were in the vicinity of the fort several times. But the fort's usefulness ended with the war, and it was in ruins by the American Revolution.

The museum here features an excellent exhibit, "George Washington and the West." The displays highlight Washington's experience as a young surveyor, his dealings as an army commander with Indians and back country settlers, and the Virginia frontier during the

**Washington directed the war effort from this office.**

French and Indian War. A number of relics are displayed here— including artifacts recovered from an archaeological dig at the site of Fort Loudoun, a cannon from Fort Loudoun mounted on the museum grounds, and a piece of timber from Fort Pleasant, near modern-day Moorefield, West Virginia. The center room of the building was Washington's headquarters from 1755-56. Two wings were added to the building at later dates. The museum is open daily from April through October, (Mon.-Sat. 10 a.m. to 4 p.m., Sun. 12-4 p.m.) Phone 540-662-4412.

## ABRAM'S DELIGHT — WINCHESTER, VIRGINIA

*Directions: From I-81, take Exit 313 onto Route 50 west to intersection of Millwood Avenue and Pleasant Valley Road. Take first right off Pleasant Valley Road. Watch for blue and white signs to visitor center.*

Abraham Hollingsworth, part of a migration of Quakers who came to the Shenandoah Valley in the 1730s, was the patriarch of a family that put down deep roots in Virginia. Like many early settlers, Hollingsworth was attracted by the rich farmland in this valley west of the Blue Ridge Mountains. He spotted some prime land near a bountiful spring and called it a "delight to behold." Thus, the name Abram's Delight is bestowed on one of Winchester's major tourism attractions. Abraham built a log cabin and grist mill on the property and then brought his family from tidewater Maryland. Five generations of Hollingsworths called the property home.

In 1754, Abraham's son Isaac built the sturdy limestone house that still stands, considered to be the oldest house in Winchester. The walls are two and one-half feet thick, reflecting the family's need for a stronghouse on the perilous frontier. A wing was added to the house in 1830.

*Abram's Delight, the oldest house in Winchester.*

When Hollingsworth came to the area in the 1730s, he took title to a tract of 580 acres. But only 35 acres are left in the park surrounding the house now. Abram's Delight stayed in the Hollingsworth family through the Civil War and World War I. But then the house fell vacant for three decades. In 1943, the city of Winchester purchased the decaying house. The Winchester-Frederick Historical Society restored it, starting in 1951 and opened it to the public in 1961. Most of the furnishings in the house are period pieces gathered from the region. The door locks are original to the house.

The Cooper log cabin on the west land was not part of the original Hollingsworth homestead. But it dates to the 1750s and was relocated from its original site near George Washington's restored office museum in downtown Winchester.

Abram's Delight is open April 1 through October daily. Guides give a tour of the house. The Winchester-Frederick County visitor center is located next door in the renovated Hollingsworth Mill House which dates to 1833.

## LORD FAIRFAX TOMB — WINCHESTER, VIRGINIA

A fair number of barons, counts, and other members of European nobility sought a new life on the American frontier. Some came looking for fortune, others to found new settlements. But Thomas 6th Lord Fairfax was unique in seeking to transplant a semi-feudal society to America. Fairfax, 1693-1781, was heir to the Fairfax Proprietary, a royal land grant from King James II of 5 million acres between the Rappahannock and Potomac Rivers in northern Virginia. This territory extended from Alexandria to the Ohio territory.

Fairfax differed from his ancestors in that he came to Virginia from England in 1745 to personally look after his holdings. In 1749, he moved to the frontier establishing Greenway Court, a manor house and cluster of buildings, near the modern village of White Post, Virginia. He rented land in 100-acre lots to settlers, offering leases that could be renewed annually, or so-called "three lives" leases to last the lifetime of a couple and their youngest son. The leaseholders were expected to cultivate the land and pay Fairfax an annual rent.

Fairfax tangled with Joist Hite, one of the Shenandoah Valley's earliest settlers, over land ownership. The two were involved in a famous lawsuit that dragged on for decades, with a final verdict coming down in Hite's favor after both men were dead. Fairfax was a patron to the young George Washington, employing him as a surveyor on a 1748 trip through lands west of the Shenandoah River. He expanded Greenway Court over the years to include a smithy, arsenal, powder magazine, cobbler's shop, land office, guest houses, and servants quarters.

*Tomb of Lord Fairfax, frontier landowner and defender.*

During the French and Indian War, Lord Fairfax played an active role in the defense of the Virginia frontier from his base at Greenway Court. Sir John St. Clair, General Braddock's quartermaster general, visited Greenway Court in 1755 to ask Fairfax to provide logistical support for the British army. Fairfax also formed ranger companies and raised militia units to guard the frontier during the Indian raids after General Braddock's defeat. He served as a justice of Frederick County and set a reassuring example by remaining at Greenway Court rather than fleeing east like so many other settlers.

Fairfax was considered personable and lacking the arrogance of nobility, but his paternalistic concept of land ownership was an anachronism on the freewheeling frontier. The Fairfax proprietary was doomed with the American Revolution. Lord Fairfax died several months after the surrender of the British army at Yorktown.

The Fairfax tomb is marked with a tablet, and is located in a small courtyard beside Christ Episcopal Church at Washington and Boscawen Streets in downtown Winchester. This is the third burial site for Fairfax. He was initially buried at Greenway Court, then reburied at a Winchester church. When that church was torn down in 1828, Fairfax was buried at the present location.

At Greenway Court off of Route 658, the stone-built land office and two outbuildings survive, but are on private property and not visible from the road. A state highway marker for Greenway Court is on Route 340, two miles north of Millwood. At the village of White Post, a reminder of Fairfax is visible, for White Post takes its name from the white wooden column erected by Fairfax as a direction sign. The town keeps the tradition alive with a white post at Route 255 and Route 340.

# MT. HEBRON CEMETERY—WINCHESTER, VIRGINIA

*Directions: From Exit 313 on I-81. West on Routes 50/522. Right onto Pleasant Valley Road. At the first stoplight, turn left onto Cork Street, go to railroad tracks. Turn right on East Lane. Enter cemetery at stone gate. Once inside the gate turn left and follow sign to Morgan's grave.*

This antebellum cemetery was dedicated in 1844, but it contains several older cemeteries as well as the grave of frontiersman Daniel Morgan. On the cemetery grounds is an ivy-covered stone wall with four arches, the ruins of a Lutheran church dating to 1764. Morgan's grave is located in the shadow of these ruins. A monument depicting Morgan in a hunting shirt stands next to his flat tombstone. "Patriotism and valor were the prominent features of his character," is the testimonial given by the citizens of Winchester to Morgan.

Morgan (1735-1802), son of Welsh immigrants, came to Winchester at age eighteen from New Jersey. He gained fame fighting in the French and Indian and Revolutionary Wars. At age 20, Morgan was a teamster in Braddock's campaign to attack Fort Duquesne. He got into a fight with a British officer and was sentenced to a harsh whipping. This episode left him bitter toward the British.

*Morgan's grave in Winchester Cemetery.*

Stationed with the rear guard, Morgan survived the rout of Braddock's army. He then served as a member of Capt. John Ashby's ranger company. In 1756, Morgan was enroute to Fort Edwards on the Cacapon River when he was ambushed by a party of Shawnee. Morgan was wounded, but made it to the fort. A year later, he was among the fort's garrison when it held off another Shawnee attack.

Following the war, Morgan farmed in the Winchester area and hauled trade goods to markets in the east. But it was as a Revolutionary War general that Morgan made his reputation. Adept at backwoods fighting, he commanded a corps of crackshot Virginia riflemen. Morgan was made a British prisoner after a disastrous assault on Quebec in 1775, but he was paroled. He played a major role in the decisive American victory at Saratoga and won a stunning victory against the British under Banastre Tarleton at Cowpens.

In the 1790s, Morgan led troops to put down a rebellion of western Pennsylvania farmers against federal whiskey taxes and served in Congress. He died in Winchester in 1802. Morgan was first buried in the old Presbyterian Church graveyard and then reburied in Mt. Hebron Cemetery in 1865.

## MORGAN CABIN
### WEST OF BUNKER HILL, WEST VIRGINIA

*Directions: Northbound on Route 11 from Winchester. At town of Bunker Hill, left at blinking light. Go three miles west on Runnymede Road. Past antiques dealer and Christ church. Follow this winding country road as it crosses I-81. At three-way stop intersection, look for small sign saying Morgan Cabin 1/2 mile. Look for highway marker and cabin on left.*

Morgan Morgan, a Welsh immigrant turned trailblazer, is honored as the first European settler of West Virginia. His cabin has been rebuilt with some of its original logs to give visitors an idea of pioneer life.

Morgan (1688-1766) left Wales at age 25 and went to Christiana, Delaware, where he married and became a local magistrate. But by 1728 he and his large family struck out for the lands west of the Blue Ridge. He received a 1,000-acre grant from Virginia officials eager to encourage settlement on the frontier. Morgan built a cabin on a knoll situated near a spring in 1731-32. His homestead was near an Indian trail that eventually became known as the Great Wagon Road, the route for thousands of German and Scots-Irish settlers migrating from Pennsylvania into Virginia.

On the frontier Morgan once again took on civic duties. Along with Joist Hite, he was appointed a justice of Orange County in 1734. He also held ranks as a captain,

major, and colonel in the local militia. In 1736 Morgan helped lead a petition drive to create Frederick County, and eventually served the county as a justice and militia officer. He was also the county's first licensed tavernkeeper and helped establish the first church known as Morgan Chapel. Morgan's sons fought in the French and Indian War and founded Morgantown, West Virginia.

Morgan's cabin was rebuilt on its original site in 1975 as a bicentennial project. The cabin's south wall contains original logs. A push-button audio box mounted near the door tells the story of this first settler. The cabin is open Sunday afternoons during the summer. A state historical marker is by the road.

The grave of Morgan and his wife Catherine at Christ Church is located west of intersection of Runnymede Road and Route 11. The brick church is the third built at the spot since 1740. Morgan's grave is in third row of cemetery west of church. Next to the original faded headstone is a small white monument imprinted with the state seal of West Virginia.

## GENERAL ADAM STEPHEN HOUSE
### MARTINSBURG, WEST VIRGINIA

*Directions: Adam Stephen House is on the east side of Martinsburg. Take Exit 12 off I-81, then Route 45 to Queen Street. Turn right off Queen Street onto East John Street. Go on East John Street for two blocks past Water Street. Look for state historical marker. Home is on left, on other side of railroad tracks and Tuscarora Creek.*

Adam Stephen, a Scottish doctor who immigrated to America in 1748, was in the thick of the fighting on the Virginia and Pennsylvania frontiers during the French and Indian War. Stephen (1718-1791) participated in the key battles for control of the Ohio Valley, commanded troops at several forts, and built military roads through the wilderness. His home is preserved as a historic site by the city of Martinsburg.

Before he came to America, Stephen saw brief combat as a surgeon with a British naval expedition against France. In America, he practiced medicine in the Fredericksburg, Virginia, area. But Stephen felt the tug of the west, and engaged in land speculation in the Shenandoah Valley. He purchased a farm on Opequon Creek near Winchester in 1753.

Stephens' military experience, however short, was valued when Virginia raised troops under Col. George Washington to resist French designs on the Ohio Valley. Commissioned a captain in the Virginia force that went to the Ohio Forks, in May 1754 he led a wing of the attack on the small French force camped at Jumonville Glen on Chestnut Ridge. He fought in the doomed defense of Fort Necessity several weeks later.

During the tense months of 1754-55 after the British were expelled from the Forks of the Ohio, Stephen commanded Virginia troops stationed at the advance post of Fort Cumberland. He led Virginia rangers during the Braddock expedition. At the battle on the Monongahela River, he and his rangers formed a rear guard. Stephen suffered minor wounds covering the retreat, but his brother Alexander was seriously wounded.

In 1755-57, while Washington organized a defense of the Virginia frontier, Stephen again commanded Virginia troops at Fort Cumberland. He faced a difficult task protecting area settlers from the terror of Indian raids, and on one occasion, a large party of raiders fired on the fort itself.

In the spring of 1757, Stephen got a change in scenery when he led two companies of Virginia soldiers to South Carolina to participate in a campaign against pro-French Creek Indians. But the campaign stalled, and the Virginians spent ten months in idle duty. In June 1758, Stephen led several companies of Virginia troops to join the Forbes expedition at Fort Loudon in Pennsylvania. Stephen and his men opened some of the toughest sections of Forbes Road. They opened the road along a hilly and stony stretch from Fort Loudon to Raystown; they bridged Edmunds Swamp east of Laurel Hill; and they hacked the way through a dense thicket known as the Shades of Death. At one point, Stephen asked Col. Henry Bouquet to send cross cut saws to replace the axes that broke apart on fallen logs.

By this time, Stephen had been promoted to colonel. But he got into a fight with British quartermaster general, Sir John St. Clair, that led to his brief military arrest. Afterward, he helped build the fort at Loyalhanna (later Fort Ligonier) and other redoubts along Forbes Road.

Stephen was commander at Fort Ligonier in 1759 after the British gained control of the Ohio forks. In later adventures, he led Virginia troops on a campaign in the Ten-

nessee country against the Cherokees in 1761. But peace talk was in the air and Stephen negotiated a treaty with a faction of the Cherokees.

In 1770, Stephen acquired land along Tuscarora Creek north of Winchester and began to develop the town of Martinsburg. He built a limestone house, completed in 1789, and operated a mill and other businesses. The town was located along the Great Wagon Road, a major thoroughfare for settlers headed south into the Shenandoah Valley.

Stephen served as a major general in the American Revolution, but he took issue with the leadership of his old commander, George Washington. Washington eventually court-martialed Stephen. Later in life, Stephen was a strong supporter of Virginia's ratification of the Constitution.

Today the Tuscarora Creek flows at the foot of the hill on which Adam Stephen's limestone house still stands. The house is furnished with 18th century furniture, artifacts and paintings, including a rare one for American homes of British General Lord Cornwallis. A number of the objects were possessions of Stephen and his family. A letter that Stephen wrote in 1758 from the "camp at Loyalhanna" is on display. The home is situated on two acres of land. Across the street is another museum with exhibits on Martinsburg history. The house is open Saturday and Sunday afternoons from 2 p.m. to 5 p.m., May 1 through Oct. 31. For information call 304-267-4434.

## FORT EDWARDS—CAPON BRIDGE, WEST VIRGINIA

---

*Directions: Look for state highway marker for Fort Edwards, 1/2 mile north of Route 50 bridge over Cacapon River. Turn right on Springfield Grade Road and follow 1/4 mile to visitor center on right.*

---

Daniel Morgan won fame for his exploits in winning the battles of Saratoga and Cowpens for the American side during the Revolutionary War. But for Morgan, the road leading to those victories began two decades earlier at a log stockade named Fort Edwards, located at the modern town of Capon Bridge. At age 20, Morgan served as a wagon driver on the 1755 Braddock expedition, but was out of range of fire at the Battle of the Monongahela. He came to know real combat one year later outside the gates of Fort Edwards.

Fort Edwards was built in 1754 by Joseph Edwards, who owned land along the Cacapon River on the main road between Winchester and Fort Cumberland. The fort was a two-story log blockhouse surrounded by a stockade.

Morgan was a member of Capt. John Ashby's ranger company during the fall of 1755. Among his duties was escorting militia units between Fort Edwards and Fort

*Adam Stephen House.*

Ashby on Patterson's Creek. On April 16, 1756, Morgan and a companion were enroute to Fort Ashby from Fort Edwards when they were ambushed by Shawnee warriors. Morgan was shot in the face and his companion killed. With one of the raiders pursuing him, Morgan turned his horse and galloped back to Fort Edwards. He made it safely back to the fort, though delirious and in shock.

The attack on Morgan came two days before a group of 40 Shawnee and French soldiers routed Virginia militia commanded by Capt. John Mercer in a bloody fight near the fort. Mercer had left Winchester with 100 men to look for the enemy. He stopped at Fort Edwards when Shawnee were sighted nearby. Mercer left with 40 men to search for the enemy and was himself ambushed about one mile from the fort. His command returned fire, but they were eventually surrounded. Reinforcements were sent from the fort, but their effectiveness was undercut somewhat when Sgt. Nathan Lewis ordered a retreat after concluding the effort was futile. Mercer and fifteen of his soldiers were killed in the fight. Fort Edwards itself then came under siege. Powder supplies ran low, but the fort held until the attackers withdrew.

In the spring of 1757, Fort Edwards came under attack again by a group of 40 Shawnee and several French officers. This time Morgan was part of the fort's garrison. When the Shawnee gave signs of lifting this siege, Morgan and a group of defenders left the fort and routed the enemy.

The Fort Edwards Foundation, a non-profit organization based in Capon Bridge, owns a twenty-three acre tract of land on the site of Fort Edwards and Joseph Edward's home along the Cacapon River. The foundation is actively engaged in efforts to protect the site and provides interpretive displays at a visitors center dedicated in September 2000. Recent archaeological digs have yielded evidence of the fort stockade, coat buttons, ceramics, and musket balls.

## Fort Ashby — Fort Ashby, West Virginia

*Directions: From Romney, take Route 28 north to town of Fort Ashby. At town's main intersection with a traffic signal, take Route 46 east to Cemetery Road. Fort is across the street from Fort Ashby grade school.*

Captain John Ashby had a close call one spring day in 1756 when he wandered away from a log stockade on the banks of Patterson's Creek. Approaching a nearby summit now known Cemetery Hill, he encountered several hostile Indians. Unarmed, Ashby began a headlong dash back to the fort pursued all the way by the warriors. He made it back inside the gates unscathed. Ashby's flight became frontier lore; he gave his name to the fort and small town that later grew up around it.

Fort Ashby is the only survivor of a chain of forts built along the Virginia frontier under orders of Colonel Washington. In Washington's 1755 defense plan, Fort Ashby was slated for a garrison of 60 soldiers and was situated about ten miles from Cocke's Fort and Parker's Fort. Located along a tributary of the South Branch of the Potomac River, Fort Ashby occupied a strategic position along the road linking Fort Cumberland and Fort Loudoun in Winchester. The fort also provided shelter to settlers in the Patterson's Creek area.

Washington might find it ironic that Fort Ashby alone of his Virginia defenses survives almost 250 years later. At one point, he gave commanding officers the option of blowing up the post and retreating to Fort Cumberland if surrounded. Fort Ashby had proved something of a headache to the young commander. The soldiers there lacked discipline and were prone to flight, as one skirmish in 1756 illustrated. A party of militia was sent from the fort under command of Lt. Robert Rutherford to escort a military courier to Fort Cumberland. The soldiers ran into an ambush and they fled back to the fort ignoring Rutherford's pleas to stay and fight.

Fort Ashby survives today because it was used as a schoolhouse and residence until the 1920s when the Daughters of the American Revolution acquired the property and restored it. The DAR's Fort Ashby Chapter now maintains the fort as a museum. The fort is unique architecturally for having a double chimney that is fourteen feet wide and four feet thick. Also noteworthy are the original woodwork, wrought iron hinges, and a hidden stairway to a basement crawlspace.

Write Fort Ashby, Box 248, Fort Ashby, WV, 26719.

*Fort Ashby.*
**This is the lone survivor of Washington's defense plans.**

## INDIAN MOUND CEMETERY/FORT PEARSALL, ROMNEY, WEST VIRGINIA

*Directions: Take Route 50 just west of Romney. Right turnoff to cemetery is near highway marker for Indian mound. Tower is at entrance.*

On a high bluff overlooking the South Branch of the Potomac River, prehistoric Indians built a burial mound, and the location later became a crossroads for two major Indian footpaths. The migratory Shawnee tribe used these trails.

During the French and Indian War, South Branch settlers built a log stockade in this area. Located along the military road connecting Forts Cumberland and Loudoun, Fort Pearsall became an important part of Virginia's frontier defenses. Today all traces of Fort Pearsall are gone, but from the vantage point of the cemetery that has developed around the seven-foot high Indian mound, the area's strategic location is evident. According to local historians, Fort Pearsall was located north of Route 50, between the cemetery and the river.

The first white settler attracted to the area was Job Pearsall who built a cabin there in the 1730s. When border tensions flared in 1754-55, Pearsall and his neighbors built a log stockade for defense.

*Cemetery on site of Fort Pearsall.*

By 1756 Virginia officials had taken notice of this strategic spot and enlarged Pearsall's fort. In May 1756, Colonel Washington assigned Capt. Robert McKenzie, five officers, and 45 enlisted men to garrison the fort; some accounts refer to the post as McKenzie's fort. At one point, the garrison swelled to about one hundred men, and the soldiers were often called upon to escort military convoys.

Fort Pearsall was also a way station for warriors of southern Indian tribes—Catawba and Cherokee—allied with the British. Washington cautioned McKenzie about giving away too many of the fort's horses to these warriors. Fort Pearsall did not come under direct attack, but raiding parties in the vicinity claimed some victims.

Today a stone tower marks the entrance to Indian Mound Cemetery. Local tradition says that the cemetery contains graves of some of the fort's defenders, but cemetery officials say no pioneer graves have ever been located. Civil War soldiers are buried in the cemetery, including sixteen unknown Confederates buried together.

## FORT PLEASANT—OLD FIELDS, WEST VIRGINIA

*Directions: At the small village of Old Fields on Route 220 in Hardy County, look for state highway marker for Fort Pleasant. Just south of the marker on a local road that runs east of Route 220 stands an antebellum mansion with a two-story porch supported by Corinthian columns. This privately owned house is on the site of Fort Pleasant. The ridge that helps form The Trough is visible to the east behind the house.*

A Dutch fur trader, John Van Meter, was one of the first Europeans to explore the rich bottomlands along the South Branch of the Potomac River. He came to the region in 1715 in the company of Delaware Indians who were trading with the Cherokee and Catawba tribes in the southern Appalachians. Van Meter's son Isaac arrived in 1735 to stake a claim to a portion of the rich lands his father had explored. Isaac settled in 1744 at an abandoned Shawnee village known as Indian Old Fields. When Virginia constructed a network of forts in 1756 after the onset of hostilities, Van Meter's property was selected as a key defense post in the South Branch Valley.

Fort Pleasant was built by militia captain Thomas Waggoner, acting on orders from Colonel Washington. The fort was named for a small stream that flowed nearby. The South Branch of the Potomac flows a half mile east of the site, one and one-half miles south of The Trough, a rugged canyon where the South Branch flows between two mountainous ridges and the scene of a fierce fight between Virginians and the Shawnee. Fort

Pleasant is also called Fort Van Meter, Fort Hopewell, and Town Fort in some contemporary accounts. Today a Greek Revival mansion with white columns, built in 1832, stands on the fort site.

Fort Pleasant did not come under direct attack, but fighting occurred in the surrounding vicinity. The fort's garrison ranged from 30 to 60 militia during 1756-58, the period of greatest activity. The fort consisted of a log stockade with blockhouses occupying one and one-half acres. Within the stockade were soldiers' huts, a powder magazine, stables, and a commissary. The troops were assured safe access to water via a palisaded enclosure that led to Pleasant Creek.

## BATTLE OF THE TROUGH
## OLD FIELDS, WEST VIRGINIA

*Directions: To drive above the east side of The Trough along South Branch Mountain, from Romney take Route 50 west. Make a left turn onto South Branch River Road or Route 8. Watch for a sign for Wappocomo Campground at turn. Turn is near the Romney sewage treatment plant.*

*By train: A three-hour scenic rail excursion through The Trough on the Potomac Eagle is offered from spring through fall. The train depot is located one mile north of Romney on Route 28. For more information, write to Potomac Eagle, P.O. Box 657, Romney, WV, 26757.*

The Trough is a wild, remote, and inaccessible place even today. In 1756, it was the scene of a desperate battle between local militia and a band of Shawnee warriors. The Trough is a narrow canyon where the South Branch of the Potomac River squeezes between two steep mountain ridges. The Shawnee called the river the Wappatomaka, possibly for the white or snow-covered ground found in the mountain elevations. The Shawnee had cultivated the rich bottomland north of The Trough, and Old Fields takes its name from the old corn fields they planted. The first white settlers came to the area in the 1730s. "The Trough is a couple of Ledges of Mountains Impassable, running side and side together for 7 or 8 miles, and ye River running down between them," wrote a young George Washington when he visited the area during a surveying trip in 1748.

When hostilities broke in 1755, South Branch settlers built forts. Some like Fort Pleasant and Fort Buttermilk became part of Colonel Washington's frontier defense line. Others like Fort VanMeter were private strongholds fitted with loopholes where settlers could seek shelter on short notice.

The Battle of The Trough started when a party of Shawnee captured a white woman at her home near the

***The south branch of the Potomac passes through The Trough, the scene of an 1756 skirmish.***

vicinity of Old Fields. She escaped and alerted men in the nearby forts. A party of militia entered The Trough and engaged in heavy fighting with the Shawnee. But the Shawnee eventually gained the upper hand and the surviving militia escaped by jumping in the river and swimming north. There are conflicting accounts in early histories about this battle.

Traveling through The Trough today offers a strong sense of what it was like to live on the frontier's edge. At one spot, ten miles south of Romney, a small stone building stands next to a farmhouse and octagonal barn. This is Fort VanMeter, 19 feet long and 12 feet high; the stones were spaced at intervals to create loopholes for defenders to aim through and fire. No roads lead through The Trough, but a bird's eye view of Fort VanMeter is possible by taking South Branch River Road. The fort can be spotted from the highway about one mile south of The Trough General Store. Or, go through The Trough at river level by riding the Potomac Eagle excursion train.

## SPRINGDALE—NORTH OF STEPHENS CITY, VIRGINIA

*Directions: North on Route 11 from Stephens City, look for intersection of Springdale Road and Valley Road. Look for highway marker. Springdale is visible from right side of road.*

Virginia's colonial governors enticed German and Scots-Irish settlers to the Shenandoah Valley in the 1730s and 1740s with offers of land. They saw settlement of the land west of the Blue Ridge as a buffer against French expansion from the Ohio River.

Joist Hite and his family of eight children were among the first to take up the offer. They settled on land a few miles south of modern-day Winchester in 1732. Hite and his wife Anna Maria came from the Alsace region of Germany. They settled first in New York then moved to Germantown, Pennsylvania, where Hite built a grist mill. Hite led sixteen families on his migration to the Shenandoah. It was in Hite's interest to do so, for he and a partner had received a grant of 100,000 acres provided that 100 families would be settled on the tract within two years.

Hite's original home, known as Hite's Fort, served as a fortified stronghold in times of danger. Hite also faced a legal challenge to his land from Lord Fairfax, the proprietor of vast holdings in northern Virginia. Fairfax contended that the colonial governor and his council did not have the right to grant land that was part of his holdings. The case dragged on for years and was finally settled in favor of Hite's heirs after the American Revolution.

Hite's son John built an impressive grey fieldstone house called "Springdale" in 1753 near the family homestead. The house stands today and, while privately owned, is identified by a state historical marker. Ruins of Hite's Fort still stand nearby on private property.

Of nearby interest: Belle Grove, a mansion on the Cedar Creek Civil War battlefield, built in 1794 by Maj. Isaac Hite, grandson of Joist Hite. Route 11, south of Middletown. Belle Grove is open April-October.

## HUPP HOMESTEAD—STRASBURG, VIRGINIA

*Directions: The Hupp house is located on the west side of Route 11 at the northern end of Strasburg. A state historical marker titled "Frontier fort" also stands in front of the house.*

Thousands of German immigrants migrated to the Shenandoah Valley in the 1720s and 30s. From families that had left the principalities of western Germany to escape religious wars, many settled first in Pennsylvania where William Penn's heirs preached religious toleration.

But stories about available land in a rich river valley in Virginia beckoned many of the Germans. They headed south through Pennsylvania's Cumberland Valley along the "Great Wagon Road." The entire migration often took two or three generations to complete. The German families settled primarily along an eighty-mile stretch of the valley from Winchester to Staunton. In time, the Germans who tenaciously clung to their ancestral language became known as the Valley Dutch.

The Hupp family was part of this great migration. They came to America in the late 1600s, settled in Philadelphia, and then headed westward to Lancaster and York. The family came to the Shenandoah Valley in 1732.

In 1755, as the threat of war darkened the Virginia frontier, the Hupps built a solid limestone house that doubled for use as a private fort. The barnlike structure still stands today, supported by walls 22 inches thick, with several loopholes to allow defenders to return gunfire from a protected position. The Hupp house is also situated next to a water supply—an important consideration if the fort had ever come under siege.

The house remains in the hands of the Hupp family 240 years later, and thanks to a descendant, travelers along Route 11 can learn about the family. A tablet put up by Frank Hupp provides details about the Hupps and the house they built. The family's land holdings once included Hupp's Hill, site of Union trenches dug during the Civil War. A Civil War museum stands on this site eight-tenths of a mile north of Strasburg on Route 11.

## FORT HARRISON—DAYTON, VIRGINIA

*Directions: Take Exit 245 off I-81 into Harrisonburg. Go west several blocks to Route 42, turn left, then Business Route 42 to intersection with Route 732, Daniel Harrison House on southwest corner.*

When Daniel Harrison built a house in the Shenandoah Valley in 1749, he took care to do two things right. He selected a rise of land near Cook's Creek to build on, and he used solid fieldstone as the building material for the house. These advantages made Daniel Harrison's house, or Fort Harrison as it was called, a natural defense point and refuge for settlers when Indians raided the area during the 1750s. Fort Harrison is reputed to have sheltered survivors of the Fort Seybert massacre in the spring of 1758. Tradition says that Harrison erected a wooden palisade around the house and dug an underground passage to a nearby spring when troubles came.

Daniel Harrison was the brother of Thomas Harrison, the founder of Harrisonburg, Virginia. Born on Long Island, he migrated to the Shenandoah Valley in 1738. He settled first in Augusta County and a decade later purchased a 120-acre tract along Cook's Creek. The property remained in the Harrison family until 1821.

Subsequent owners added a brick section to the rear of the stone house. In 1978, the property was purchased by Fort Harrison Inc., a non-profit corporation formed by the Harrisonburg-Rockingham Historical Society. The Daniel Harrison House is a museum open during weekend afternoons from May to October. Nearby, the historical society operates the Shenandoah Valley Heritage Museum and Research Center, 382 High Street, Dayton.

*Augusta Stone Church.*

## AUGUSTA STONE PRESBYTERIAN CHURCH FORT DEFIANCE, VIRGINIA

*Directions: The church is located eight miles north of Staunton, on Route 11 at intersection with Fort Defiance Road.*

Many settlers in the Shenandoah Valley fled eastward after the first wave of attacks by Delaware and Shawnee warriors in the fall of 1755. But the Scots-Irish residents in the settlement called Beverly Manor in Augusta County decided to follow the advice of their dynamic pastor—Rev. John Craig—and stay to defend their homes and farms. Under Craig's direction, the settlers built a stockade around the Augusta Stone Church and gathered there for protection when war parties were spotted in the region.

Augusta Stone Church never came under direct attack, but it helped to anchor a defense line along the frontier. The limestone church was built in 1749 and is considered the oldest Presbyterian church in continuous use in Virginia. The church was established to serve the religious needs of the Scots-Irish who started migrating into the Valley of Virginia during the 1730s. The Scots-Irish left Ulster in northern Ireland in pursuit of economic opportunities and to practice their Presbyterian religion without government interference.

Many Scots-Irish settled first in Pennsylvania, attracted by William Penn's promise of religious tolerance, but population growth and land scarcity led growing numbers of them to greener pastures in the Shenandoah. They followed the Great Wagon Road into Virginia and settled on large tracts of land that the colony granted speculators to encourage settlement. One such tract was the 11,000-acre Beverly Manor granted in 1736 to William Beverly. As the numbers of Scots-Irish increased in the Manor, they petitioned the Donegal Presbytery in Pennsylvania to send ministers.

John Craig answered the call. Born in 1709 in County Antrim, Craig was educated at the University of Edinburgh and came to America in 1738. He arrived in Augusta County in 1740 and described it as a "wilderness, without

a place of worship or church order." Craig rectified that by building Augusta Stone Church, and then another one at Tinkling Spring in current-day Fisherville, Virginia. He served as pastor of the Augusta church until his death in 1774.

The Augusta church, with some later alterations, stands today in a grove of trees atop a hill. The church is noted for some unique architectural features, including drooping gables and a stone water drain around the perimeter. A museum is located in a small building next to the church. Many relics of John Craig are exhibited there, including his 1682 Bible, his autobiography and baptismal records, communion tokens, and the original deed to the land.

## VIRGINIA'S SOUTHERN FRONTIER

Virginia's vulnerable frontier extended far south of the Shenandoah Valley. In a region between the Blue Ridge and the Appalachian Mountains, the Delaware and Shawnee launched raids, militia manned a string of forts, and settlers fortified their homes during the years from 1755 to 1758.

One of the first raids by Shawnee Indians in July 1755 wiped out the Draper's Meadows settlement at modern-day Blacksburg. A state historical marker is located on Route 460 at the southern entrance to Blacksburg. Colonel James Patton, one of the leading figures in Augusta County, was ambushed and killed as he led a party of rangers to the settlement. The Draper's Meadows massacre also produced one of the most famous Indian captivity stories. Mary Draper Ingles was captured and taken to Shawnee towns in the Ohio country. She managed to escape and make her way home, by a perilous journey along the New River.

Early in the war, Virginia went on the offensive against the Shawnee. Major Andrew Lewis led the ill-fated Sandy Creek expedition in the winter of 1756 against Shawnee towns on the Big Sandy River. The expedition of 340 rangers and Cherokee warriors encountered problems with bad weather, rough terrain, and insufficient food supplies, and turned back before reaching its goal.

The failure of the offensive operation led to a renewed emphasis on defending the frontier settlements. Virginia's General Assembly authorized the building of a chain of forts from the Cacapon River to Mayo River near the North Carolina border. Colonel George Washington selected the sites; the positioning of forts on the southern front was discussed during a council of war in July 1756 at Augusta Courthouse (modern-day Staunton). Geography played a key role in deciding where the forts were located. Washington wrote, "...they are generally fixed on the heads of creeks, & extending towards the Allegany Mountains with almost inaccessible mountains between them, and are placed in the most commodius manner for securing the inhabitants of such waters."

In October 1756, Washington went on a circular inspection tour of the southern forts, leaving Augusta Courthouse to meet Col. John Buchanan at Looney's Ferry on the James River. Washington visited Fort Vause which had been overrun and burned by a war party of 200 Shawnee and 25 French commanded by Capt. Francois-Marie Picot de Belestre that previous June. Because of its strategic location, Fort Vause was being rebuilt by Capt. Peter Hogg at the time of Washington's visit (State historical marker located on Route 11, .3 mile west of Shawsville).

On his journey, Washington also visited Fort Trial (state marker on Route 56, 6 miles north of Martinsville); Fort Blackmore (state marker on Route 220, 3 miles north of Rocky Mount); Fort William, (state marker on Route 220, .3 miles south of Fincastle); Fort Young (state marker on Route 154, Covington); Fort Breckenridge (state marker on Route 220 3 miles north of Covington); Fort Dickinson (state marker on Route 42, 3 miles southeast of Milboro Springs); and Fort Dinwiddie (state marker on Route 39, five miles west of Warm Springs).

None of these forts survive today. The land they are located on is in private hands. The city of Covington has reconstructed the stockade of Fort Young in a park on West Liberty Street near original fort site.

*Highway marker for Fort Breckenridge.*

*Reconstructed Fort Young in Covington, Va.*

# 8

# Maryland Governor Sharpe Organizes Maryland Defense, 1756-1758

## INTRODUCTION

Horatio Sharpe deserves as much credit as anyone for defending Maryland's frontier during the critical years from 1754 to the fall of Fort Duquesne in 1758. Sharpe (1718-90) became Maryland's governor in 1753. He had the qualifications to lead the colony during wartime, for he had served as an officer in the British army and was familiar with fortifications and the logistics of supplying armies in the field. For a brief period he held command of British forces in the southern colonies.

The governor was active; he lobbied Maryland lawmakers to appropriate money for defense and spent his own money to equip soldiers when the legislature balked at his requests. Sharpe made inspection trips to the frontier, strengthened Fort Cumberland, and built Fort Frederick, one of the few stone forts in the colonies. He even lent his coach so Gen. Edward Braddock could ride in comfort over frontier roads.

Sharpe performed these tasks ably despite being torn by conflicting loyalties. He was the personal representative of an overseas proprietor, Lord Calvert, yet he shared the power of the purse with an elected assembly. Sharpe was thwarted in early efforts to mount a defense when the Assembly voted to dedicate revenues from licenses granted to peddlers to the war effort. These monies had traditionally gone to the Calverts; the proprietor instructed Sharpe to block the measure.

Sharpe was genuinely concerned about the plight of the frontier settlers, yet the French threat seemed remote in the colony's more populated tidewater areas. Furthermore, Maryland stood to gain nothing from frontier expeditions since Virginia and Pennsylvania claimed the Ohio territory to the west. Sharpe was also a servant of King George II; he requisitioned wagons and supplies and recruited soldiers for service with Braddock's army.

After Braddock's defeat in the fall of 1755, the seriousness of the war threat hit home in Maryland. Frontier settlements were left deserted. Even residents of tidewater Annapolis panicked at the thought of French armies at their doorstep. Sharpe ordered the construction of Fort Frederick and satellite outposts (Tonoloway Fort or Stoddert's Fort at the Tonoloways, Fort Mills, Baker's Fort, Shelby's Fort) to guard the North Mountain area. He formed ranger companies to patrol the countryside and credited them with limiting the destruction of Indian raids.

On the frontier, Jonathan Hager was a fur trader who served as a ranger captain. His house was a frontier stronghold and is now a museum in Hagerstown. Thomas Cresap was a land speculator and trader who supplied goods to Braddock's army from his trading post at Oldtown, located on the site of an old Shawnee village. Cresap's son Michael built a stone house there which is now a museum.

SITES AT A GLANCE—This map will give you a feel for the general locations of sites in this chapter. Some sites overlap and are not shown on this map.

Fort Frederick
Jonathan Hager House
Fort Cumberland
Cresap House
Pack Horse Ford

## JONATHAN HAGER HOUSE HAGERSTOWN, MARYLAND

*Directions: Take Exit 6A off I-81. Go east to Hagerstown. Follow Washington Avenue (Route 40 east) to light at Walnut Street, and turn right. Look for brown and white Hager House signs. Look for City Park. Go right on Key Street to house.*

Starting in the 1730s, a flood of German settlers poured into the western frontier of Maryland. One of them was Jonathan Hager, a native of Westphalia who first landed at Philadelphia in 1736 and then moved to Maryland. In 1739, Hager purchased a tract of 200 acres from Daniel Dulany, Maryland's great land speculator and attorney general, and named the site Hager's Fancy.

Hager earned his living as a trader. He built a fieldstone house in the German architectural style where he could shelter his family and conduct business. The house was easily converted into a stronghold. The walls were built over a fresh spring that flowed through an opening in the basement. This meant that Hager had a protected water supply in case of attack. The walls were 22 inches thick and strong enough to withstand a hail of bullets. Hager served as a ranger captain during the French and Indian War, but it is uncertain whether his house ever came under attack.

Hager founded the town of Hagerstown in 1762, was elected to the Maryland General Assembly in 1771, and was accidentally killed in 1775 while overseeing the building of a church. He was fatally injured when a heavy beam fell on him.

The city of Hagerstown acquired ownership of the Hager House in 1954 and began extensive restoration work. Today the city operates the house as a museum in Hagerstown's City Park. The rooms are filled with many authentic and interesting pieces of German furniture and tools from the 17th and 18th centuries. One room is maintained as a trader's storehouse with guns, fur pelts, and a bear claw bracelet. The spring still flows in the cellar with the water staying at a cool 40 degrees year-round.

The Hager House was the site of extensive archaeological digs and many of the finds are exhibited in a small museum on the grounds. The artifacts displayed include trade beads, gorgets, bullets, animal bones and pottery. Special events are held throughout the year.

*Jonathan Hager House.*

The house is open April-December, Tuesday-Saturday 10 a.m. to 4 p.m., Sunday 2 p.m. to 5 p.m. Admission is charged. Call 301-739-8393.

## PACK HORSE FORD
## C&O CANAL NATIONAL HISTORICAL PARK
## ROUTE 34, MARYLAND

*Directions: Head west from Sharpsburg on Route 34. As you near the river look for Maryland historical marker on left for "Swearingen Ferry—Pack Horse Ford." Turn left on Canal Road. Continue to canal towpath with parking lot. Pack Horse Ford is one-half mile south. The location in the river is marked by an irregular pattern of rocks forming a double "V." Follow Route 34 over the river to Shepherdstown, West Virginia.*

Pack Horse Ford is a historic crossing point on the Potomac River, first used by Indians enroute to or from the Susquehanna River. Later traders with goods loaded on pack horses forded the river here. When German and Scots-Irish settlers migrated from Pennsylvania into Maryland and Virginia during the 1730s, they found this the only good crossing point for miles around.

In 1755 Thomas Swearingen started a ferry service across the Potomac at the location of the modern highway bridge. Across the Potomac is Shepherdstown, the oldest town in West Virginia. Thomas Shepherd settled here in the 1730s and built a grist mill. The town was established in 1762 and initially named Mecklenburg. The name was changed in 1798 in honor of the founder. The mill built by Shepherd still stands on Mill Street in Shepherdstown and is marked on walking tour maps. The mill is located on private property. Foliage obscures the view from Mill Street in summer.

## FORT FREDERICK—BIG POOL, MARYLAND

*Directions: West on I-70 from Hagerstown, take Exit 12 for Route 56 near Big Pool. Take Route 56 one mile east to fort. Look for signs.*

Fort Frederick, Governor Horatio Sharpe's contribution to the defense of Maryland, was the strongest British fort in the mid-Appalachian region until Fort Pitt was built near the close of the French and Indian War. Sharpe built his fort of stone because he thought it stood a better chance of withstanding assaults than the log-and-earthen forts that were common on the frontier. The governor was particularly alarmed by the fall of wooden Fort Granville in Pennsylvania to a raiding party of Delaware and French in July 1756. He wrote, "Fort Cumberland and the little places of Defence that have been built in the Neighboring Colonies are by no means such as I would have built on the Frontiers of this Province."

*Aerial view of Fort Frederick.*

Fort Frederick's sandstone walls are 17 feet high with a width ranging from three feet to four and one-half feet. The walls are bolstered with four diamond-shaped bastions where cannon were mounted. Larger than most frontier forts, Fort Frederick covered one and one-half acres on a bluff just north of the Potomac River. Inside the fort's walls were two barracks built to house 400 provincial soldiers, headquarters, a parade ground, and at least one drinking well.

Sharpe oversaw work on the fort from 1756 to 1758. A construction project of that scope was an expensive proposition for Maryland. Sharpe had a running battle with the provincial assembly to obtain appropriations. Fort Frederick was situated at North Mountain near settlements that had been raided by the Delaware and Shawnee, but no attacks were made on the fort itself.

Fort Frederick served as a rendezvous point for Cherokee warriors and provincial troops headed to join the 1758 Forbes expedition. The fort was a refuge for settlers during Pontiac's War in 1763-64. The fort was in American hands during the American Revolution and Hessian prisoners were lodged there. The fort was also garrisoned by Union troops during the Civil War.

By the late 19th century, the fort's walls had crumbled and the parade ground was a grazing area for cattle. The state acquired the fort site for a park in the 1920s. The Civilian Conservation Corp rebuilt the stone walls during the 1930s and the two barracks were reconstructed later.

Today Fort Frederick provides an authentic setting for French and Indian War reenacts. The barrack rooms are furnished to illustrate period use.

Fort Frederick has undergone many archaeological digs. The finds are displayed in exhibits on the upper floor of the barracks to the right of the fort gate. The visitor center near the entrance to the park features a video and uniform displays of the soldiers stationed there. The park also features a campground, and hiking along the Chesapeake and Ohio Canal. Contact Fort Frederick State Park, 11100 Fort Frederick Road, Big Pool, Md., 21711. Phone 301-842-2155.

*British camp at a Fort Frederick reenactment.*

## FORT MILLS—LICKING CREEK, EAST OF PECTONVILLE, MARYLAND

*A Maryland highway marker for Fort Mills is on Route 40 on the west side of a bridge over Licking Creek. The fort site is several miles north of sign. Look for turnoff for Licking Creek Road east of bridge. Licking Creek Road leads to creek bottomlands, but the area is heavily posted with no trespassing signs.*

The settlers along Licking Creek, a tributary of the Potomac River, were vulnerable to attack in the months following Braddock's defeat. Delaware and Shawnee raiders stalked isolated homesteads as an exhibit at Fort Frederick illustrates. One of area's settlers, Thomas Mills, built a private fort at his plantation on the east shore of Licking Creek. Maryland forces later used Fort Mills as a base and delivered supplies of ammunition there. Governor Horatio Sharpe listed Fort Mills as one of several in the North Mountain area. In April 1756, Indian raiders fought a skirmish with local militia in the vicinity of Fort Mills.

## FORT COOMBE—NORTH OF HANCOCK, MARYLAND

*Directions: From Route 144 in Hancock, Md. Turn north on Pennsylvania Avenue. Turn left on Resley Street or SR 3001 for three miles crossing I-70 and state border, and sharp left bend south of Warfordsburg, Pa. White farmhouse on left side of bend. Look for old abandoned road to right. In the distance is an interstate sign for Pa. Welcome Center. Park here and walk 300 feet down old road to Fort Coombe monument. Monument is near the ruins of a burnt farmhouse and overlooks I-70.*

Fort Coombe was a private stockade built in 1755 by brothers Andrew and Joseph Coombe. It was part of Maryland's defenses, but boundaries shifted with the postwar surveying of the Mason-Dixon line. Today the site of the fort is located in Pennsylvania along an old road cut off by a modern interstate highway.

Fort Coombe was a refuge for settlers of the Tonoloways or Conolloways, as the southern end of the Great Cove was called. The area was settled in the early 1750s by squatters who illegally occupied Delaware lands. The Great Cove was the target of one of the first Delaware attacks on the English frontier after General Braddock's defeat, and the Tonoloway settlement was not spared. Fort Coombe came under siege by the Delaware at one point in the fall of 1755. In early 1756 the Delaware raided the area twice again, burning isolated homesteads and killing the inhabitants. Fort Coombe was a refuge; at one point Maryland militia found over 40 people huddled in the fort while the enemy stalked the woods. When a building inside the fort was set afire, the defenders used soap suds to put out the flames. Patrols from Fort Frederick were periodically sent out to Fort Coombe, but the need for this post declined as the Forbes campaign got underway in 1758.

In 1935, a memorial monument was erected at the location of Fort Coombe. The public ceremony was typical of many in the 1920s and 1930s honoring colonial shrines. Descendants of early settlers, local lawmakers, clergy, and the Daughters of the American Revolution participated. Ivy was planted around the stone boulder used for the monument. The tablet's inscription reads:

Fort Coombe. The scene of Indian massacres of early Conolloway settlers in 1755 and 1756. This tablet erected by the Franklin County Daughters of the American Revolution and the Fulton County Historical Society.

The efforts of an earlier generation to honor the fort's defenders are jeopardized. The fort site is a half-forgotten backwater. The monument was along the main Hancock-Warfordsburg Road of the 1930s, but today the road has been cut off by I-70. That makes Fort Coombe tricky to find.

## KING OPESSA'S TOWN—OLDTOWN, MARYLAND

In a pattern repeated many times on the frontier, white settlers staked claims on land that had been an Indian village site. This is true of Oldtown, the location of Thomas Cresap's trading post. In the early 1700s, Shawnees lived here in a village known as King Opessa's Town. The village occupied a key location at a ford on the Potomac River. Countless generations had passed by this spot along a branch of the Warrior's Path, a north-south trail connecting the Iroquois tribes in the north with the Cherokee and Catawba tribes in the south. This particular branch ran from Standing Stone along the Juniata River, skirted east of Raystown, and followed mountain summits and gaps to reach the Potomac Ford at Opessa's town.

The Shawnee occupied this spot for about 50 years from the 1690s to 1740s. The most prominent Shawnee was Opessa who settled here about 1711. Opessa was one of the chiefs who agreed to a peace treaty with William Penn in 1701. At the time, Opessa lived at Pequea east of the Susquehanna River. Within a few years, he voluntarily abdicated his leadership position and moved north to join a Delaware tribe. He eventually moved west and settled at the town that bore his name. He died in the 1720s and his descendants moved west of the Alleghenies. Cresap found the town abandoned when he arrived in 1741.

### THOMAS CRESAP

Thomas Cresap was called "Big Spoon" by the Indians and "Rattlesnake Colonel" by Gen. Braddock's British regulars. He provoked border hostilities between Pennsylvania and Maryland in the 1730s, and he lived to see the territorial dispute resolved thirty years later when Charles Mason and Jeremiah Dixon surveyed the boundary line between the two colonies.

Thomas Cresap (1694-1790) is a prime example of the hardy breed of individualists living on the frontier. Cresap's first fight came when he established a ferry operation across the Susquehanna River at present day Wrightsville, Pennsylvania. Cresap's ferry was located on land granted to him by Maryland.

But Pennsylvania also claimed the land, and Cresap became a thorn in the side of provincial authorities. Several attempts were made to drive him off his property. Finally in 1736, a county sheriff gathered a group of men and lay siege to Cresap's fortified house. Captured after the house was set afire, he was taken prisoner to Philadelphia where he angered citizens by proclaiming the city one of the prettiest towns in Maryland.

After his release from jail, Cresap moved west to Oldtown, Maryland, the site of a former Shawnee village and ancient fording spot on the Potomac River. Cresap built a fort near the river and became a fur trader, trail blazer, and land speculator. He offered food and hospitality to Indians using the north-south Warrior's Path, hence the name "Big Spoon." His home was also a way station for surveyors, land agents, and fur traders headed west. George Washington, Christopher Gist and George Croghan all stopped by his place.

Cresap helped blaze the path to the Forks of the Ohio that eventually became known as Braddock's Road. He supplied goods to Braddock's army, but some officers felt his business practices were unsavory, hence the name "Rattlesnake Colonel."

During the French and Indian War, Cresap moved his base of operations to Conococheague along the Potomac. After the fighting ended, Cresap lived for three more decades, long enough to see the frontier pass by. Mason and Dixon stayed overnight at his house in 1767 while drawing the boundary that resolved the dispute between Pennsylvania and Maryland.

The colonel's son, Michael Cresap, built a stone house still standing in Oldtown. Michael fought in Lord Dunmore's War, a 1774 border conflict with the Indians, and in the American Revolution.

## MICHAEL CRESAP HOUSE — OLDTOWN, MARYLAND

*Directions: Follow Route 51 west to left turnoff for Oldtown, about 14 miles from Cumberland, Md. Look for Oldtown sign. The turnoff takes a sharp curve under a railroad bridge. Keep right on Main Street to Cresap House. Look for historical marker.*

The Michael Cresap House, built in 1764, is a focal point in this historic crossroads town along the Potomac River. Oldtown's strategic importance dates back to the days when it was a Potomac fording place on the Great Warrior's Path, the north-south trail that connected the Iroquois tribes in the north with the Cherokee and Catawba tribes in the south.

In the early 1700s, a Shawnee tribe lived here. The village was called King Opessa's Town for their chief. Thomas Cresap bought land at the site of the abandoned village and built a stockade there in 1741. His son Michael Cresap built a two-story stone house in 1764 on Main Street, now maintained as a museum. The brick addition to the house was added in 1781. Michael Cresap was an explorer and frontiersman like his father. He led a militia unit in 1775 to Boston to join the Continental Army.

For two hundred years a succession of families lived in Cresap's house. The house was purchased and restored in the 1960s by Irvin Allen, a local minister. The exhibits in the house include displays of Indian stone artifacts, Cresap family heirlooms, tools and guns, and railroad and canal town memorabilia.

Cresap's house sits on a slight embankment above Lock 70 of the Chesapeake and Ohio Canal. Follow the short road from the house straight to the canal bed which is maintained by the National Park Service. A 184-mile hiking trail parallels the entire length of the C & O Canal bed from Washington D.C. to Cumberland, Maryland. The site of Thomas Cresap's log stockade and mill are located on park land between the canal bed and Potomac River.

Contact Allegany County Visitors' Bureau, c/o Western Maryland Station Center, 13 Canal Street, Cumberland, Md., 301-777-5905 to obtain information about Cresap house visiting hours or write: Michael Cresap Museum, c/o Irvin G. Allen, Main Street, Route 1, Box 4, Oldtown, Md., 21555.

*Michael Cresap House built in 1764.*

## FORT CUMBERLAND — CUMBERLAND, MARYLAND

*Directions to Fort Cumberland: From I-68 west, take Exit 43B (Downtown) at Cumberland. Left on Harrison Street. Right on South Mechanic Street. Left at Baltimore Street and park at visitors center in railroad station. Walk across Baltimore Street. bridge over Will's Creek to start walking tour in Riverside Park.*

The city of Cumberland has done an imaginative job telling the story of Fort Cumberland. The fort site on a hill overlooking the Potomac River is covered by a 19th century neighborhood, but a good sense of the fort's main features can be gained by following a walking trail that covers several city blocks. Fort Cumberland was an important rendezvous for British and provincial troops embarking on expeditions into the Ohio country.

The fort's story is told on 28 plaques installed at points along the walking tour. The fort's perimeter can be traced by following the white markers set in the cobblestone walkway. In Riverside Park just below the hill, the restored log cabin headquarters of one-time fort commander Col. George Washington, and a reconstructed section of the fort palisades, are visible. Riverside Park overlooks the juncture of the Potomac River and Wills Creek, a strategic point for the fur traders and scouts who came here in the 1750s.

When the Shawnee lived in the area, they called this spot Caiuctucuc, meaning "the meeting of the waters of many fishes." But the migrating Shawnee were gone from the area when the Ohio Company, an English land company, established a trading post here in 1750. Several years later the company built a storehouse on the south side of the Potomac at Ridgeley, West Virginia.

The first move to fortify this spot came in 1754 when colonial militia built Fort Mount Pleasant. Later that same year Maryland Gov. Horatio Sharpe expanded the outpost into a more substantial fort.

Fort Cumberland was named for a son of King George II, the Duke of Cumberland. The fort was large enough to contain a parade ground, barracks for soldiers, officers' quarters, hospital, magazine, and storehouses. It was a hub of activity with the arrival in the spring of 1755 of Gen. Edward Braddock's army. Braddock spent a month at the fort gathering supplies and dealing rather unsuccessfully with Indian allies. After Braddock's defeat at the forks of the Ohio, the remnants of the army under Col. Thomas Dunbar bypassed Fort Cumberland and headed to comfortable quarters in New York.

Fort Cumberland was in a vulnerable position during the period from 1755 to 1758 when Delaware and Shawnee raiding parties devastated the frontier. The fort was considered too exposed by Washington to offer much protection to area settlers. The fort came under fire from raiding parties hidden on the nearby McKaig's Hill to the north and Knobley Mountain on the south side of the Potomac. A group of militia marched out from the fort one night in July 1756 to attack Indians on McKaig's Hill.

Although a Crown fort, Fort Cumberland was often undermanned; Virginia and Maryland officials bickered over the cost of its maintenance. By late 1758 with the success of the Forbes expedition, Fort Cumberland was something of a backwater post. Yet British troops maintained a garrison here until 1765.

Today the fort site encompasses the eastern part of Washington Street, which includes the Emmanuel Episcopal Church and Allegany County Court House, site of the parade grounds. The church was built between 1848 and 1851 in the Gothic revival style. Underneath the church's ground floor are old cellars or tunnels, said to be the only remaining traces of Fort Cumberland. The tunnels were once earthworks that were covered over when the church was built, though some area historians dispute this. One of the entranceways to the tunnels is visible from the steps of the Masonic Temple, just south of the church.

The church has a model replica of Fort Cumberland. Contact the church about touring the tunnels. Walking tour brochures of Fort Cumberland and the Washington Street Historic District are available at the nearby Allegany County Visitor's Center, Western Maryland Station, Harrison and Mechanic Streets, Cumberland, Md., 21502. Call 1-800-872-4650.

## GEORGE WASHINGTON'S HEADQUARTERS CUMBERLAND, MARYLAND

*Directions: From Baltimore Street in downtown Cumberland, turn left on Greene Street to Riverside Park. Cabin on right side of street.*

George Washington commanded troops at Fort Cumberland at both the start and end of his military career. The first time, Washington was a young colonel placed in charge of Virginia's defenses by a royal governor; the second, he was an aging president determined to exert federal power to put down a rebellion of farmers in western Pennsylvania.

When President Washington reviewed troops on Fort Cumberland's parade ground in 1794, he no doubt thought of his first command at the fort in 1755 during the French and Indian War. But his memories may not have been pleasant. Fort Cumberland proved to be a headache for young Washington. Virginia Gov. Robert Dinwiddie placed the fort under Washington's command, but a complicated jurisdictional dispute threatened that command.

Fort Cumberland was located in Maryland and considered a Crown fort. Troops from Virginia and Mary-

*Washington's Headquarters.*

land were stationed there, and for a time, a Marylander, Capt. John Dagworthy, was the ranking officer at the fort. Since Dagworthy held a commission in the British royal army, and Washington did not, the Virginian was concerned about being outranked if he ventured to the fort. Washington even journeyed to Boston to make his case for undisputed command of the fort to the British Army commander. He obtained only partial satisfaction.

Therefore, Washington spent relatively little time at his log cabin headquarters which is preserved in Riverside Park. He based his operations at Winchester, Virginia, where another of his headquarters is also preserved. Washington's longest stay at Fort Cumberland was during the winter of 1756. He also was based here in early 1758 while the Forbes expedition gathered strength for their march on Fort Duquesne.

During the dangerous days of 1756 when the French and their Indian allies were raiding the frontier at will, Washington actually lobbied Dinwiddie to abandon Fort Cumberland. He wanted to relocate the troops posted there to beef up outposts closer to the frontier settlements on the South Branch of the Potomac River. But Dinwiddie said Fort Cumberland could only be abandoned on the King's orders.

Washington returned to Fort Cumberland in October 1794 at the head of a 3,000-man army mobilized to crush the Whiskey Rebellion. The rebellion broke out in the Pittsburgh area when farmers objected to a federal tax on whiskey.

Today Washington's one-room headquarters is maintained by the city and the Cresap Chapter of the Daughters of the American Revolution. The cabin initially stood inside the fort at the top of the hill. But in 1844 it was moved to a farm in the area. The cabin was relocated to Riverside Park in 1921. The log timbers are original except for the bottom two rows. Inside are exhibits featuring period uniforms, a musket made at Fort Cumberland, and a cannonball found in the area. The cabin is open on Washington's birthday and the city's Heritage Days Festival in mid-June. Contact the DAR about making an appointment to visit the cabin.

# 9

# The Forbes Campaign: British Victory at the Ohio Forks, May–November 1758

## INTRODUCTION

By 1758, the British were ready to make another attempt to expel the French from the Forks of the Ohio. General John Forbes, the commander assigned to this task by London, vowed to avoid the mistakes that doomed General Braddock's expedition in 1755. Forbes decided on a slow methodical advance. He believed the best way to cross the Alleghenies was in stages. He sent road crews ahead to fell trees and cut a road through the Pennsylvania wilderness. The advance guard under command of Col. Henry Bouquet, a Swiss mercenary in the British service, followed and erected a string of forts to secure communications and stockpile supplies for the main army. This string of forts was an insurance policy. If the British were defeated in a wilderness battle, the army could regroup at the rear bases and prepare for a second try.

There would be no pell-mell retreat to Philadelphia as the remnants of Braddock's army had done. Forbes, unlike Braddock, also recognized that securing the alliance or at least the neutrality of the Native Americans in the Ohio Valley was essential to British victory. Much of

SITES AT A GLANCE—This map will give you a feel for the general locations of sites in this chapter. Some sites overlap and are not shown on this map.

Ft. Ligonier
Ft. Bedford
Cowans Gap
Ft. Pitt
Carlisle
Somerset Historical Center

Forbes' success resulted from diplomatic efforts to lure the Delaware and Shawnee away from the French. The efforts of a courageous Moravian missionary, Christian Frederick Post, and the signing of a peace treaty with the Delaware at Easton in October 1758 were crucial in this regard.

Still the inexorable advance of a 6,000-man army towards the Forks moved the peace talks along. Forbes' army crossed five mountains to reach its goal, but the route taken through southern Pennsylvania was more direct and shorter than Braddock's Road through Virginia and Maryland.

Forbes was mainly concerned with selecting the best military route, but everyone realized that trade and commerce would eventually follow the path of the soldiers. Representing Virginia's interests, Col. George Washington lobbied for the reopening of Braddock's Road, but the prospect of crossing several rivers and the lack of good roads along the Potomac River mitigated against that route. Still, Virginia troops put on a show of clearing the underbrush from Braddock's Road to keep the French guessing.

Philadelphia merchants lobbied for cutting a new road across Pennsylvania. Forbes and Bouquet kept their options open until mid-summer, but they came to the conclusion early on that it was easier to supply the troops and find forage for the horses using the Pennsylvania route. The discovery of a pass through the formidable Allegheny Mountain sealed the decision in favor of Pennsylvania.

As with the Braddock expedition, a number of distinguished colonial figures served on the Forbes campaign. Bouquet learned the lessons of wilderness warfare that he applied effectively five years later at Bushy Run on this campaign. Washington commanded the Virginia troops. Washington's colleague Col. Adam Stephen led work details on some of the roughest stretches of the road. Colonel James Burd commanded at Fort Ligonier when it came under attack. Colonel John Armstrong of Kittanning fame was another campaign veteran.

There were two jumping off points for the Forbes campaign: the Carlisle encampment where Pennsylvania troops and British regulars from New York gathered, and Fort Cumberland where troops from the southern colonies rendezvoused.

In the east, Fort Loudon and Fort Lyttelton served as communications and supply posts. A five-mile stretch of Forbes Road from Cowans Gap State Park to Burnt Cabins is preserved as a hiking trail in this area. The British built a fort at Juniata Crossings to safeguard a river ford. Fort Bedford was where the two sections of the army joined together. The army camped at an old traders' post known as Shawnee Cabins. A stretch of Forbes Road can be hiked at that site in Shawnee State Park.

From this point onward, the army faced the challenge of crossing Allegheny Mountain (elev. 3,000) and Laurel Hill (elev. 2,795). The discovery of a hidden pass eased the passage over Allegheny Mountain. A cluster of army camps at Fort Stony Creek, Edmund's Swamp Redoubt, Clear Fields, and Tomahawk Camp helped the soldiers prepare for the ascent over Laurel Hill. A portion of Forbes Road can be hiked in Laurel Ridge State Park. Just west of Laurel Hill, Forbes Road is marked at Thomas Crossroads. A stretch of Forbes Road fronts the restored Revolutionary War settlement of Hannastown, north of modern Greensburg.

Fort Ligonier served as the forward base from which the final assault on Fort Duquesne was launched. But Fort Ligonier came under attack by a force of French and Indian on October 12. The British beat off the attack, but lost many of their horses.

The Forbes campaign was a slow-moving affair with troops strung out along the route. One officer described the road building as diabolical work. Forbes himself was incapacitated by illness during the entire campaign, but he struggled through to victory only to die several months later back in Philadelphia. Forbes deliberately slowed his advance, waiting for diplomats to deprive the French of their Indian allies. But in late October, word came of the Treaty of Easton. By then, however, it was late in the season and many of Forbes officers wanted to call off the campaign for the year and leave a garrison at Fort Ligonier.

In mid-November, a small party of French and Indians staged a raid to nab more British horses, and one soldier was captured. He provided information that Fort Duquesne was undermanned and most of the Indians had departed. Forbes gave the go-ahead for the final assault and within two weeks a British army approached the Forks. They raised the British flag over the smoking ruins of Fort Duquesne. The French had blown up the fort and departed without a fight.

During the next several years, the British built a larger, grander fort on the site, and named it Fort Pitt in honor of British Prime Minister William Pitt. Today modern Route 30 parallels much of Forbes Road with some variations. A series of stone tablets erected by the Pennsylvania Historical Commission in the 1930s marks key forts and army camps along the road. The westernmost tablet stands next to the 1764 Fort Pitt Blockhouse at Point State Park in downtown Pittsburgh.

## CARLISLE ENCAMPMENT & OLD GRAVEYARD CARLISLE, PENNSYLVANIA

During the early years of the French and Indian War, the town of Carlisle served as a place of refuge for settlers fleeing the raiding parties to the west. Carlisle became the key defense post west of the Susquehanna River and in 1757, British regulars and provincial troops under command of Col. John Stanwix arrived here to build a fortified encampment northeast of town.

This encampment on the site of modern U.S. Army Carlisle Barracks was not a fort in the traditional sense; troops camped in a cleared area surrounded by earth ramparts and entrenchments. Supplies were housed in storage sheds and cattle and horses clustered in pens.

The encampment served as the starting point for Gen. John Forbes' campaign in 1758. Units of the Royal American regiment arrived here, as well as garrisons from provincial forts along the Blue Mountains. For a time, several hundred Cherokee warriors gathered here until many tired of the campaign's slow pace and headed back home to the southern Appalachians.

Forbes arrived at Carlisle in early July and supervised arrangements for pack horses and wagon trains needed to keep his army supplied. By early August, Forbes had left Carlisle for the army's big rendezvous at Fort Bedford. Carlisle remained an important supply depot and later was designated British Army headquarters for the Southern District. During Pontiac's War in 1763-74, Col. Henry Bouquet organized his expeditions here.

The encampment grounds continue in military use as the Carlisle Barracks, home of the U.S. Army War College and U.S. Army Military History Institute. Exhibits in the Hessian Powder Magazine and Museum on the Barracks grounds trace the post's colorful history from the Stanwix encampment through the American Revolution, Civil War, and modern times. The powder magazine was built in 1777 to store gunpowder. Hessian prisoners may have done some of the construction work. The museum is located on Guardhouse Lane in the Carlisle Barracks, one mile northeast of Carlisle on Route 11 and is open on weekend afternoons. Remember you are entering an active military post and should obey posted rules.

### Old Graveyard, Hanover and South Streets

Two veterans of Forbes' campaign are buried a short distance from each other in Carlisle's Old Graveyard on the south side of town. Colonel John Armstrong (1717-1795) led the 1756 expedition that destroyed the Delaware village of Kittanning and commanded the First Battalion of Pennsylvania troops on the Forbes campaign. He also served as a brigadier general in the American Continental Army during the Revolution. Armstrong, a Scots-Irish immigrant from Ulster, arrived in the Cumberland Valley in the 1730s. The inscription on his flat tombstone reads: "General John Armstrong, eminently distinguished for patriotism, valor and piety." Armstrong's grave is located near the South Street entrance on the cemetery's northeast side. Turn left after that entrance and walk diagonally past a half dozen rows of gravestones. Armstrong's grave is on a slight elevation under a pine tree.

Robert Callender (1726-1776) served as a company captain under Armstrong. His upright tombstone is several paces north of Armstrong's grave. Callender packed a lot of activity into his 50 years. He was one of the Indian traders in the Ohio region during the 1750s and had operations at Pickawillany and Logstown. Callender was a sutler in the Braddock expedition and also helped Forbes with supply arrangements. After the war, Callender became the owner of what today is called the Jean Bonnet Tavern west of Bedford at the intersection of the Forbes and Burd Roads or modern Routes 30 and 31. Callender was also a part owner of the trade goods destroyed on Sideling Hill by James Smith's Black Boys in 1765. This band of black-faced Conococheague Valley residents, angry that the traders were selling arms to the Delaware and Shawnee in western Pennsylvania, waylaid the traders' pack train in a challenge to British Indian policy.

Near the cemetery's west gate is a sandstone boulder with a tablet listing colonial and Revolutionary war veterans buried here. The grave that draws the most attention is that of Mary Hays McCauley, better known as "Molly Pitcher," the heroine of the Revolutionary War battle of Monmouth. A statue of Pitcher holding a gun staff and a cannon mark her grave.

## CHEROKEES AT FORT LOUDON
## FORT LOUDON, PENNSYLVANIA

In 1758, the British worked diligently to line up Native American allies for the march on Fort Duquesne. The lack of such allies was recognized as a major handicap to the Braddock expedition of 1755, and the British turned to the Cherokee and Catawba tribes for help. These two southern highland tribes had fought on the British side before, in regional wars in North Carolina and Georgia.

The Cherokees were one of the most populous of the southern tribes, numbering 10,000. They had a long-standing rivalry with the northern Iroquois; the various Warrior's Trails that traversed the valleys of Pennsylvania, Maryland, and Virginia got their name from the war parties of Cherokees and Iroquois that moved north and

south along them. On the surface, the Cherokees appeared to be just the right British counterbalance against the pro-French Delaware and Shawnee. But things did not work out that way. Within two short years after the Forbes campaign, the situation deteriorated to the extent that the British and Cherokees were at war against each other.

There was talk of Cherokee warriors coming to the support of Braddock's army, but that prospect soon faded. Small bands of Cherokees—some 250 altogether—assisted the British in 1757 along the Virginia and Pennsylvania frontiers. The Cherokees scored some successes that year—surprising a party of Shawnee and Delaware near Raystown, and ambushing a French patrol 20 miles east of Fort Duquesne.

But problems emerged. A party of 60 Cherokees entering Pennsylvania's Conococheague Valley in pursuit of pro-French Indians was mistaken for enemy raiders themselves. They lodged for the night in a house at a trading post known as Black's Town (modern Mercersburg) near Fort Loudon. A suspicious resident alerted the fort's garrison and a tragedy was only averted when white traders accompanying the Cherokee spotted the danger in time to clear up the misunderstanding. The Cherokees were also disgruntled by the lack of gifts to compensate them for their services.

By 1758, British Indian agents had laid plans for a more efficient system to distribute presents, and some 400 Cherokee warriors journeyed north. Cherokee scouts kept Fort Duquesne under close watch; some scouts went as far north as Fort Presque Isle along Lake Erie. But presents could not make everything alright.

The Cherokees and backcountry settlers in Virginia clashed over ownership of horses that often roamed loose on the frontier. Armed fights between Cherokee parties headed north and settlers erupted in May at the Virginia settlements of Otter Creek and Bedford. The fighting alarmed the Cherokee head warrior Wawhatchee, who was already at Carlisle, Pennsylvania. He headed home to cool things down.

In late June, Col. Henry Bouquet spoke at a council with Cherokee and Catawba warriors at Fort Loudon, a key depot along Forbes Road. He warned the warriors that the French would try to take their land: "That Rapacious Nation is already in Possession of all the Lakes and Rivers and of the best hunting Country but it is not enough yet for them, they would Sweep us from the Earth, and drown us at once in the Waters of the great Lake."

But the alliance was unraveling even as Bouquet spoke. General Forbes' slow methodical approach to the campaign frustrated warriors accustomed to quick and decisive military actions of several months or less. The Cherokees, gathered at Carlisle, Fort Loudon, and Fort Lyttelton, drifted away back home and by July only 50 Cherokee scouts remained with Forbes' army.

A last chance for understanding came in October when the head Cherokee Chief Attakullakulla, or Little Carpenter, met with Forbes at Raystown. The meeting did not go well. The two were at odds over the amount of gifts being distributed to the warriors. Forbes was disappointed that Little Carpenter would not commit his warriors for the final advance against Fort Duquesne. For his part, Little Carpenter had gotten word from the Shawnee that the French were prepared to abandon the fort and he headed home.

Border incidents between the Cherokees and the white settlers in the Carolinas soon aggravated matters in 1759. French agents as well as emissaries from the neighboring Creek tribe who were pro-French stirred up discontent. A war party from the Cherokee town of Settico went raiding in North Carolina, killing nineteen settlers. The British demanded extradition of the killers and then took several Cherokee leaders hostage.

In 1760, British veterans of the Forbes campaign were dispatched to the Cherokee frontier. The Cherokees beat back the expedition and captured the isolated British post of Fort Loudoun near Chota in Tennessee. In 1761, Lt. James Grant led a second expedition that destroyed fifteen Cherokee towns. Little Carpenter agreed to peace terms.

The Cherokees had gone from being allies of the British to foes in a few short years. The British effort to forge a friendship with a major native tribe was a complete failure.

## FORBES ROAD TRAIL
## COWANS GAP STATE PARK, PENNSYLVANIA

---

*Directions: To reach Cowans Gap State Park from Route 30, take Route 75 north of Fort Loudon to Richmond Furnace. Watch for park sign. Take Richmond Road west up mountain slope to Aughwick Road at park entrance. Turn right on Aughwick Road until it becomes Allen Valley Road. Look for trailhead sign for Forbes Road on left.*

---

The first mountain barrier encountered by Forbes' army was Tuscarora Mountain (elev. 2000) to the west of Fort Loudon. Fortunately, Col. James Burd found a way to surmount this obstacle when he built his road for the Braddock expedition in 1755. Burd widened portions of the Raystown Path, an old Indian trading route, and he found that the trail led over a gap in Tuscarora Mountain at a lower elevation of 1,200 feet. Forbes Road followed the course of Burd Road.

In the vicinity of the modern town of Fort Loudon, Forbes Road skirted along the southern base of Parnell's Knob, a distinctive landmark, and turned north into Path Valley and through the pass in Tuscarora Mountain now known as Cowans Gap. From Cowans Gap, Forbes Road followed the course of Little Aughwick Creek through a narrow valley between Tuscarora Mountain and Cove Mountain to the site of the old squatters camp at Burnt Cabins. Today the Boy Scouts maintain this 2.8-mile section of Forbes Road as a public hiking trail.

The dirt trail passes through a wooded area along the slope of a hill to the west of Little Aughwick Creek. The trail is situated above several marshy areas because road builders located the grade higher than the soft ground and springs where possible. Because of the terrain and the darkness in this forested mountain valley, walking this trail offers as good a sense as possible of what British soldiers must have experienced as they headed into the wilderness. The hiking trail starts at the north end of Cowans Gap State Park, a scenic 1,000-acre park that offers swimming, camping, and boating, and enters the Buchanan State Forest. The trail comes out at the Old Mill in the modern town of Burnt Cabins.

The Mason-Dixon Council of Boy Scouts based in Hagerstown, Maryland, has also traced Forbes Road along a route that follows modern roads and trails for the 25-mile stretch between Burnt Cabins and Ray's Hill Mountain in Bedford County. At Cowans Gap State Park, the Brightbill Interpretive Center off Aughwick Road has excellent exhibits about the hardships faced by travelers crossing the Alleghenies and the roads they took. The center also has exhibits about wildlife and how Cowans Gap was formed over the eons by wind erosion. The story of the Samuel Cowans family who settled in the area after the American Revolution is told. The center is open for several hours each day during the summer months and on weekends in the spring and fall.

## FORT LYTTELTON (OR LYTTLETON)
## EAST OF FORT LITTLETON, PENNSYLVANIA

Fort Lyttelton was built as a provincial post in 1755 and it served as an important supply post during the Forbes campaign three years later. Indians and traders traveling the Raystown Path called this area Sugar Cabins for its abundance of maple syrup trees. In the early spring, temporary camps were set up here to boil maple sap into syrup.

Fort Lyttelton was the westernmost of four defense posts built under orders of Pennsylvania Gov. Robert Hunter Morris after Braddock's defeat. The Indian trader George Croghan oversaw construction of this log fort, selecting a location along the newly opened Burd Road. Morris named the fort in honor of Sir George Lyttelton, the British Chancellor of the Exchequer. The fort was garrisoned by provincial troops, and while it did not come under direct attack, plenty of skirmishes and raids occurred in the vicinity. Survivors of the Sideling Hill battle found refuge here in 1756. In June 1757, a girl milking a cow was scalped and killed by Indian raiders within sight of the fort.

*Fort Lyttleton marker sits along Forbes Road.*

During the Forbes campaign, British and provincial troops were stationed here. This was a rendezvous point for Cherokee warriors coming north to join the campaign. Colonel Henry Bouquet arrived here in mid-June 1758 with the advance guard of Forbes' army. General Forbes passed this area in mid-September enroute to Fort Bedford. Two months earlier in a letter to British Prime Minister William Pitt, Forbes described Forts Lyttelton and Loudon as having two or three houses each enclosed by a stockade 100 feet square. The size of the garrison at Fort Lyttelton was reduced after the British capture of Fort Duquesne. The fort was staffed during Pontiac's War, but it was reported in ruins by 1764.

The fort site is located on the north side of Route 522 one-half mile east of the modern town of Fort Littleton. Route 522 parallels Forbes Road in this stretch. A state historical marker notes the site at the base of a small hill. A stone monument erected here in 1924 has this inscription: "Begun in 1755 by George Croghan, named by Governor Morris, after Sir George Lyttelton, then Chancellor of the Exchequer. Garrison variously by Provincial and regular troops, as well, local volunteers in 1763. By 1764 it was reported in ruins."

## Juniata Crossings
### west of Breezewood, Pennsylvania

*Directions: The exact site of the fort is unknown, but it is believed to be about one-half mile north of the Juniata Crossing Bridge on Route 30. A state historical marker for "Forbes Road (Fort Juniata)" is on the north side of Route 30. Traffic moves by fast on this section of Route 30 which is divided by a median strip. Driving west on Route 30, there is access to a public fishing area at the bridge. Look for the parking area at northeast corner of bridge. Take path to river.*

In June 1758 British engineers built an odd-shaped fort to guard the one major river crossing on Forbes Road. Fort Juniata or Juniata Crossing Fort was situated on both sides of a ford on the Raystown branch of the Juniata River. The river makes a bend at this point. Soldiers waded the river here when the water was low, but a ferry was also established to haul men and supplies across. The main fort with four bastions, barracks, and storehouses was located on the east bank of the river. On the west bank, an extended L-shaped log structure sheltered rows of tents, animals, and wagons. By the time of Pontiac's War, this fort was in serious disrepair.

The Juniata crossing served as a major gateway to the west during the 18th and 19th centuries. Ferry boats, covered toll bridges, and later, the concrete spans of Route 30, have all helped travelers cross here. A 19th century inn still stands at this location.

## Fort Bedford Museum
### Bedford, Pennsylvania

*Directions: Take Exit 11 off Pennsylvania Turnpike. Go south on Route 220 to Pitt Street (Route 30) in downtown Bedford. Go west one block. Turn right on Juliana Street to museum.*

Colonel Henry Bouquet built Fort Bedford in the summer of 1758 on an elevation overlooking the south branch of the Juniata River. Bedford, initially called the fort at Raystown, was one of the rendezvous points and supply depots for the Forbes expedition. Raystown took its name from John Ray, an Indian trader who had a post here. Fort Bedford was a pentagon-shaped wooden fort with an unusual feature: a covered stairway that extended down a slope to the river so the garrison could obtain fresh water without being exposed to enemy fire. The fort had five bastions with mounted swivel guns, firing platforms, and two redoubts on the south and west sides.

At the peak of the Forbes campaign, over 6,000 troops gathered here from posts in Virginia and Pennsylvania. They were spread out in a grand encampment surrounding the fort. A number of buildings were erected at the encampment, including hospitals, storehouses, and charcoal ovens.

Fort Bedford was formally named for the Duke of Bedford after the fall of Fort Duquesne and was maintained for another decade. Despite being weakly manned, Fort Bedford did not come under attack during Pontiac's War in 1763-64. But raiding parties were active in the area. In 1769 Fort Bedford played a role in the controversy between the British Crown and frontiersmen over trading practices with the Ohio tribes.

*Fort Bedford overlooks the Juniata River.*

James Smith and the "Black Boys" briefly occupied the fort in a bloodless raid. They acted to free comrades jailed at the fort for destroying gunpowder destined for the Indian trade. Several months later, Smith himself was captured and jailed at Fort Bedford. He was tried on charges at Carlisle and acquitted.

Today downtown Bedford covers much of the fort site. During the fort's bicentennial in 1958, the town built a blockhouse-style structure to serve as a museum. The museum contains a scale model of the fort, and exhibits on Indian artifacts, flintlock rifles, cannonballs, and tools excavated from the fort, period documents, and replica British flags, as well as items covering other periods of area history. The museum is open 10 a.m. to 5 p.m. May through October, except for Tuesdays in May, September and October.

## WEST OF FORT BEDFORD TO SCHELLSBURG, PENNSYLVANIA

*Directions: Shawnee State Park can be reached by turning south on Route 96 on the west side of Schellsburg. To reach the Forbes Road trail, turn left off Route 96 at the park entrance, bear left past the park office and look for picnic area on right side of road near lake. A Forbes Road sign marks the trailhead by the picnic area.*

The Forbes expedition basically followed a road blazed by Col. James Burd in 1755 until a point four miles west of Fort Bedford or Raystown. Burd in turn had widened the Raystown Path, a main east-west path for Indians and English traders venturing into the Ohio country. As the British army headed west from Fort Bedford, they encountered vestiges of the traders' commerce network.

The point where Forbes Road split off from Burd Road is known as The Forks. Today this is the intersection of

Routes 30 and 31 and the location of the 18th century Jean Bonnet Tavern. The route used by Forbes' army parallels Route 30 here. The Burd Road veered more to the southwest through an area known as The Glades. A stone tablet at the intersection in front of the Bonnet Tavern has the inscription: "The Forks. The Road cut by Col. James Burd 1755 and the Forbes Road diverge here. Forbes Road leading southwest to Shawnee Cabins."

An Indian village once was located here. In 1762, Robert Callender, an Ohio trader and veteran of the Forbes campaign, acquired the land and started to build the stone tavern that stands here today. In 1780, the tavern was licensed to Jean Bonnet as a public house. The Jean Bonnet Tavern is a public restaurant today as well as a bed and breakfast. Patrons dine in a room with a massive stone fireplace and frontier art prints on the walls.

The next army encampment was at Shawnee Cabins, in today's Shawnee State Park south of Schellsburg. A portion of Forbes Road is preserved as a hiking trail through the park. Shawnee or Shawanese Cabins was located eight miles west of Fort Bedford on Shawnee Creek. It began as a stopover for migratory Shawnee. Indian traders enroute to the Ohio Valley mention staying here at a cabin, but the place was apparently deserted when war broke out in 1755.

For Forbes' soldiers, this was a resting place before experiencing the rigors of the road between Allegheny Mountain and Laurel Hill. Today the terrain of the bottomland along Shawnee Creek has been altered by a dam which created Lake Shawnee in the middle of the state park.

The Forbes hiking trail skirts the southern lakeshore, crosses the dam, and heads in a southeast direction paralleling Shawnee Creek. Some believe the actual site of Shawnee Cabins was located on a small island or spot of high ground in the lake where the regional park office stands.

On Route 30 just west of Schellsburg are state highway markers for Shawnee Cabins and Forbes camp. The Pennsylvania Historical Commission erected a stone tablet on the north side of Route 30 in this vicinity. The inscription reads: "Shawnee Cabins encampment. At this point the Forbes Road leads southwestward to the eastern slope of the Allegheny Mountain."

*One of the distinctive Forbes Road markers.*

## FROM ALLEGHENY MOUNTAIN TO LAUREL HILL
### JENNERSTOWN, PENNSYLVANIA

*Directions to Fort Stony Creek: From Route 30, take Route 403 north. As you enter the small town of Kantner, Route 403 is called Forbes Road. Follow Route 403/ Forbes Road to the east side of Kantner. Look for tablet in front of elementary school on knoll. Route 403 crosses Stony Creek (which is still stony) to the east. Just east of Stony Creek is Oven Run valley. The run is named for the army's stone bake ovens that were built there. Local historians report the ovens remained until the 1870s. After crossing the bridge over Stony Creek on Route 430, turn right on SR 1010 and cross a smaller bridge over Oven Run.*

The soldiers building Forbes Road faced their greatest challenge along the section between Allegheny Mountain and Laurel Hill. Scaling these two heights was difficult enough; building a road across the plateau linking them required strenuous labor. The terrain featured swamps and laurel thickets that were hard to penetrate. In August 1758, some 1,200 advance troops under command of Col. Henry Bouquet set to work. Allegheny Mountain (elev. 3,000) loomed as the first hurdle.

Luckily for the expedition, British engineer Ensign Charles Rhor discovered a pass at an elevation 400 feet lower. Discovery of Rhor's Gap sealed the decision by Gen. Forbes to take an all-Pennsylvania route to Fort Duquesne rather than using Braddock's Road. The army built a small earthen fort called Fort Dewart on top of Allegheny Mountain along a stream known today as Breastwork Run. A state historical marker on Route 30 at the summit notes the fort site is about one-half mile north. The fort site is marked by a stone tablet, but it is on private property and difficult to reach.

After descending Allegheny Mountain, the army crossed a plateau filled with swamps and thickets. Today, some of that terrain—and Forbes Road sites—have been altered by strip coal mining and land reclamation. Crossing Edmunds Swamp proved exceedingly difficult. Road builders called it the Shades of Death for the dense foliage and underbrush that blot out the sunlight. A camp and later an earthen redoubt were built in the middle of the swamp.

Lieutenant Colonel Adam Stephen used classical language to describe the task facing him and his road builders from Virginia. In an August 8 letter to Bouquet from the Camp at Edmunds Swamp, Stephen wrote: "This morning has set the men to work about bridging the Swamp, and goes my Self with a party to reconnoitre the Shades of Death, a dismal place! and wants only a Cerberus to represent Virgils gloomy description of Aeneas's entering the Infernal Regions." In Greek and Roman mythology, Cerberus was the three-headed dog that guarded the gate to Hades, so Stephen's gloom is evident. A state historical marker for Forbes Road/Edmunds Swamp is located on Route 30 at Buckstown.

Fort Stony Creek served as a supply depot during the Forbes campaign and for several years afterward. The fort consisted of a redoubt and storage sheds and was situated on an elevation overlooking the aptly named Stony Creek. General Forbes stayed here briefly in late October. A stone tablet, located at North Star East Elementary School, erected by the Pennsylvania Historical Commission, marks the fort site. The inscription reads: "Stony Creek encampment. The Ovens. Supply headquarters. Fortifications were erected a few rods (one road equals 16.5 feet) northeast of this site. The Forbes Road heads northward to the encampment at the foot of Laurel Hill."

Encampments were also located near the eastern slope of Laurel Hill. A state historical marker for "Forbes Road/ The Clear Fields" is on the north side of Route 30, 1.3

miles west of Jennerstown. The British valued the "clear fields" or meadows; they provided forage for horses. The army also built an entrenchment called Fort Dudgeon in the area, but the works were destroyed by strip mining. The Tomahawk encampment was located on the slope just west of the Clear Fields. A stone tablet erected here by the Pennsylvania Historical Commission marks the site with this inscription: "Tomahawk Encampment. At foot of Laurel Hill. The Forbes Road leads northwestward to Fort Ligonier. 35.5 miles from Fort Bedford."

*Directions to Tomahawk Encampment: West of Jennerstown, take Route 30 and make right onto Klines Mill Road. Go west on Klines Mill Road for one mile. At intersection of SR 4012 and Sliding Rock Road, look for stone tablet in shade of pine tree.*

## SOMERSET HISTORICAL CENTER
### NORTH OF SOMERSET, PENNSYLVANIA

*Directions: Take Exit 10 off Pennsylvania Turnpike at Somerset. Take Route 601 north until it becomes Route 985. Watch for signs. The center is located on left side of road. The center is open Wednesday through Saturday 9 a.m. to 5 p.m.; Sunday, Noon to 5 p.m. Admission charged. Call 814-445-6077.*

This state-owned site is known as western Pennsylvania's rural heritage museum. It depicts the transformation of southwest Pennsylvania in the Allegheny Mountains region from wilderness to farm belt. The center traces life from the 1760s to the 1890s and

*The Somerset Center presents pioneer story.*

features numerous restored buildings moved from other locations. Buildings on the extensive grounds range from a 1773 log cabin to an 1876 general store. From the visitor center, look north for a panoramic view of the spot ten miles away where a trace of Forbes Road crosses Laurel Ridge, a major mountain barrier on the way to the Ohio region.

The visitor center also shows a good video, "Patterns of the Land," that depicts how the culture of the Native Americans and traders gave way to that of the pioneers and small farmers. Throughout the year, the Somerset Historical Center schedules special events ranging from 18th century military encampments to mountain craft and harvest days where traditional rural customs are celebrated.

## CROSSING LAUREL HILL
### LAUREL RIDGE STATE PARK, PENNSYLVANIA

*Directions: The Forbes Road trail is 1.6 miles north of Route 30. Hikers start at a parking lot on the south side of Route 30 near the state park sign. The parking lot leads to the Laurel Highlands Trail that crosses Route 30. This trail is considered moderate in terms of difficulty, including some switchbacks up and down small hills and log walks over Pickings Run. A trail shelter and mileposts are found in this stretch. Depending upon the hiker's physical condition and stamina, it can take one hour or one-and one-half hours to walk from the parking lot to the Forbes Road trail at a steady clip.*

British soldiers cut through dense laurel thickets to get across Laurel Hill, but as with other mountain barriers in their way, they found a gap that allowed passage at a lower elevation. The Forbes Road followed an area between two small streams now known as Pickings Run and Card Machine Run. Colonel James Burd and an advance guard of 1,500 troops crossed Laurel Hill in early September 1758, enroute to fortify a post at Loyalhanna, later Fort Ligonier. A diorama in the Fort Ligonier museum gives a realistic view of a horse-drawn army wagon negotiating a boulder strewn mountain road.

Today the section of Forbes Road over Laurel Hill is preserved as a dirt jeep trail and is a landmark along the 70-mile Laurel Highlands Trail from Ohiopyle State Park to Johnstown, Pennsylvania. Like the part of Forbes Road preserved as a hiking trail through Cowans Gap, hiking along the Forbes Road trail in Laurel Ridge State Park offers a glimpse into the British soldiers' experience in 1758. But it should be noted that while the British waded through impenetrable laurel thickets, the modern hiker will find the trail leading through a second-growth and third-growth forest that still has patches of laurel, but is more open and lets more sunlight in.

Reaching the Forbes Road trail, there is a wooden sign, "Forbes Road 1758." The forest in the vicinity is relatively open and there is little underbrush. Driving up the hill along the jeep trail is not advisable because it passes through private property. Look sharply; there are still signs of wagon ruts in the woods and even spots where wagon wheels cut a groove in the rocks. Travelers used this stretch of Forbes Road for decades after Forbes' army passed through.

West of Laurel Hill in the Ligonier Valley, visitors can drive along a paved stretch of Forbes Road to modern Thomas Crossroads where a stone monument is located. The blue tablet on the small monument says: "Original course of Forbes Road 1758 through Ligonier Valley. Erected 1958 by the Ligonier Valley Chamber of Commerce."

---

*Directions: To reach this monument, turn right onto Laughlintown-Watertown Road at the intersection on Route 30 by the Compass Inn Museum. Follow the Laughlintown Road north past Hall Road and Penrod Road to SR 1010, also known as Old Forbes Road. Turn left onto SR1010. Look for road sign showing left fork in road. Pass the Lebanon United Methodist Church along this road. Follow several miles to Thomas Crossroads at the intersection of SR 1010 and SR 1017 (or Gravel Hill Road and Kinsey Farm Road). A blue Forbes Road sign and the monument are on west side of intersection. Look east from here and get a good view of the gap over Laurel Hill where the army crossed.*

---

***Forbes Road monument at Thomas crossroads.***

## FORT LIGONIER—LIGONIER, PENNSYLVANIA

---

*Directions: Drive west on Route 30 to junction with Route 711 (South Market Street). Turn right on Route 711 to reach fort entrance.*

---

The British regarded Fort Ligonier as the key to the West during the 1758 Forbes campaign. The fort was designed to provide Forbes' army with something the 1755 Braddock campaign lacked—an advance base to fall back on should a direct attack on Fort Duquesne fail. Fort Ligonier served its purpose well. Fort Ligonier was built at a strategic point along Loyalhanna Creek near the site of the Delaware village of Loyalhanna. Loyalhanna, a village settled by migrating Delaware in the 1720s, was at the juncture of the Raystown and Catawba paths.

In July 1758, Col. John Armstrong scouted the area and recommended it to Gen. John Forbes as the site to build a fort about 50 miles east of Fort Duquesne. Armstrong called attention to the abundant grasslands that would provide forage for the army's horses. By September, Col. James Burd arrived with 1,500 advance troops to build the fort. Burd built a substantial log fort with four bastions and a unique outer retrenchment topped with sharpened log pickets. It was named for British Field Marshall John Ligonier.

The fort served as the launching point for Capt. James Grant's ill-fated reconnoitering mission to Duquesne. When Grant met with disaster, all was not lost because the rest of the advance troops had the fortified position at Ligonier. Before the bulk of Forbes' army arrived, Fort Ligonier was attacked in October by a force of 500 French Canadian soldiers led by Capt. Charles Aubry, a veteran officer from the Louisiana territory. Although the attackers were outnumbered 3-1 by Burd's garrison, the battle was hard-fought. The British had the advantage of training cannon fire on the attackers, but in the end the French made off with the garrison's horses.

By November 1, the ailing Forbes arrived at Fort Ligonier and took up residence in the officers' hut. A smaller force of 250 French soldiers approached the area in mid-November. Colonel Washington and a force of 1,000 Virginians went out to meet them, but two groups of Virginians accidentally fired on each other in the dark woods, killing fourteen. Washington stopped the fusillade when he realized what was happening, but barely escaped getting shot by his own men.

Forbes decided to march on Fort Duquesne despite the late season, but the heavily outnumbered French blew up the fort and fled north as his army approached.

Fort Ligonier continued service as an important supply link through the French and Indian War. The fort was at-

*Fort Ligonier was an
imposing structure.*

*The reconstruction at Fort
Ligonier goes back 40 years.*

tacked twice during Pontiac's War in 1763; Colonel Henry Bouquet made it a stopping point on his march to relieve the besieged Fort Pitt that same year.

Today Fort Ligonier has been elaborately reconstructed. The site was the subject of an extensive archaeological dig in the 1950s and 1960s. Fort reconstruction in the 1960s was financed by Pittsburgh's Mellon banking family. The fort and a museum featuring many artifacts found in the dig are operated by the Fort Ligonier Association, a non-profit group. The association is preparing to complete the reconstruction work. This was made possible when two neighboring properties were acquired several years ago.

## THREE REDOUBTS — HISTORIC HANNA'S TOWN, NORTH OF GREENSBURG, PENNSYLVANIA

*Directions: Take Route 119 north of Greensburg for three miles. Watch for Hanna's Town sign and state historical marker, then left on SR 1032 that follows the old Forbes Road. This road passes by Hanna's Town. The site of the Three Redoubts is located about 1 1/2 miles west of Hanna's Town at the intersection of SR 1032 and Route 819. The earthen redoubts are long gone, but this is still a rural area and largely undeveloped.*

An army encampment called Three Redoubts was located just west of this reconstructed frontier settlement.

The highway that runs by Hanna's Town follows the course of Forbes Road. Hanna's Town was founded in 1773, fifteen years after Forbes' army passed through, but it illustrates the importance of Forbes Road to future western trade and settlement. Robert Hanna, a justice of the peace, laid out his town along the road built by British army engineers just as Col. George Washington and others had foreseen. Hanna's Town was the first county seat established west of the Allegheny Mountains. In 1775, as tensions heated between the colonies and the mother country, the town residents drafted the "Hanna's Town Resolves" expressing their opposition to the acts of the British Parliament. A fort was built here during the American Revolution. The stockade provided shelter to the residents when the town was raided and burned by a party of pro-British Senecas and British sent out from Fort Niagara in 1782. The county seat was moved to Greensburg in 1786 and Hanna's Town was abandoned.

Archaeological digs starting in 1969 have uncovered the location of many structures and artifacts. The Westmoreland County Historical Society has reconstructed the courthouse, palisaded fort, and other log houses. The town is open Tuesday-Saturday 10 a.m. to 4 p.m. and Sundays 1 p.m. to 4 p.m. from Memorial Day through Labor Day and on weekends in May, September, and October.

## THE FALL OF FORT DUQUESNE
## POINT STATE PARK, PITTSBURGH, PENNSYLVANIA

*Directions: Point State Park is reached from east and west by I-376 and I-279, by Route 8 from the north and Route 51 from the south.*

At a council of war at Fort Ligonier on November 11, 1758, Gen. John Forbes and his officers decided to halt the campaign on Fort Duquesne until the next spring. The snow covered the tops of the Alleghenies, many of the soldiers were near the end of their enlistments, and the British still lacked good intelligence about the strength of the French forces at the fort.

The next day, a small force of French soldiers approached the fort. Virginia troops went out to meet them, but instead of confronting the foe they blundered into a confusing crossfire against each other in the woods. Still, the Virginians captured several prisoners, including an Englishman who had defected to the French. He provided information that only 500 French troops were left at the fort and their Indian allies had left.

Encouraged, Forbes ordered an immediate advance on Fort Duquesne. About 2,500 troops set out, divided into three brigades commanded by Col. Henry Bouquet, Col. George Washington and Col. Archibald Montgomery. They made several camps during a nine-day march across

Chestnut Ridge and through what is now the Pittsburgh metropolitan area. The advance guard halted at Turtle Creek and waited for Forbes and the rest of the army to catch up.

On November 24, as scouting parties approached the French fort, they reported the sound of explosions. French commander Capt. Francois-Marie Le Marchand Sieur de Ligneris had ordered the destruction of the fort and evacuation of French forces north to Fort Machault on the Allegheny River. Forbes and his army conquered the ruins on November 25, held a thanksgiving service, and sent out details to bury the dead of Grant's fiasco and Braddock's defeat of three years before.

Point State Park in downtown Pittsburgh marks the finale of the Forbes campaign. The park includes an outline of Fort Duquesne and exhibits on the Forbes expedition in the Fort Pitt museum. The westernmost tablet of the Forbes Road monuments put up by the Pennsylvania Historical Commission is located in front of the museum. The inscription reads: "Fort Duquesne. End of Forbes Road. His victory determined the destiny of the Great West and established the Anglo-Saxon supremacy in the United States."

**Note:** The landscape of Forbes Road through the Pittsburgh region has been greatly altered by development and thus is not covered in this book.

## THE GENERAL AND THE MISSIONARY

General John Forbes and Christian Frederick Post made an unlikely pair. Forbes, (1710-1759) a Scotsman, advanced through the ranks in the British army. Post, (1710-1785) a Moravian missionary from the German province of East Prussia, came to America in 1742 and learned the Delaware language. Their names are linked in history because it is generally recognized that the British won control of the Ohio Forks in 1758 through a combination of military (Forbes) and diplomatic (Post) tactics.

As Forbes directed his 6,000-man army on a methodical advance on Fort Duquesne, Post made two journeys west to talk peace with the Delaware and Shawnee in the Ohio region. Post even delivered his peace message within view of the French guns at Fort Duquesne.

A third name should also be mentioned here. Pisquetomen, a prominent Delaware and brother of Shingas and King Beaver, made an important trip as an envoy of the Ohio Delaware to Philadelphia in July 1758. It was during this visit that Pennsylvania Gov. William Denny asked Post to visit the Ohio tribes and persuade them to make peace. The missionary had got his feet wet in diplomatic dealings with Teedyuscung, the eastern Delaware leader, who had reached an uneasy peace with the British in 1757 and was in contact with the Ohio Delaware. The Ohio Delaware, in turn, were well aware of the Forbes expedition and sensed the tide of war turning with British victories at Louisbourg and Fort Frontenac. Pisquetomen accompanied Post on his trips to the Ohio region and kept him safe from harm by the French and their hardcore allies among the western tribes.

On the first journey in July-September 1758, Post asked the Delaware and other tribes to attend a peace conference at Easton, Pennsylvania. Forbes and Post met just twice at Raystown and Loyalhanna in the fall of 1758, but the general was well aware of the importance of Post's work. If the Ohio tribes could be persuaded to make peace with the British or even declare their neutrality, the French position at the Forks would be severely undermined and the job of taking Fort Duquesne made much easier.

Forbes worried in early September that a precipitous blow by his army might jeopardize the success of the pending conference at Easton. But timing his army's advance to the pace of peace talks was a delicate matter. By October, Forbes had to be concerned about supplying an army in the wilderness, with winter only weeks away. He lost the assistance of those British mercenaries from the South, the Cherokee warriors, who became disgruntled with the slow pace of the campaign.

The peace conference at Easton in October 1758 proved to be a success. On November 9 from Loyalhanna, Forbes sent an open letter to the Delaware and Shawnee urging them to evacuate their people from Fort Duquesne:

> As I am now advancing, at the Head of a large Army, against his Majesty's Enemies, the French, on the Ohio, I must strongly recommend to you to send immediate Notice to any of your People, who may be at the French fort, to return forthwith to your Towns, where you may sit by yr Fires, wth yr Wives and Children, quiet and undisturbed, and smoke your Pipes in safety.

Post and Pisquetomen were back in the Ohio region by this time, delivering news of the Easton conference and urging the tribes to leave the French. Faced with the approach of a large British army and the loss of Indian allies, the French abandoned Fort Duquesne. Pisquetomen subsequently expressed concerns about British construction of Fort Pitt at the Forks and other intrusions into the Ohio region. After the war, Post traveled widely in his missionary work and died in Germantown, Pennsylvania, in 1785.

Throughout the 1758 campaign, Forbes was afflicted by an ailment that left him weak and unable at times to walk or ride a horse. The nature of Forbes' illness is not certain, but in any event the general carried on all the way to the ruins of Fort Duquesne. He hoped to regain his health, but he died in March 1759 in Philadelphia.

# The Building of Fort Pitt — 1759-1764
## Point State Park, Pittsburgh, Pennsylvania

*Directions: Point State Park is reached from east and west by I-376 and I-279, by Route 8 from the north and Route 51 from the south.*

Once the British had control of the Forks of the Ohio, they meant to keep it. Several hundred Virginia soldiers under Col. Hugh Mercer spent the winter of 1759 at the Forks. They built a log fort known as Mercer Fort's on the Monongahela River side. In those early months, the threat of counterattack from the French based at Fort Machault was very real. The Virginians were at the end of a long, uncertain supply line and their fort could not withstand cannon fire.

But London had grand plans for that strategic point, named Pittsburgh for British Prime Minister William Pitt. Starting that spring, workmen and supplies headed west on Forbes Road to build a great fortification known as Fort Pitt, intended to give the British undisputed control over the Ohio region.

The French were preparing to launch an attack on the Forks in July when word came that a British army was at the gates of Fort Niagara, their supply point. French troops at Fort Machault headed to the relief of Niagara and were defeated at the battle of La Belle Famille. With the fall of Niagara, the French threat virtually ceased.

Still, construction of Fort Pitt continued at a breakneck pace. The British established an early industrial works with a saw mill, coal mines, stone quarries, and limestone and brick kilns. Completed, Fort Pitt encompassed eighteen acres, dwarfing the size of Fort Duquesne. It was pentagonal-shaped with earthen ramparts. The ramparts facing the east or landbound side were faced with brick and fronted by stone. The barracks could lodge up to 1,000 soldiers. The commandant's quarters, workshops, and powder magazines were also located within the fort ramparts. Outside the fort was an extensive King's Garden and a burgeoning Low Town.

The British also improved the fort's supply lines. In 1759, Col. James Burd built a fort along the Monongahela River at modern Brownsville, Pennsylvania. He had just finished building a new road from the site of Gist's Plantation to the Monongahela. Fort Burd served as a supply depot for goods shipped via waterways to the Forks.

Fort Pitt suffered severe flood damage in 1762 and 1763; the all-earth Ohio bastion was almost swept away by floodwaters. The defenders of the fort constructed a makeshift defense at this bastion when Pontiac's warriors besieged the fort in the summer of 1763. This was the only

*Fort Pitt blockhouse built by Colonel Bouquet in 1764.*

time the fort came under hostile fire. While Pontiac's warriors lacked cannon needed to pound the fort into submission, they were able to cut off food and supplies until Col. Henry Bouquet's relief expedition scored a victory at Bushy Run.

Bouquet built several brick and wood redoubts to strengthen Fort Pitt's defenses in 1763-64. One of these redoubts—the Fort Pitt Blockhouse—survives today. It is a focal point of Point State Park, a 36-acre park of fields, walkways, fountains, and historical markers. The five-sided blockhouse is built of brick and has a tablet over the entrance with the legend "A.D. 1764 Col. Bouquet." The blockhouse is adjacent to the Fort Pitt Museum in the restored Monongahela Bastion. The museum has two stories of exhibits, dioramas, and models exploring the history of the region.

Visitors entering the park from the east at Commonwealth Place will encounter the restored Music and Flag Bastions. These bastions were excavated by archaeologists in the early 1950s. The ground around the Music Bastion has been excavated to show the foundation of the original brick masonry. A walkway circles the bastion. Point State Park was created in the 1960s in an area cleared of slums and warehouses.

*The monument marks the end of the Forbes Road. One of Fort Pitt's bastions is also visible.*

# 10

# Pontiac's War,
# 1763–64

## INTRODUCTION

It was a dream that recurred over the course of American history. What if the different tribes could coalesce into a pan-Indian uprising to drive the European intruders back into the sea? Perhaps Pontiac, an Ottawa chief who waged war against the British in 1763-64, came closest to making that dream a reality.

Pontiac, (c. 1720-1769) chose to strike at a moment when a great shift in power was underway in North America. Vanquished in the Seven Years' War, the French in 1763 ceded Canada to the British, Louisiana to the Spanish, and gave up their claims to the Ohio Valley. The French, left with two tiny islands off Newfoundland, were no longer an American power.

British troops fanned out to take control of French forts on the Great Lakes and tributaries of the Ohio River. With the Union Jack flying above the scattered outposts, the tribes of the region—the Delaware, Seneca, Ottawa, Shawnee, Potawatomis, Hurons and Chippewas—lost their ability to play one European power against each other. And the tribes soon discovered they lost more tangible benefits since British imperial policy differed quite significantly from the French.

The British army commander Sir Jeffrey Amherst sent out stern orders blocking the tribes' access to liquor, gunpowder, and blacksmiths. The British frowned on contact between soldiers assigned to the posts and women from neighboring tribes. Even more jarring to the sensibilities of Pontiac and his allies, the British held a different view of land ownership than the French. They believed that the eastern half of the continent belonged to the British by virtue of a treaty signed in Paris and they did not have to give presents to the various tribes to possess it.

Pontiac tapped the energies unleashed by a spiritual revival among the Delaware and other tribes. Since the period of first contact in the 16th and 17th centuries, the tribes had grown steadily more dependent on European-made goods. They used iron kettles instead of clay pots, guns instead of stone projectile points, and cloth instead of animal skins. But while the Indians desired the European goods, they did not develop the technology to make the goods themselves. A new breed of spiritual leaders preached that the Indians would only find greatness again if they cast off the evil European influences and reverted to traditional ways.

One of the most prominent leaders was Neolin or Delaware Prophet, (ca. 1725-1775) who lived in the Ohio Valley. He had an unusual manner of crying while he spoke, but Neolin's message was a powerful one to a people dispossessed of their lands. He prophesied that the tribes would unite to wage war against all whites.

Pontiac spread word of Neolin's preachings, while making an important distinction—the tribes should unite to drive out the English, but not the French. Indeed, Pontiac hoped that the French king would send troops back to America to help out once the tribal uprising began. But he underestimated the extent of the French defeat. The commandants at the remaining French forts in Illinois waited only for the word to go home.

Nevertheless, the uprising that Pontiac helped guide pushed the British out of the Upper Great Lakes and Upper Ohio Valley. During the spring of 1763, a string of British outposts fell and two strategic posts, Fort Pitt

SITES AT A GLANCE—This map will give you a feel for the general locations of sites in this chapter. Some sites overlap and are not shown on this map.

Devil's Hole

Ft. Presque Isle

Ft. Le Boeuf
Ft. Venango

Scots-Irish settlement

Ft. Pitt

Bushy Run

Conestoga

Enoch Brown Park

and Fort Detroit, were besieged. Pontiac conducted the siege at Detroit, one of the longest on record for an Indian force. Frontier settlements and homesteads in Pennsylvania, Maryland, and Virginia, felt the terror of raids by the Delaware and Shawnees. The British engaged in an early form of bacterial warfare—by distributing blankets infected with smallpox to the warriors outside Fort Pitt.

British relief forces eventually raised the sieges at Detroit and Fort Pitt. A British victory at Bushy Run in western Pennsylvania broke the uprising's momentum and opened the way for punitive expeditions against tribal villages in the Muskingum Valley. In an effort to remove the reasons for the uprising, the British government issued a proclamation declaring the Alleghenies the western limit of white settlement. But this order of the Crown was widely ignored.

The uprising eventually petered out as various tribes made their own separate peace. Pontiac met a fate that befell other Indian leaders who led resistance. He had lost much of his influence in the years after 1765. While visiting the Peoria village of Cahokia in 1769, he was assassinated by a Peoria brave acting on the decision of a tribal council.

## PONTIAC'S WAR SITES—1763-1764

The pan-Indian uprising known as Pontiac's War covered a wide geographic area from Lake Michigan to Pennsylvania's Blue Mountains. Warriors from the Ottawa, Huron, and Potawatomi tribes struck the first blow against British rule at Fort Detroit in May 1763, but the fort's garrison held out during a prolonged siege. Pontiac's allies had greater success capturing a string of British posts along the Great Lakes and Illinois Country. Within the month the Shawnee, Delaware, and Seneca joined Pontiac and destroyed British posts at Fort Presque Isle, Fort Le Boeuf, and Fort Venango in western Pennsylvania. Fort Pitt, the great British bastion at the Forks of the Ohio, was surrounded for several months by a force of warriors representing a half-dozen tribes.

During the summer of 1763, Pontiac's uprising continued to build momentum. Along Forbes Road in Pennsylvania, raiding parties launched a strong attack on Fort Ligonier and killed several settlers in the vicinity of Fort Bedford. Fort Bedford served as a refuge for frightened families. Settlers along the Juniata River were attacked. Farther east, white refugees overran the town of Carlisle. Frontier settlements in Maryland and Virginia suffered from hit-and-run attacks too. In July 1763, raiders attacked and killed neighbors of trader Thomas Cresap at Oldtown, Maryland. In southern Virginia, homesteads in Augusta County and the Greenbrier area came under attack.

The British counterattack began with expeditions to lift the sieges at Fort Detroit and Fort Pitt. In July Col. Henry Bouquet led an army of 450 soldiers westward from Carlisle along Forbes Road. The army stopped at Fort Ligonier to pick up supplies.

At a small post known as Bushy Run on August 5-6, Bouquet's army came under attack. The warriors had broken off their siege of Fort Pitt to stop Bouquet's advance; instead Bouquet scored a decisive victory and relieved Fort Pitt. This was a major turning point in Pontiac's War, but elsewhere the British suffered defeat. In September, Seneca warriors ambushed a British wagon train moving north on the portage road around Niagara Falls in western New York. The wagoneers and their horse teams were thrown into the depths of the Niagara Gorge at a spot known as Devil's Hole.

Although communications were restored with Fort Pitt in western Pennsylvania, warfare erupted throughout the Blue Mountains in eastern Pennsylvania in the fall of 1763. The Wyoming Valley had been in turmoil since the mysterious death of the Delaware leader Teedyuscung in a cabin fire in April. As settlers from Connecticut poured into the valley, Teedyuscung's son Captain Bull and the remaining Delaware moved to Great Island along the west branch of the Susquehanna River. An expedition under Col. John Armstrong burned this village in September; in retaliation Captain Bull led devastating attacks in October on the Connecticut settlers at Wyoming and the Scots-Irish settlement in Northampton County.

Captain Bull's raids put the Moravian Indian converts in the region in peril, for they were not trusted by either side. The Moravian converts living at Wechquetank in the Poconos and Nain, a village outside Bethlehem, were evacuated to Philadelphia where they spent many months in virtual confinement.

Stories of Indian massacres infuriated the Paxton Boys, a band of frontier militia and ruffians who wrought vengeance on the peaceful remnant of the Conestoga tribe. The Paxton Boys raided Conestoga in Lancaster County in December 1763 and killed the old men, women, and boys they found there. Survivors were given refuge in the Lancaster County jail, but the Paxton Boys raided the jail and killed them on the spot.

Bloody raids continued sporadically into 1764. Delaware warriors struck a shocking blow in July when they raided the Enoch Brown schoolhouse in Pennsylvania's Conococheague Valley, killing the schoolmaster and ten students.

In the fall of 1764, the British sent new expeditions to the west. Colonel Bouquet marched into the Ohio country and forced the Delaware and Shawnee to sue for peace and give up their captives. In December, Bouquet escorted 200 former captives to Carlisle's Public Square where many were reunited with their families for the first time in eight or nine years. It was on this occasion that Regina Leininger, taken captive at the Penn's Creek massacre in 1755, recognized her mother only after hearing her sing the words of a German lullaby.

## Forts Le Boeuf and Venango
## Waterford and Franklin, Pennsylvania

*Directions: The Fort Venango monument is in a residential neighborhood bordering the Allegheny River. The monument is located in front of a vacant lot and across from Evangelical Lutheran Church. A similar monument for Fort Machault is at 616 Elk Street. Take Route 322 into downtown Franklin. Turn left on Elk Street and follow east past Washington Crossing Road (Routes 8/62) and Eighth Street Bridge to curbside monuments.*

When the British took control of the upper Ohio Valley in 1759-60, they built new forts near the sites where French outposts once stood. These forts were wooden blockhouses surrounded by earth embankments. Fort Le Boeuf shared the same name as its French predecessor on the portage road. Fort Venango was located on the Allegheny River near the mouth of French Creek and close to the ruins of Fort Machault, burned by the French in 1759. These British forts were poorly manned when Pontiac's War suddenly erupted in the spring of 1763. British commanders had ordered a reduction in the size of the garrisons a year before when conditions in the region appeared peaceful. This left the garrisons unprepared when Seneca warriors launched surprise attacks.

Fort Venango was struck on June 16, and the small garrison was massacred. Fort Le Boeuf was the next post to come under attack on June 18. Ensign George Price and his command barricaded themselves in the blockhouse and put out the fires caused by burning arrows. Price and seven soldiers escaped from the blockhouse at nightfall and made their way to Fort Venango. They found that post in ruins and continued on to safety at Fort Pitt. Seneca, Chippewa, Huron and Ottawa warriors captured the British post at Presque Isle on Lake Erie on June 22.

The Fort Le Boeuf museum at Waterford has exhibits on Pontiac's War and the attack on Fort Le Boeuf by the Seneca. The museum is on the east side of Route 19 at the south end of town. The museum is open some weekend afternoons in the summer and fall, but it is best to call ahead for a schedule. To arrange a tour, call the Department of Sociology, Anthropology and Social Work, Edinboro University, Edinboro, Pa. 814-732-2573.

A small stone monument marking the site of Fort Venango is located in Franklin at the curb at the intersection of 8th and Elk Streets. The inscription reads: "Site of Fort Venango 1760. Taken and burned by Indians 1763."

## Bushy Run Battlefield
## East of Harrison City, Pennsylvania

*Directions: From Route 30, take Route 66 north to Route 993. Go west on Route 993 for several miles to park entrance. Watch for park signs.*

The Battle of Bushy Run with its desperate fighting and surprise military maneuvers is one of the more dramatic encounters between British soldiers and Native Americans during a period of conflict from 1755 to 1764. Thanks to a modernized visitors center at this state-owned historic site, Bushy Run is also one of the best places to get an understanding of the clash of cultures that marked the last phase of this conflict—Pontiac's War.

In June 1763, word reached New York and Philadelphia of the Fort Pitt siege, and the loss of frontier forts to Pontiac's warriors. British authorities turned to Col. Henry Bouquet to lead a relief expedition to western Pennsylvania. Bouquet had earned his spurs in frontier warfare during the Forbes campaign in 1758; five years later he led an army of 450 men westward along the familiar path of Forbes Road to reassert British control. Bouquet's force consisted of two regiments of Scottish Highlanders and the Royal Americans, a British unit made up of colonials. Bouquet sent units to reinforce the garrisons at Fort Bedford and Fort Ligonier. The army carried surplus barrels of flour in wagons to feed the settlers taking refuge at Fort Pitt.

By August 2, the army reached Fort Ligonier where the wagons were left behind. The flour was transferred from wooden barrels and placed in sacks atop pack horses for easier transport. Bouquet detoured off Forbes Road enroute to a small communications post at Bushy Run. He

*This monument marks Bouquet's defensive position.*

*British troops during a reenactment at Bushy Run .*

planned to rest there before marching through the Turtle Creek area where the army was vulnerable to ambush.

Before he reached that spot, Bouquet's army was attacked on August 5 by a force of several hundred warriors representing a half-dozen tribes. This force, most likely under the command of the Mingo chief Guyasuta, interrupted the siege of Fort Pitt with word of Bouquet's approach. After hours of fighting and the loss of 50 soldiers, Bouquet's troops retreated to a hill where they established a defense position, using the flour bags to shelter the wounded. Water rations grew scarce and Bouquet feared the worst with the expected resumption of the battle next morning.

On August 6, the battle resumed. Bouquet believed his force would eventually be overwhelmed unless some dramatic action was taken to alter the course of battle. He devised a strategy where two companies of soldiers were withdrawn from the south portion of the British line. Guyasuta's warriors attacked this position, thinking the British were about to crack. However, Bouquet had sent the two companies undetected through a small valley. They emerged to fire on the warriors' unprotected flank. Caught unaware and without an opportunity to reload their guns, the warriors fled. Bouquet's army marched on, fending off smaller attacks, and several days later relieved Fort Pitt. Bouquet's victory is credited with stabilizing the British presence in the west until a larger army could be sent into the Ohio Valley in 1764.

Bushy Run Battlefield today is a 162-acre park run by the Pennsylvania Historical and Museum Commission. The park features a walking trail that gives a realistic look at the battlefield topography. A portion of the original frontier road remains. The hillside site of Bouquet's flour bag entrenchment is marked by a stone monument and concrete replicas of flour bags. A neighboring hill has markers indicating the burial site of the British soldiers who fell in battle. The visitor center has exhibits that ex-

pertly tell the story of the battle, and the underlying events that led Pontiac's warriors to attempt to drive the British out of the lands west of the Allegheny Mountains.

## DEVIL'S HOLE—LEWISTON, NEW YORK

*Directions to Devil's Hole State Park: From Niagara Falls, take Robert Moses Parkway north. Exit at Devil's Hole and park in parking lot. Take a pedestrian bridge to cross the parkway to the state park.*

The attack was sudden and swift. The result was bloody with British wagoneers, teams of horses, and wagons thrown into the depths of the Niagara Gorge far below.

Devil's Hole—the name conjures a forbidding place. It refers to a deep cave in the rock-strewn rapids of the Niagara River. Indian folklore holds that an evil spirit dwelled there. On the morning of September 14, 1763, Devil's Hole gained new notoriety when several hundred Seneca warriors ambushed a lightly guarded British wagon train moving north on the portage road around Niagara Falls. The 25 wagons and escort of 30 soldiers were quickly overwhelmed at a spot that became known as Bloody Run. The portage road closely followed the east rim of the gorge. The Senecas threw their victims into the gorge. And for good measure, they threw in the draft horses and their gear, too. The rapids of Devil's Hole were 300 feet below. Only two members of the wagon train convoy escaped. One of them was John Stedman, the portage master.

A relief column of British soldiers heard the din of battle two miles away at a spot on the river known as the Lower Landing. They marched to the rescue under command of Lt. George Campbell and they, too, were ambushed. Eighty soldiers died in that rout.

The Devil's Hole massacre came during the height of Pontiac's War, the pan-Indian uprising to drive the British out of the Great Lakes region and Ohio River Valley. In the fall of 1763, all the British outposts in the west had fallen to the warriors under the banner of the Ottawa Chief Pontiac with the exception of Pitt, Niagara, and Detroit.

The Niagara portage was a lifeline from Fort Niagara to Fort Detroit. That lifeline held despite the massacre at Devil's Hole. In a matter of weeks, supplies and goods were moving over the portage again. A relief ship eventually reached besieged Fort Detroit. Pontiac and his warriors gave up the siege.

For seventy-five years, first the French and then the British used the portage around Niagara Falls to move troops and supplies to the west. Senecas had been hired as porters to haul goods up the Niagara escarpment at present day Lewiston and then along the eight-mile portage road to Fort Little Niagara (later Fort Schlosser) just south of Niagara Falls.

Some historians attribute the Seneca attack to anger at losing portage jobs when the British switched to transporting goods by wagon train. Others note the Devil's Hole massacre as the worst defeat suffered by British forces during Pontiac's War. Within a year, the British strengthened security along the portage road by building blockhouses at strategic points. The portage started at the Niagara escarpment, the old shoreline of an ancient lake. The Senecas called this place "Crawl-on-all-Fours" in recognition of the tough climb.

In 1764, the British built one of the first crude railroads or lift-elevators for hauling goods up the 350-foot escarpment from the Lower Landing. This machine, called the "cradles," was in use for forty years. The site of the cradles is at Artpark, a state performing arts park at Lewiston.

The site of the Devil's Hole massacre is at Devil's Hole State Park, one of a chain of parks along the Niagara Gorge. The park consists of a greenway along the rim of the gorge and hiking trails that descend into the gorge. One trail follows the rim. Another descends into the gorge along a series of switchbacks and stone steps. Another trail follows an old railroad bed along Devil's Hole gulch. The Schoellkopf Geological Museum in Niagara Falls, New York, sells a "Walker's Guide to the Niagara Gorge," that provides directions to the trails.

## Scots-Irish Settlement Graveyard
## Old Allen Township Presbyterian Church,
## Howertown, Pennsylvania

*Directions: From Northampton, east on Route 329 to Howertown intersection with SR 3017. Continue east for one mile on Route 329. Pass East Allen Township Ambulance Association building on left side, then look for church in grove of trees. Look sharply here, for church building is unmarked. Park on gravel driveway.*

Pontiac's War spread with a vengeance to the Blue Mountain region of eastern Pennsylvania in October 1763, and 50-year-old Jane Horner, a member of Northampton County's Scots-Irish settlement, fell victim to the rampage. Horner was walking to a neighboring house on the morning of October 8 when she was spotted by a party of Delaware raiders from the Wyoming Valley and quickly killed. Horner (nee Kerr), a native of northern Ireland, emigrated to America in 1734 and moved with her husband James to the enclave of Scots-Irish who had settled on the west bank of Hockendauqua Creek.

The main target of the raiders was a local tavern owned by James Stenton. A company of soldiers from Fort Allen had stayed overnight at the tavern and took the brunt of the Delaware attack. There are conflicting accounts as to how many tavern inhabitants and raiders were killed.

*Grave of Jane Horner, victim of a 1763 raid.*

Delaware warriors also attacked other homesteads in the area and caused refugees to flee to Bethlehem.

Jane Horner's grave is located in the old Presbyterian burial ground of the Scots-Irish settlement. The letters on her flat tombstone are faded, but the Bethlehem Chapter of the Daughters of the American Revolution erected a bronze tablet with the inscription: "Jane Kerr, wife of James Horner, who suffered death by the hands of the Indians. Oct. 8, 1763 aged 50 years."

The grave of her husband, who died in 1793 at age 83, is nearby in the Horner family plot located in the middle of the graveyard near the west side. The cemetery is a peaceful, tree-shaded place surrounded by a stone wall. The graveyard is set back from the c. 1813 Presbyterian Church, a white frame building with black shutters. Look for a mowed path to the right of the church leading to the graveyard.

## Paxton Boys

One of the most controversial frontier episodes erupted in December 1763 when a group of vigilantes from Pennsylvania's Paxtang area massacred a peaceful tribe of Indians living behind the lines of white settlement. This attack that wiped out the Conestoga tribe came at the height of Pontiac's War.

For the Conestoga who had settled on land in Lancaster County granted them by the Penn family, the outbreak of Pontiac's War meant trouble, and put them in a precarious position. Many had adopted Christianity and other English ways, but were viewed by frontier settlers as a fifth column that gave aid to Indian raiding parties. The Conestoga massacre also exposed fault lines between the Scots-Irish who had lost relatives and neighbors in Indian border raids, and Quakers who controlled the provincial government in Philadelphia. Indeed, the massacre's aftermath brought the province to the brink of civil war.

The pacifist Quakers had adopted a largely defensive response to the Indian raids on the frontier; the Scots-Irish wanted a more aggressive war against the tribes allied with Pontiac. The Paxton rangers, a militia outfit, had raided cornfields in the Wyoming Valley to deprive the Delaware of food supplies in the fall of 1763 despite disapproval from Governor John Penn.

The frontiersmen contended that Indians converts living in Moravian missions in the Bethlehem area were trading with the Delaware. The presence of the Conestoga was also a sore spot in the rift. Community leaders like Rev. John Elder of Paxton Church urged Gov. Penn to move the Conestoga closer to Philadelphia; the requests were ignored.

The first act of violence occurred on December 14, 1763. A group of 50-odd men from Paxtang burned the Conestoga village to the ground and killed the six villagers there. Among those slain was Chief Shehaes, an aged veteran of land dealings with the Penn family, as well as women and children. The fourteen surviving Conestoga were then sheltered in the jail at nearby Lancaster; the General Assembly voted for funds to transport them to Philadelphia. But on December 27, an armed party of 100 Paxtang men raided the jail and killed all fourteen. A detachment of British soldiers in Lancaster did not intervene.

The killings spurred Gov. Penn to offer rewards for the capture of the Paxton Boys and merge the militia unit, the Paxton Rangers, with other detachments. The Moravian Indians were moved to Philadelphia for their own protection, but a number of them died of disease brought on by living in crowded barracks.

The frontier vigilantes' wrath now turned on Philadelphia. The Paxton Boys, their numbers swelled by recruits, marched on the provincial capital in March 1764. They were met outside the city by a delegation that included Benjamin Franklin. The groups' spokesmen presented a list of demands and grievances, then returned home. Just one of their demands—for a bounty on Indian scalps—was granted.

## PAXTON CHURCH—PAXTANG, PENNSYLVANIA

*Directions: From Harrisburg, take I-83 north toward Hershey. Take Paxtang exit. Turn left on Route 322. Turn left at Paxtang Ave. and follow through Cameron Park to Derry Street, and right on Derry Street. Turn left on Wilhelm Street just before historical marker for church. Continue on Wilhelm Street past several stop signs. Church on left side at Wilhelm and Elder Streets.*

The Paxton Church was the spiritual center of the Paxtang community on Pennsylvania's frontier. The Scots-Irish immigrants who settled this area brought their Presbyterian religion with them. The first log church here

*Paxton Church dates to 1740.*

was built in the 1720s. The existing limestone church dates back to 1740, making it the second oldest Presbyterian church in continuous use in the United States. A replica of the original log church was built in 1950 on the church grounds.

One of the church's more prominent ministers was Rev. John Elder, known as the "Fighting Parson" for his role in organizing the Paxton Rangers militia unit during Pontiac's War. A native of Scotland, Elder (1706-92) served as church pastor from 1738 to 1791. Elder emerged as a spokesman for the frontier Scots-Irish in their efforts to persuade the Quaker-dominated government to take stronger measures against Indian incursions. Elder was in the thick of the controversy surrounding the massacre of the Conestoga tribe. He urged provincial officials to move the Conestoga away from the frontier, to no avail. He also sought to dissuade the vigilante group known as the Paxton Boys from attacking the Conestoga.

Elder is buried in the northwest corner of the Paxton Church graveyard. Two of his sons are buried nearby. A tablet on the cemetery gate lists the names of Paxtang's frontier defenders. Also buried in the northwest corner are two other prominent veterans of the French and Indian War: John Harris Jr. (1726-91) founder of Harrisburg, and William Maclay (1734-1804) who later became a U.S. senator and wrote a famous journal about the early days of Congress.

## CONESTOGA—INDIAN MARKER ROAD
### SOUTH OF WASHINGTON BORO, PENNSYLVANIA

*Directions: Take Route 441 south of Washington Boro until it becomes River Road. Follow the winding River Road for several miles, then left on Indian Marker Road. Follow Indian Marker Road 1.9 miles to intersection with Safe Harbor Road. Conestoga Monument is at intersection.*

As the 18th century began, Conestoga was an important Indian town on the east bank of the Susquehanna River. Several Pennsylvania governors visited here; Indian traders gathered at this center of commerce. Three centuries later, Conestoga is remembered as a dark chapter in American history. Conestoga, as the state monument bluntly states, is where an ancient Indian tribe was exterminated in 1763 when passions aroused by Pontiac's War spilled into bloodshed.

The Susquehannock tribe had occupied the region for generations. English explorer John Smith visited one of their forts in 1608 when he sailed up Chesapeake Bay into the lower reaches of the Susquehanna. The Susquehannocks were powerful until defeated by the Iroquois in the 1670s. The Susquehannocks were scattered in defeat; a remnant of the tribe established themselves at Conestoga, and became known as the Conestoga Indians.

William Penn purchased the lands along the Susquehanna from the Iroquois. When Penn heard of the Conestogas' dissatisfaction with the sale, he signed a peace treaty with them in 1701 and granted the tribe a tract of 414 acres to live on. Successive governors held councils here and bestowed gifts on the Conestoga.

The Conestoga lived here peacefully for several decades. But as white settlement spread westward, the size of the tribe declined until only twenty people were left. They were reduced to selling hand-made brooms and baskets to their neighbors for a livelihood.

With the renewal of Indian raids during Pontiac's War in 1763, the position of the Conestoga became perilous. A frontier vigilante group known as the Paxton Boys threatened their lives. Several frontier leaders asked that the Conestoga be moved to Philadelphia for their own protection, but the request was ignored. On December 14, 1763, a party of 57 Paxton Boys surrounded the village of Conestoga and murdered the three men, two women and one boy they found there.

Among those slain was the aged Chief Shehaes, who had met Penn in 1701. The fourteen remaining Conestoga were away from the village selling their brooms and baskets and doing other errands. The local sheriff located them and lodged them temporarily in the jail in nearby Lancaster for their other protection. But on December 27, a party of 100 Paxton men broke into the jail and killed the last of the Conestoga as they kneeled down protesting their innocence.

The 1852 Fulton Opera House on North Prince Street, Lancaster, is on the old jail site. A state historical marker has been erected to note the opera house. The site of Conestoga is on rolling farmland about two miles east of the Susquehanna River. The Pennsylvania Historical Commission and Lancaster County Historical Society erected a stone monument in 1924, with the inscription: "The tribe was exterminated by the Paxton Boys in 1763." The site of the 1763 village lies south of the monument.

## MARTIN AND PETER CHARTIER

*Directions to Martin Chartier monument: Take Route 441 south of Columbia to Washington Boro. Monument is at intersection of Route 441 and Charlestown Road. Go to right side of the Susquehanna River and parallel railroad tracks. Monument next to grove of pine trees and artillery piece.*

This father and son are representative of a distinctive type in 18th century America: the restless venturing Indian trader who bridged the gap between white and Native American cultures and owed few allegiances to any distant crown. Both Martin and Peter Chartier were associated with the Shawnee, a tribe that made peripatetic journeys between the Ohio Valley and the Susquehanna Valley in the early decades of the 18th century. Martin Chartier, a French Canadian, first surfaces as a member of French explorer Rene-Robert La Salle's expedition down the Mississippi River in 1679. Among a garrison stationed at a French fort in Illinois, Chartier also was reportedly among a group of soldiers who deserted their post.

In 1692, Chartier suddenly appeared at the head of a band of Shawnees that migrated to Maryland. He moved with the Shawnee in 1698 when they settled near the Conestoga village in the Susquehanna Valley. Chartier assisted William Penn in his negotiations with various tribes. He was an interpreter at major conferences at Conestoga. Chartier was awarded a 300-acre land tract north of Conestoga at modern-day Washington Boro, Pennsylvania, and settled here late in life.

Chartier's son Peter, a half-breed son of a Frenchman and Shawnee woman, was a trader in his own right. In the 1730s, he lived with a Shawnee band that settled where Yellow Breeches Creek enters the Susquehanna River at modern-day New Cumberland, Pennsylvania.

Within a few years, Chartier and the Shawnee moved westward to the Allegheny River. During King George's War from 1744 to 1748, Chartier openly sided with the French and robbed several English traders. During the next twelve years, he and his band of Shawnee moved among various locations in the Ohio and Mississippi valleys. Chartier's trail fades out in the Illinois territory about 1760, the same place where his father Martin made his entrance on the American stage.

The Pennsylvania Historical Commission and Lancaster County Historical Society erected a stone monument to Martin Chartier in 1925 in Washington Boro at the site of his land grant. The plaque reads:

Martin Chartier Died 1718. Noted Indian trader and interpreter in early Pennsylvania and Maryland. Frenchman from Canada who resided at Ft. St. Louis of the Sier de la Salle in present Illinois, 1684-90. A leader thence of the Shawnee Indians to Maryland, 1692, and to Susquehanna River at Pequea Creek, now Lancaster County, Pennsylvania, 1697.

Agent in William Penn's treaties with the Indians of the Susquehanna. Settler here in later years at the site of Washington Borough on a 300 acre tract granted to him by Penn. Father by his Shawnee wife of Peter Chartier, the Indian trader and interpreter.

## ENOCH BROWN MEMORIAL PARK
### NORTH OF GREENCASTLE, PENNSYLVANIA

*Directions: Take Route 11 north of Greencastle for three miles. Turn left on Williamson Road, then right on Stone Bridge Road. Turn left on Enoch Brown Road to park. Watch for brown/white park signs.*

This was a remote spot when three Delaware raiders attacked the log schoolhouse that stood here on July 26, 1764. The raiders massacred a teacher and ten of his students and quickly moved on. For the victims of the raid, this quiet hollow is their final resting place.

The massacre of schoolmaster Enoch Brown and ten students, near the close of Pontiac's War, was shocking. By 1764, the Conococheague Valley had experienced nine years of deadly raids dating back to the aftermath of Gen. Braddock's defeat. The Enoch Brown massacre was one of the last of those raids, but it is among the best known because of the image of young children killed and scalped while pursuing their studies. The attack embittered the Scots-Irish settlers against any prospects of peaceful coexistence with the Delaware and Shawnee who once hunted those lands.

The attack on Brown's schoolhouse came suddenly. The raiding party killed its victims before local residents sensed anything wrong. One student, ten-year old Archie McCullough, survived with a scalping wound to the head.

Local tradition says Brown's body was discovered with a Bible clasped in his hands. Brown is said to have gone on his knees to beg that the children be spared.

Today the schoolhouse site is preserved as a memorial park. An 1884 monument on the schoolhouse site is dedicated to "pioneer martyrs in the cause of education and Christian civilization." A tombstone marks the common grave of the victims. The names listed are: Enoch Brown, Ruth Hart, Ruth Hale, Eben Taylor, George Dunstan, Archie McCullough (the survivor) and six unknown.

*Common grave for teacher and students slain in 1764 massacre.*

# Sources

## The British, French, and Native Americans Move into the Ohio Valley, 1720s–1759

George Washington, *The Journal of Major George Washington* (Williamsburg, Virginia: The Colonial Williamsburg Foundation, 1991) 4, 13, 17, 22.

T. V. Welch, A. F. Andrews, L. R. Dressler, *The Old Stone Chimney* (Buffalo, NY: Denton, Cottier & Daniels, 1891) songsheet.

Brian Leigh Dunnigan, *A History and Guide to Old Fort Niagara* (Youngstown, NY: Old Fort Niagara Association, 1985) 61.

Paul A. W. Wallace, *Indian Paths of Pennsylvania* (Harrisburg, PA: Historical and Museum Commission, 1971) 200-212.

Robert C. Alberts, *A Charming Field For An Encounter: The Story of George Washington's Fort Necessity Campaign* (Washington, D.C.: United States Department of Interior/National Park Service, 1975) 16.

## Braddock's March to Disaster, March–July 1755

Peter Shaw, ed., *The Autobiography and Other Writings by Benjamin Franklin*, (NY: Bantam Books, 1989) 129.

Walter S. Hough, *Braddock's Road Through The Virginia Colony*, Vol. III, Winchester-Frederick County Historical Society (Strasburg, VA: Shenandoah Publishing House, 1970) 15-50.

Fairfax Harrison, ed., "With Braddock's Army, Mrs. Browne's Diary in Virginia and Maryland," *The Virginia Magazine of History and Biography* (Oct. 1924) Vol. XXXII, No. 4, 316-318.

Ralph Andrist, ed., *The Founding Fathers: George Washington, A Biography in His Own Words* (New York: Harper & Row, 1972) 55-56.

## Raids on the Conococheague Valley 1755-1758

John H. Nelson, *Frontier Forts of Fulton County, Pennsylvania*, Vol. 14 (Fulton County Historical Society, 1992), 3.

Hayes Eschenmann, *The Elusive Fort Morris* (Shippensburg, PA: Beidel Printing House Inc., 1987) 95-113.

S. K. Stevens, Donald H. Kent, and Autumn L. Leonard, eds., "The Papers of Henry Bouquet," Vol. II, *The Forbes Expedition* (Harrisburg, PA: The Pennsylvania Historical and Museum Commission, 1951) 73.

James E. Seaver, *The Life of Mary Jemison* (New York: The American Scenic and Historic Preservation Society, 1982) 30.

## Attack and Counterattack in Central Pennsylvania, 1755-1756

Charles Fisher Snyder, "The Penn's Creek Massacre," *Northumberland County Historical Society Proceedings and Addresses*, Vol. II (July 26, 1939) 154-55.

William A. Hunter, *Forts on the Pennsylvania Frontier 1753-1758* (Harrisburg, PA: The Pennsylvania Historical and Museum Commission 1960) 385.

## Moravian Missions Attacked—Benjamin Franklin Organizes Defense, 1755-1757

Franklin, *Autobiography*, 134-136.

The Rev. William H. Rice, "The Gnadenhuetten Massacres," *The Pennsylvania German*, Vol. 3, No. 1 (January 1906) 29.

"The Dansbury Diaries 1748-1755," *Old Dansbury and the Moravian Mission*, The Moravian Archives and Monroe County Historical Society, (Camden, ME: Picton Press, 1994) 209.

John Bartram, *Travels in Pennsylvania and Canada* (Readex Microprint Corp.: 1966) 31.

## Pennsylvania Germans Defend Blue Mountain Region, 1756-1757

Bartram, *Travels*, 10, 12.

Wallace, 162-163.

Ralph S. Shay, ed., "The Journal of Lieut. Philip Marzloff at Fort Swatara Aug. 128, 1757," *The Lebanon County Historical Society*, Vol. XIII, No. 7 (1964) 318.

## George Washington Defends Virginia Frontier, 1755-1758

Charles Morrison, *Wappatomaka: A Survey of the History and Geography of the South Branch Valley* (Parsons, WV: McClain Printing Co., 1971) 16.

Elizabeth Barry Brown, *Augusta Stone Presbyterian Church*, Fort Defiance, VA: 1993. (leaflet)

F. B. Kegley, *Kegley's Virginia Frontier* (Roanoke, VA: The Southwest Virginia Historical Society, MCMXXXVIII) 244.

Margaret T. Peters, *A Guidebook to Virginia's Historical Markers*, Virginia

Historic Landmarks Commission (Charlottesville, VA: University Press of Virginia, 1989) 212-213.

## Maryland Gov. Horatio Sharpe Builds Fort Frederick, 1756-1758

Exhibit text at Fort Frederick and Allan Powell, *Maryland and the French and Indian War*, (Baltimore MD: Gateway Press, 1998) 95.

## The Forbes Campaign: British Victory at the Ohio Forks, May–November 1758

*Bouquet Papers*, 98, 341.

Alfred Proctor James, ed., *Writings of General John Forbes Relating to his Service in North America* (New York: Arno Press and The New York Times, 1971) 251-252.

## Pontiac's War, 1763-1764

Schoellkopf Geological Museum, *Walkers' Guide The Niagara Gorge Trails Along the American Side*, (Niagara Falls, NY: Niagara Frontier State Parks Commission, 1989).

# Selected Bibliography

Alberts, Robert C. *A Charming Field for an Encounter*. Washington D.C.: National Park Service, 1975.

Albright, S. C. "Graves That Tell a Tale." Vol. III. No. 2. Lebanon County Historical Society, n.d. 43-86.

Alden, John Richard. *Robert Dinwiddie Servant of the Crown*. Charlottesville, VA: The Colonial Williamsburg Foundation. University Press of Virginia, 1973.

Alderfer, E. G. *The Ephrata Commune An Early American Counterculture*. Pittsburgh, PA: University of Pittsburgh Press, 1985.

Alderfer, Gordon E. *Northampton Heritage: The Story of an American County*. Easton: The Northampton County Historical and Genealogical Society, 1953.

Allen, Irvin G. *Historic Oldtown, Maryland*. Parsons, WV: McClain Printing Co., 1983.

Anderson, Niles. "The General Chooses a Road." *Western Pennsylvania Historical Magazine*. Vol. 42. (1959): 109-138; 241-258; 383-401.

_____, *The Battle of Bushy Run*. Harrisburg, PA: Pennsylvania Historical and Museum Commission, 1966.

_____, "New Light on the 1758 Forbes Campaign." *Western Pennsylvania History Magazine*. Vol. 50. No. 2 (April 1967): 90-103.

Andris, Ralph K., ed. *George Washington: A Biography in His Own Words*. New York: Harper & Row Publishers, 1972.

Ansel, William H., Jr. *Frontier Forts Along the Potomac and Its Tributaries*. Parsons, WV: McClain Printing Co., 1984.

Appel, John C. *A Return to the Monroe County Frontier*. Monroe County Historical Society, 1975.

Baker, Richard A. "Indian Forts in Berks County." *The Historical Review of Berks County*. Vol. XVIII. No. 2. (Jan.-March 1953): 49-63.

Bartram, John. *Travels in Pensilvania and Canada*. Readex Microprint Co., 1966.

Baucher, Richard. "Indian Forts in Berks County." *The Historical Review of Berks County*. Vol. XVII. No. 2. (January-March 1953): 49-63.

Bethlehem Chamber of Commerce. *Bethlehem of Pennsylvania: The First Hundred years, 1741 to 1841*. Bethlehem: 1968.

Beyer, George R. *Guide to the Historical Markers of Pennsylvania*. Harrisburg, PA: Pennsylvania Historical and Museum Commission, 1991.

Biddle, Gertrude B. and Sarah D. Lowrie, eds. *Notable Women of Pennsylvania*. Philadelphia: University of Pennsylvania Press, 1939.

Bowers, O. C. "Col. Patrick Jack." *Kittochtinny Historical Society*. Vol. 9 (1921), 509-533.

Brown, Stuart E., Jr. *Virginia Baron: The Story of Thomas 6th Lord Fairfax*. Berryville, VA: Chesapeake Book Co., 1965.

Burkhart, William H., ed. *The Shippensburg Story 1730-1970*. Shippensburg, PA: Shippensburg Historical Society, 1970.

Cassady, John C. *The Somerset County Outline*. Scottdale, PA: The Mennonite Publishing House, 1932.

Champion, Walter T. "Christian Frederick Post and the Winning of the West." *Pennsylvania Magazine of History and Biography*. CIV, No. 3. July 1980, 308325.

Chidsey, A. R., Jr. *A Frontier Village: Pre-Revolutionary War Easton*. Easton, PA: The Northampton County Historical and Genealogical Society, 1940.

Colley, David. *Two Hundred Years of Life in Northampton County Military History*. Vol. X. Easton, PA: Northampton County Bicentennial Commission, 1976.

Conrad, W. P. *From Terror to Freedom in the Cumberland Valley*. Greencastle, PA: Lillian S. Besore Memorial Library, 1976.

Corkran, David H. *The Cherokee Frontier: Conflict and Survival*. Norman, OK: University of Oklahoma Press, 1962.

Currie, William J., III, ed. *A Hiker's Guide to the Laurel Highlands Trail*. 4th edition. Pittsburgh: Sierra Club, Pennsylvania and Western Pennsylvania Conservancy, 1992.

Dohme, Alvin. *Shenandoah, The Valley Story*. Washington, D.C.: Potomac Books Inc., 1973.

Donehoo, George P. *Indian Villages and Place Names in Pennsylvania*. Baltimore, MD: Gateway Press, 1977.

Donovan, Frank, ed. *The George Washington Papers*. New York: Dodd, Mead & Co., 1964.

Dunnigan, Brian Leigh. *A History and Guide To Old Fort Niagara*. Youngstown, NY: Old Fort Niagara Association, 1985.

_____. *Siege 1759: The Campaign Against Niagara*. Youngstown, NY: Old Fort Niagara Association, 1986.

_____. "Portaging Niagara." *Inland Seas Quarterly Journal of the Great Lakes Historical Society*. Vol. 42. No. 3. Fall 1986, 177-183.

Eschenmann, Hayes R. *The Elusive Fort Morris*. Shippensburg, PA: Beidel Printing House Inc., 1987.

_____. *Indians Indians*. Shippensburg, PA: Whipperwhill Publications, 1992.

Farley, G. M. "The Battle of the Trough." *Wonderful West Virginia*. Vol. 46. No. 11. January 1983, 6-9.

Feldstein, Albert L. *The Guide to Historic Sites in Allegany County, Maryland*. Cumberland, MD: Cumberland Press Printing Co., 1993.

Finarock, John L. *Notes on Franklin County History*. Chambersburg, PA: Kittochtinny Historical Society, 1942.

Fort Ligonier Association. *War for Empire in Western Pennsylvania*. 1993.

Gallup, Andrew, and Donald P. Shaffer. *La Marine The French Colonial Soldier in Canada. 1745-1761*. Bowie, MD: Heritage Books, 1992.

George, Michael J. "The French and Indian War in Berks County: The early months from October 1755 to March 1756." *The Historical Review of Berks County*. Vol. XLII. No. 3. Summer 1977, 88-115.

Geyer Alan R. and William H. Bulles. *Outstanding Scenic Geologic Features of Pennsylvania*. Harrisburg, PA: Commonwealth of Pennsylvania, 1979.

Giddens, Paul H. "The French and Indian War in Maryland." *Maryland Historical Magazine*. Vol. 30. No. 4. Dec. 1935, 281-309.

Hark, J. Max. "Meniolagomeka Annals of a Moravian Indian Village 130 Years Ago." *Transactions of the Moravian Historical Society*. Vol. II. No. 3. 1877-86, 129-144.

Harrison, Fairfax, ed. "With Braddock's Army: Mrs. Brownes's Diary in Virginia and Maryland." *The Virginia Magazine of History and Biography*. Vol. 32. No. 4. Oct. 1924, 305-320.

Henning, D. C. "Tales of the Blue Mountain." *Schuylkill County Historical Publications*. Vol. 3. 1911, 40-48.

Hough, Walter S. *Braddock's Road Through the Virginia Colony*. Vol. VIII. Strasburg, VA: Winchester-Frederick Historical Society, 1970.

Hunter, William A. "The Ohio, The Indian Land." *Pennsylvania History*. Vol. XXI. No. 4. October 1954. Reprint. Pennsylvania Historical and Museum Commission.

_____. "Victory at Kittanning." *Pennsylvania History*. Vol. XXIII. No. 3. July 1956. Reprint. Pennsylvania Historical and Museum Commission.

_____. *The Provincial Fort at Carlisle, 1755-1758*. Carlisle, PA: Hamilton Library and Historical Association of Cumberland County, 1956.

_____. *Forts on the Pennsylvania Frontier, 1753-58*. Harrisburg, PA: The Pennsylvania Historical and Museum Commission, 1960.

_____. "Our First Invasion." *Dauphin County Historical Review*. Vol. XII. No. 1. December 1964, 19-24.

_____. *The Walking Purchase*. Historical Pennsylvania Leaflet. The Pennsylvania Historical and Museum Commission, 1972.

_____. *Peter Chartier Knave of the Wild Frontier*. Cumberland County National Bank and Trust Co., 1973.

Huntingdon County Historical Society. *Sesqui-Centennial Celebration of Huntingdon County, 1787-1937*, 1937.

James, Alfred Proctor, and Charles Morse Stotz. *Drums in the Forest*. Pittsburgh: The Historical Society of Western Pennsylvania, 1958.

James, Alfred Proctor, ed. *Writings of General John Forbes Relating to his Service in North America*. New York: Arno Press and the New York Times, 1971.

Jennings, Francis. *Empire of Fortune Crowns Colonies and Tribes in the Seven Years War in America*. New York: W. W. Norton & Co., 1988

Kent, Barry, Janet Rice, and Kakuko Ota. "A Map of 18th Century Indian Towns in Pennsylvania." *Pennsylvania Archaeologist*. Vol. 51. No. 4, 1981.

Kent, Barry. *A Revised Plan for the Reconstruction of Fort Loudon*. Fort Loudon Historical Society, 1990.

Kent, Donald H. *The French Invasion of Western Pennsylvania, 1753*. Harrisburg, PA: The Pennsylvania Historical and Museum Commission, 1981.

Kittochtinny Historical Society. *Papers Read Before the Society October 1950 to May 1957*. Vol. XIII, n. d.

_____. *Papers Read Before the Society 1963-1970*. Vol. XV. Chambersburg, PA: 1970.

_____. *Papers Read Before the Society 1971-1978*. Vol. XVI. Mercersburg, PA: 1978.

Koontz, Louis K. *The Virginia Frontier 1754-1763*. Bowie, MD: Heritage Books, 1992.

Lacock, John Kennedy. "Braddock Road." *Pennsylvania Magazine of History and Biography*. Vol. 37. 1914, 1-38.

Lancaster County Historical Society. "The Site of Conestoga Indian Town and the Historic Conestoga Indians." Vol. XXVIII. No. 9. Nov. 7, 1924, 132-138.

Lewis, Thomas A. *For King and Country The Maturing of George Washington 1748-1760*. New York: Harper Collins Publishers, 1993.

MacKinney, Gertrude, ed. *Pennsylvania Archives. October 15, 1753–Sept. 24, 1756*. Eighth Series. Volume 5. Harrisburg, PA: Pennsylvania Department of Property and Supplies, 1931.

Mason Dixon Council Boy Scouts of America. *The Forbes Road Historic Trail*. Hagerstown, MD: 1972.

McCardell, Lee. *Ill-Starred General: Braddock of the Coldsteam Guards*. Pittsburgh, PA: University of Pittsburgh Press, 1958.

McConnell, Michael N. *A Country Between The Upper Ohio Valley and Its Peoples 1724-1774*. Lincoln: University of Nebraska, 1992.

Mish, Mary Vernon. "Springfield Farm of Conococheague." *Maryland Historical Magazine*. Vol. 47. 1952, 314-333.

Mish, Mary Vernon. *Jonathan Hager Founder*. Hagerstown, MD: Hagerstown Bookbinding and Printing Co., 1987.

Montgomery, Thomas Lynch, ed. *Report of the Commission to Locate the Sites of the Frontier Forts of Pennsylvania*. Vol. One. Second Edition. Harrisburg, 1916.

The Moravian Archives and Monroe County Historical Society. *The Dansbury Diaries 1748-1755, Old Dansbury and the Moravian Mission*. Camden, ME: Picton Press, 1994.

Moravian Historical Society. "Gnadenhuetten on the Mahoning 1746-55." *Transactions of the Moravian Historical Society*. Vol. VII. Part 5. 1906, 349397.

Moravian Historical Society. "Wechquetank 1749-1760." *Transactions of the Moravian Historical Society*. Vol. VIII. Part 1. 1907, 1-24.

Morgan, Capt. John. "Life in a Frontier Fort." *Pennsylvania Magazine of History and Biography*. Vol. 39. No. 2. 1915, 186-191.

Morrison, Charles. *Wappatomaka: A Survey of the History and Geography of the South Branch Valley*. Parsons, WV: McClain Printing Co., 1971.

Mulkearn, Lois. "Half King, Seneca Diplomat of the Ohio Valley." *The Western Pennsylvania Historical Magazine*. Vol. 37. No. 2. Summer 1954, 65-81.

Mulkearn, Lois, and Edwin V. Pugh. *A Traveller's Guide to Historic Western Pennsylvania*. Pittsburgh, PA: University of Pittsburgh Press, 1954.

Murray, Elsie. *Teaoga Annals of a Valley*. Athens, PA: Tioga Point Museum, 1939.

Myers, Elizabeth L. "The Upper Places Nazareth, Gnadenthal and Christian's Spring." *Northampton County Genealogical and Historical Society*. 1929. 1-10.

Nelson, John H. "Frontier Forts of Fulton County." *Fulton County Historical Society*. Vol. 14. 1992.

Netherton, Ross. *Braddock's Campaign and The Potomac Route to the West*. Falls Church, VA: Winchester-Frederick Historical Society, 1989

Niagara Frontier State Parks Commission. *Walkers Guide: The Niagara Gorge Trails Along The American Side*. Niagara Falls, NY: 1989.

Nixon, Lily L. *James Burd, Frontier Defender*. Philadelphia PA: University of Pennsylvania Press, 1941.

Nolan, J. Bennett. *General Benjamin Franklin: The Military Career of a Philosopher*. Philadelphia, PA: University of Pennsylvania Press, 1936.

Northampton County Historical and Genealogical Society. *The Scotch-Irish of Northampton County*. Vol. 1. Easton, PA: 1926.

Northumberland County Historical Society. *Early Events in the Susquehanna Valley*. Millville, PA: 1981.

Olberly, Lawrence R., Jr. and James A. Wright. "The Wilson Blockhouse." Northampton, PA: 1974.

Older, Curtis L. *The Braddock Expedition and Fox's Gap in Maryland*. Westminster, MD: Family Line Publications, 1995.

O'Meara, Walter. *Guns at the Forks*. Pittsburgh, PA: University of Pittsburgh Press, 1979.

Peckham, Howard. *Pontiac and The Indian Uprising*. Detroit: Wayne State University Press, 1994.

Peters, Margaret T. *A Guidebook to Virginia's Historical Markers*. Virginia Historic Landmarks Commission. Charlottesville, VA: University Press of Virginia, 1989.

Powell, Allan. *Fort Frederick: Potomac Outpost*. Parsons, WV: McClain Printing Co., 1988.

_____. *Fort Cumberland*. Parsons, WV: McClain Printing Co., 1989.

_____. *Fort Loudon Winchester Defense in the French and Indian War*. Parsons, WV: McClain Printing Co., 1990

_____. *Maryland and the French and Indian War*. Baltimore, MD: Gateway Press, 1998.

Quarles, Garland R. "George Washington and Winchester Virginia 1748-1758." *Winchester-Frederick County Historical Society Papers*. Vol. VIII, 1974.

Randall, Williard Sterne. *A Little Revenge Benjamin Franklin at War With His Son*. New York: Quill/William Morrow, 1984.

Rice, Otis K. *The Allegheny Frontier West Virginia Beginnings 1730-1830*. Lexington, KY: The Univ. Press of Kentucky, 1970.

Rice, Rev. William H. "The Gnadenhuetten Massacres." *The Pennsylvania German*. Vol. 7. March 1906, 71-79.

Rouse, Patrick Jr. *The Great Wagon Road: From Philadelphia to the South*. Richmond, VA: Dietz Press, 1992.

Schoenfeld, Max. *Fort De La Presquile*. Erie, PA: Erie County Historical Society, 1989.

Schnure, W. M. "The Penns Creek Massacre of 1755." *The Snyder County Historical Society Bulletin*. Vol. 1. No. 2. Jan. 23, 1914, 21-24.

Seaver, James. *The Life of Mary Jemison*. New York: The American Scenic and Historic Preservation Society, 1982.

Severance, Frank H. *An Old Frontier of New France The Niagara Region and Adjacent Lakes under French Control*. Vols. I and II. Bowie, MD: Heritage Books, 1958.

Shay, Ralph J. "The Journal of Lieut. Philip Marzloff at Fort Swatara Aug 1-28, 1757." *Lebanon County Historical Society*. Vol. XIII. No. 7. 1964, 307-327.

Sipe, C. Hale. *The Indian Wars of Pennsylvania*. New York: Arno Press and New York Times, 1971.

_____. *The Indian Chiefs of Pennsylvania*. Lewisburg, PA: Wennawoods Publishing, 1994.

Snyder, Charles Fisher. "Pilger Ruh." *Northumberland County Historical Society*. Vol. 16. 1948, 28-33.

Stegmaier, Harry Jr., David Dean, Gordon Kershaw, and John Wiseman. *Allegany County: A History*. Parsons, WA: McClain Printing Co., 1976.

Stevens, Sylvester K. and Donald H. Kent, eds. *Wilderness Chronicles of Northwestern Pennsylvania*. Harrisburg, PA: Pennsylvania Historical Commission, 1941.

Steven, Sylvester K., Donald H. Kent, and Autumn L. Leonard, eds. *The Papers of Henry Bouquet: The Forbes Expedition*. Vol. II. Harrisburg, PA: Pennsylvania Historical Society, 1951.

Stotz, Charles Morse. *The Story of Fort Ligonier*. Ligonier, PA: Fort Ligonier Memorial Association, 1954.

_____. *Point of Empire Conflict at the Forks of Ohio*. Pittsburgh, PA: Historical Society of Western Pennsylvania, 1970.

_____. *Outposts of the War for Empire. The French and English in Western Pennsylvania: Their Armies, Their Forts, Their People 1749-1764*. Pittsburgh, PA: Historical Society of Western Pennsylvania. University of Pittsburgh Press, 1985.

Trudel, Marcel. *The Jumonville Affair*. Philadelphia, PA: Eastern National Parks and Monuments Association, 1989.

Vivian, Cassandra. *A Driving Tour of the National Road in Pennsylvania*. Monessen, PA: Trade Route Enterprises, 1994.

Waddell, Louis M., and Bruce D. Bomberger. *The French and Indian War in Pennsylvania 1753-1763 Fortification and Struggle During the War for Empire*. Harrisburg, PA: Pennsylvania Historical and Museum Commission, 1996.

Wagoner, Shirley A. "Captain Jack — Man or Myth." *Pennsylvania History*. Vol. XLVI. No. 2. April 1979, 99-119.

Waitley, Douglas. *Roads of Destiny: The Trails that Shaped a Nation*. Washington and New York: Robert B. Luce Inc., 1970.

Walkinshaw, Lewis Clark. *Annals of Southwestern Pennsylvania*. New York: Lewis Historical Publishing Co., 1939.

Wallace, Anthony F. C. *King of the Delawares Teedyuscung 1700-1763*. Syracuse, NY: Sycracuse University Press, 1990.

Wallace, Paul A. W. *Pennsylvania Seed of a Nation*. New York: Harper & Row Publishers, 1962.

_____. *Indian Paths of Pennsylvania*. Harrisburg, PA: Pennsylvania Historical and Museum Commission, 1971.

_____. *Conrad Weiser Friend of Colonist and Mohawk*. New York: Russell and Russell, 1971.

_____. *Indians In Pennsylvania*. Harrisburg, PA: Pennsylvania Historical and Museum Commission, 1981.

_____. *Daniel Boone in Pennsylvania*. Harrisburg, PA: Pennsylvania Historical and Museum Commission, 1987.

Ward, Harry M. *Major General Adam Stephen and the Cause of American Liberty*. Charlottesville: Univ. of VA. Press, 1989.

Ward, Matthew C. "Fighting the Old Women Indian Strategy on the Virginia and Pennsylvania Frontier 1754-1758." *The Virginia Magazine of History and Biography*. Vol. 103. No. 3. July 1995, 297-320.

Washington, George. *The Journal of Major George Washington*. Williamsburg, VA: Colonial Williamsburg Foundation, 1991.

Weslager, C. A. *The Delaware Indians: A History*. New Brunswick, NJ: Rutgers University Press, 1991.

Wheeler, Geo. "The Tulpehocken-Shamokin Trail." *Northumberland County Historical Society*. Vol. 2. 1939. 112-127.

Workman, Donald. *The War for British Empire in Alleghany County, Maryland*. Cumberland, MD: 1969.